IN THE MERDE FOR LOVE

A Year in the Merde

IN THE MERDE FOR LOVE

STEPHEN CLARKE

BLOOMSBURY

Copyright © 2005 by Stephen Clarke

Published by Bloomsbury Publishing, New York and London
Distributed to the trade by Holtzbrinck Publishers

All papers used by Bloomsbury Publishing are natural, recyclable products made
from wood grown in well-managed forests. The manufacturing processes
conform to the environmental regulations of the country of origin.

Library of Congress Cataloging-in-Publication Data

Clarke, Stephen, 1958–
In the merde for love / Stephen Clarke
p. cm.
ISBN-13: 978-159691-190-1
ISBN-10: 1-59691-190-5

1. British—France—Fiction. 2. Paris (France)—Fiction. 3. Tearooms—Fiction.
I. Title.

PR6103.L374815 2006
813′.6—dc22
2005057178

First U.S. Edition 2006

1 3 5 7 9 10 8 6 4 2
Typeset by Hewer Text Ltd, Edinburgh
Printed in the United States of America by Quebecor World Fairfield

"Everything is for the best in the best of all possible worlds."

Voltaire, *Candide*

"Hell is other people."

Sartre, *No Exit*

"I'll have some of that Voltaire, please."

Paul West, *In the Merde for Love*

CONTENTS

1

Sexe and the Country

1

FLORENCE AND I were sitting forty kilometres south of Limoges, in Corrèze, almost exactly in the centre of France. If you staked a man out Da Vinci–style on a map of the country, with his right hand in Brittany, his left in Strasbourg, and his feet in Biarritz and Monaco, then Corrèze would be the small patch where he'd wet himself.

Florence's mum had a country house in Corrèze. We'd planned to stop off there for a quick lunch and then drive on for a two-week amble around southwest France.

But things hadn't gone exactly to plan, and we were sitting in the sun beside a recently dented car. It was after ten minutes of waiting for the police or a tow-truck to arrive that Florence laid her head on my lap and uttered the fateful words.

"I suppose we'll have to spend a few days with Maman."

Of course, she didn't know then that I was going to try and kill her mother. Neither did I. We'd only been together for about two months, and if anyone had asked my opinion, I'd have said that I didn't think attempting to murder your new girlfriend's mum was a good basis for a successful relationship.

It wasn't really my fault, anyway. I blame it on the French driver.

"Connasse!" he shouted.

French insults are so wonderfully grammatical, I thought. Even in the heat of a verbal battle you have to remember to change the rude word for a male idiot, "connard," to the feminine form.

But he was being totally unfair. I was the one who'd been driving, not Florence. He was only shouting at her because she was nearer to him than I was. And he'd just made what felt like an asteroid-sized dent in the passenger-side rear door of Florence's dad's brand-new car, thereby coming within a microsecond of making a similar dent in Florence herself.

"Are you OK?" I asked her in English.

"Oui." She always answered me in French. "Et toi, Paul?"

"Yes, but I'd like to go and stuff that guy's designer sunglasses up his nose."

"No, you cannot do that, you are English. You must show your phlegm."

"My phlegm?" I hadn't heard this one before. Did the French think we Brits calmed down by spitting all over the place? They must have been watching too much of our football on satellite TV.

"Yes, you are phlegmatic. You have cold blood."

Ah, the Englishman as reptile, now we were on more familiar ground.

"No," I said, "those sunglasses have got to go."

I got out of her dad's royal-blue Renault Vel Satis and gave myself a quick frisk to see if any extremities had come loose. No, both cars had been travelling pretty slowly so I was suffering from nothing more serious than a stiff neck and a vague sensation of wanting to punch someone.

I walked round to the red Asian 4WD that had hit us. Its front headlights were not even cracked.

The driver was a bottle-blond, forty-something teenager with wraparound sunglasses so dark I was surprised he could see the sky, never mind cars ahead of him. This model of the French urban warrior watched me walking towards him, and began jabbing at the button to close the window he'd been yelling out of.

"You are blind, perhaps?" I asked, nodding at his glasses. I called him vous, of course, instead of the familiar tu or toi, because we hadn't yet been introduced.

"Et toi?" he shouted through the closed window. I forgave him his familiarity on the basis that he was a good twenty years older than me. "Don't you know la priorité à droite?"

He huffed towards his polo-shirted wife and their two skater-boy kids. They were all glowering at me venomously. It was true—by falling victim to the guy's bad driving I had screwed up his family's holiday timetable. Breakfast in Burgundy was probably on their schedule, lunch in Limoges, but not crash in Corrèze.

"La priorité à droite?" I said. This is the stupidest, most dangerous law in the Western world. It is the French law which states that a car coming from the right has right of way. You might be tooling along on what looks and feels like a major road, and if a car leaps out of a tiny hidden sidetrack without looking to see whether anything is coming, and thereby wipes out your whole family, it's perfectly legal because it was coming from the right. "There is no priorité à droite on a roundabout," I said.

"Roundabout?" The driver pulled his sunglasses down his nose and looked around as if he'd only just noticed the large, grass-covered traffic island next to his car. He also took in the distinctly circular road running around it and the four or five exits leading off in different directions.

"What a merde, these roundabouts," he moaned, expressing the view of a fair number of Frenchmen, who don't seem to know what roundabouts are for. To provide work for municipal gardeners, perhaps? "They're an anglais thing, aren't they?"

"Yes. We invented them to stop accidents. France is a technological nation, so we did not think you will have a problem with our roundabouts. After all, you can even open oysters." I took a chance including a joke with the horrifically difficult word "huîtres," but I was on a roll and it hit home.

"Et vous, vous êtes Anglais." This was his butch wife, leaning over and bellowing across the steering wheel at me. At least she called me vous. "You English don't know how to drive on the right."

"And your husband, what is his excuse?" I asked.

The wife gripped her husband's arm and whispered urgently to him. He nodded.

I guessed what she'd said when he started up his engine and hit reverse. The two cars wrenched apart like post-coital lovers whose skin has temporarily stuck together. Then the 4WD did a neat one-point turn and drove off the way it had come.

As the driver sped away I memorized his number and, pointlessly, the faces of the two long-haired boys who were grinning at me through the back window. Papa had just become the outlaw hero of their very own road movie. The French love road movies. They call them "les rod-moo-vee."

"What did you say to him?" Florence asked.

"Nothing that insulting. He probably thinks I won't know how to report him because I'm English."

"Yes, and just after lunchtime his blood is probably half wine," she said.

I went to admire the dent on her side of the car. An ugly red-and-blue bruise that wouldn't have been too serious except for the fact that the impact had bent the rear wheel arch and ripped the tyre, which was whistling goodbye to its short but high-pressured life.

There was no way I could get at the wheel to change it. We had to call out a tow-truck.

We pushed the car over to the side of the road and went to sit in the long grass looking out over a field of sunflowers that stretched back hundreds of yards. I'd never seen so many sunflowers in one place before. In my mind they grew alone, sentries watching over suburban gardens. But here, the massed ranks of five-foot-high flowers looked like an invasion of the Earth by an army of thin green aliens.

"Are you really OK?" I asked. "You didn't hit your head or anything?"

"No. I might need you to massage my neck, though." Florence flashed me a smile and ran a long finger down from her ear to the smooth, bare shoulder curving up out of her T-shirt. The first time we ever went to bed together, I'd been struck by the incredible smoothness of her skin, as if she'd spent her teenage years cocooned in coconut milk. She was half-Indian—her father was a Tamil from the volcanic French island of La Réunion, near Madagascar—and she had a body that was a perfect blend of French poise and Indian litheness.

She pushed her black bra strap out of the way and pressed her fingertips into the muscle behind her collar bone. "You're going to have to kiss me, just *there*." She groaned, finding a tender spot and rolling her eyes.

All of which sounded very promising.

Until, that is, she announced that we were going to stay with her mum.

The garagiste arrived half an hour later. When he heard that a Parisian car (that is, one with a number ending in 75) had caused the crash, he was more than happy to write an oil-stained statement testifying that we'd been in the right and that the other driver had left the scene illegally.

He also put in a good word for us with the pair of local gendarmes who came to investigate the accident. They were looking stressed in their tight trousers and old-fashioned képis. This was the first Saturday in July, when a large percentage of the French population, plus a sizeable herd of foreign tourists, was migrating southwards through the region. Boozed up, overheated, impatient, lost, and distracted by vomiting kids, loose luggage and ringing phones, the millions of drivers charging along the auto-routes would cause more accidents over the next two days than there had been in the last six months.

So when the two young gendarmes saw that we were a simple case of dent and run, they made a quick show of taking notes and drove off again in their little blue van.

Our arrival chez Maman was a bit of an anticlimax, even though her daughter had probably never turned up in a battered orange tow-truck before.

Florence opened a small white-painted gate and we walked into an empty garden. Over to our right was an overgrown lawn and a handful of mature fruit trees. I could see birds pecking busily at enormous scarlet cherries. Straight ahead was a stone barn with a moustache of moss running along the edge of its gleaming slate roof. To our left was the house, a one-storey construction made out of stone the milky-beige colour of the skin on a ripe Saint Nectaire cheese. The window shutters were painted slate-grey to go with the roof, and they were all closed, as was the front door.

"They're having a sieste," Florence whispered. "We'll wait until they wake up."

You really felt that you were in the middle of a continent here. There was the occasional breath of wind, but most of the time the air just hung there, shimmering and seething in the sun. The thick foliage and low branches of the cherry tree weren't enough to provide comfortable shade, so we went into the barn to get a parasol.

Being suddenly hidden from view gave me an idea.

Florence read my mind.

Well, perhaps I did give her a little hint by grasping her around the waist and pressing my face to her neck.

She shook herself free. "No, Paul, it is not a good idea. Look. There are just piles of logs and an earth floor. Ce n'est pas pratique." Some girls get a damn sight too pratique as soon as they're within range of their mothers, don't they? "You get the parasol," she said. "I've got a beach towel that we can lay on the grass." She turned back towards the sunlit doorway, then stopped and swore.

"What is it?" I asked.

"We left the luggage in the car."

"Oh merde."

2

B Y THE TIME we had found the garage-owner's number,
explained our problem above the noise of another accident
scene, and been told that our car was safely padlocked away in his
yard and that he for one wasn't going to go and unlock the yard
just to get some bags, there were signs of life from the house.

A small, chestnut-haired boy in blue swimming trunks ran out
into the garden and saw us lying under our parasol.

"Flo!" the boy squealed.

"My nephew," Florence explained. "My sister's boy, Semen."
Weird names they have out here in the country, I thought.

The boy flopped down on the grass to hug her. As he did so, he
eyed me suspiciously. "He's small," he said.

"Semen!" Florence hissed at him as if he'd commented on some
unmentionable affliction. At the time I didn't think any more about
it. I'm six feet tall and have no hang-ups about my height. And I
was wearing baggy shorts, so he couldn't possibly have been
commenting on any other shortcoming in my physique.

"Bonjour. Je suis Paul." I held out my hand for the little guy to
shake. His suspicion instantly doubled.

"Doesn't he want to kiss me?" he asked Florence.

"He's English," she told him.

This seemed to explain away everything strange about me, and
the boy—whose actual name, I had now worked out, was
Simon—walked around his aunt and kissed me on the cheeks.

"He is small, though, isn't he?" he whispered to Florence.

She tutted. "Where's grand-mère?"

"Still snoring."

"Is Michel here?" Florence asked. Michel was her elder brother, whom I'd heard about but never met.

"Oui. But he *never* wakes up."

We went into the kitchen to get something to drink. Little Simon leapt around Florence like a puppy who hasn't been for a walk for two days. But all the time he kept half an eye on me as if I was about to steal his favourite toy. There was still something about me that bothered him.

The kitchen was a cool relief after the oppressive sunlight of the garden. The large square flagstones on the floor were cold to the touch. I twisted the top off a stubby bottle of Kanterbräu beer and guzzled it down in one blissful gulp. I could feel the sweat condensing deliciously in the small of my back.

So it was something of a shock when I sat down at the long dinner table and fractured both of my knees.

"Ah, yes, I should have told you," Florence said. "Be careful when you sit there."

I stood up again (my knees weren't actually broken, I discovered, only as dented as the car) and examined the table.

It was about ten feet long, made of dark wood, and seemed to be of a normal height. But below the scratched table top there were deep drawers that lowered the leg room, so that only a crouching midget could have sat comfortably down to dinner.

"It is a traditional Corrèze table," Florence explained. "My great-grandfather made it when he built the house."

"Didn't he have any legs?"

"Yes. It's just that we don't have his chairs any more. They were very low too."

"Can't you cut the legs off these chairs?" I mimed amputation. "Or add a few centimetres to the table legs?"

"Oh no, Maman would not like that."

Little Simon was suddenly clinging to Florence again.

"He wants to cut our chairs?" he asked, aghast.

"No, no," Florence assured him. "It's OK, Paul, you will quickly learn to eat your dinner facing to one side."

"Ma chérie!"

A woman swept into the kitchen. She was wearing a brown kaftan-style dress that made it impossible to tell whether she was as thin as a parasol or as bulky as her dinner table. She bounded up to Florence and gave her a loud smacking kiss on each cheek. As they pressed together I saw that Madame Flo senior was very shapely in that comfy, fifty-year-old kind of way.

"Maman, je te présente Paul."

Maman turned to look at me. I stood up and smiled with all the gratitude that a boy should show to the woman whose loins had produced his lover.

She smiled back warmly and tugged on my shoulder until I was small enough for her to kiss. I tried not to let my brain register the fact that my mother-in-law's large breasts were bouncing against my ribs.

"Enchanté, Madame. Vous allez bien?"

"You can call me Brigitte," she said, promoting me instantly to a tu. "Qu'il est mignon!" she laughed, and kissed me again on the cheek. Mignon, I knew, meant cute. Though it can also be used to describe a cute guinea pig.

Brigitte was small and graceful, like her daughter, but not at all Indian. Her hair was dark red—the colour black-haired women dye their hair to cover up greyness. It was cut in a thick bob, and her skin was very fair. She had Florence's joyful smile and laughing eyes, and emanated a kind of universal love for humankind.

And I don't think it was *all* down to the Prozac.

We exchanged potted CVs. She was a primary-school teacher, an institutrice, in a town near Tours. I was a soon-to-be English-tea-room owner.

"Ah oui, Maman," Florence interrupted. "I'm leaving my job and going to work in the salon de thé."

"What?"

Suddenly I looked less mignon. I could tell that I'd mutated from the harmlessly exotic boyfriend to the corrupting influence that had persuaded Madame's poor offspring to give up a job for life. The universal love had evaporated and been replaced by raw disapproval.

"Oui, Maman, mon boulot me faisait chier." Florence's work was "making her shit," as if constipation in the office was some kind of ideal state.

She explained that her company was instigating a "plan social," offering staff a full year's salary or early retirement to leave. Even when the French economy slows down, people are rarely thrown on the rubbish heap. So she had taken the offer and was coming in with me to set up the tea room.

"And in this salon de thé, what will you do? Be a waitress? Is that why you qualified as an accountant?" Brigitte smiled wanly over at me as if to say that she wasn't implying that her daughter was too good for the likes of me. Even though she was.

"It's a small business, Maman, we'll do everything. You know, Paul was the head of marketing for a big company before giving it up for his salon de thé."

Brigitte leaned back against the polished slate mantelpiece and

this T-shirted, unshaven foreigner with the faded
.lip-flops who didn't look like the head of anything
.ybe some international association of beach bums.
rench company?"

es, and before that an English company," Florence said.

"Hmm." For some reason, Brigitte was slightly reassured by
this. "In London?"

"Yes, Maman, in London."

"They say it's the most expensive city in the world."

"It is, but luckily the salaries are in proportion," I said, drawing
myself up to my full height and almost cracking my skull on the
low ceiling beams.

Maman went to the fridge in the corner of the kitchen and took
out a large glass jug full of pink foam.

"You will have some strawberry juice?" she asked me.

"Strawberry juice?"

"Yes, we have so many, we don't know what to do with them. I
mix them up, add some water and a little sugar and lemon juice,
and voilà."

"Mmm, it must be délicieux," I said, thinking the liquid looked
like mashed sheep's brain.

We sat at the table, our knees twisted to one side, and drank
tumblers of pink frothy goo that got stuck between your teeth.
Little Simon was the only one who could sit comfortably. The rest
of us were like three Snow Whites squatting chez the dwarves.

"So where is it, this salon de thé?" Brigitte asked, with only
mild aggression.

"Near the Champs-Elysées," I said.

"The rent must be very expensive."

"I negotiated a good price."

"When do you open?"

"A la rentrée, the first of September," I said.

"Yes, Maman, Nicolas is doing the plans. You remember Nicolas?"

"Oh, oui, he was so nice, Nicolas!" Brigitte sighed fondly.

I wondered how she was so familiar with the architect who was overseeing the refit at the tea room. Florence had told me he was a young architect who'd give us a good price—a "prix d'ami"—because he was "a boy I went to school with." Parisian women are surrounded by "boys I went to school with" because so few of them leave Paris to study or find a job. The question is, of course, what did they get up to when they were at school together?

This Nicolas was quite a handsome guy if you liked the tall, pale, artistic type with impeccably casual designer clothes and an overdose of self-confidence.

It was comforting to know that a friend of Florence's was dealing with all the stuff I was linguistically incapable of: getting building permission and quotes, buying materials, scheduling in the various workmen. But I couldn't get the question about his place on Florence's sexual CV out of my mind. Wasn't there a difference between hiring an architect you knew and giving work to an ex-boyfriend?

I made a mental note to call him over the weekend to make damn sure that everything was ready to roll on Monday morning, when the guys with sledgehammers were due to go in and remove all evidence that the premises had recently been a shoe shop.

"Was he very big, Nicolas?" little Simon asked.

"Shut up, Simon," Brigitte snapped, giving me a "don't worry about him, he's just being stupid" smile.

"Wel-kum, wel-kum!"

A grinning man of about my age and size was stooping through the doorway from the lounge. This was Florence's big brother, Michel.

Like Florence, he was a perfect cocktail of French and Indian blood, a dark-eyed, long-limbed latte of a man. Unlike her, he had a lot of bodily hair, and a corresponding tendency to baldness that he attempted to hide by pulling his hair back in a short ponytail. He was shirtless, with a slight pot belly, and his shorts were even more rumpled than mine. I guessed he'd slept in them.

He kissed Florence and gripped my hand, examining with a mixture of curiosity and pity this guy who was shagging his sister.

Waving away the offer of sheep juice, he went to the fridge, where he found a bottle of fizzy Badoit water and guzzled down half of it, puffing breathlessly as the bubbles fizzed up into his nose.

"Michel, that bottle is for everyone," Brigitte told him, and he laughed, the kid who's never had to listen to what his parents told him.

Florence and I told the story of our accident, and then Brigitte announced that as we'd be staying for a few days, we could help out with the chores. A holiday at her country house wasn't a holiday, it seemed. Everything was permanently on the verge of falling down, going rotten or getting eaten by pests. I knew the feeling.

I was given several choices of how to occupy my first afternoon in Corrèze. Unfortunately, curling up with Florence wasn't one of them. There was picking lettuce, radishes, courgettes or strawberries, demossing the barn roof, or digging.

I had noticed a large, fresh hole down the slope a little from the barn.

"You are making a swimming pool?" I asked.

"No, it is for the fosse septique," Brigitte explained.

"The what?"

"You know, the reservoir for the, you know . . ."

"For the caca and pipi," Simon giggled.

"You don't have one?" I asked, envisaging dawn trips to fertilize the hedges.

"Yes, yes, but it is out of date."

"Out of date?" There was a problem with having last season's septic tank?

Florence explained, while Brigitte listened tensely. This was obviously a subject that was painfully close to her heart.

Apparently all the houses in the village had septic tanks, but none of them were "aux normes"—they didn't conform to modern building laws. It seemed that it was OK to pollute the outskirts of every town in France with hideous billboards and industrial estates, but it was illegal to have an undersized septic tank.

The ones in Brigitte's village were all basically brick chambers in the garden where waste products had been flowing and fermenting efficiently for centuries. However, with modern washing machines and dishwashers, too many houses were pumping warm water out into the roadside ditches, turning the lanes into subtropical gardens that the council had trouble keeping in check. Now the mayor had got a regional grant to fit large modern septic tanks that would hold all the waste water.

"They do not make the hole for you?" I asked.

"Yes, yes, but . . ." Brigitte shuddered.

"Maman is afraid they'll break the water pipes or cut through the roots of the walnut tree," Florence explained.

"Huh," Michel grunted. "She just doesn't want strange men digging around in her—"

"Michel!" Brigitte blushed as pink as her strawberry juice.

"Anyway," Florence went on, "Maman wants us to dig the hole ourselves."

"I think I prefer to pick courgettes," I volunteered.

"OK, you can do some digging tomorrow," Brigitte said. "You'll just have to be careful because we're quite close to breaking through to the old tank."

In short, my French vacances were in danger of getting off to a very shitty start.

3

I HAD SEEN the three or four rows of courgettes round the
back of the house, and figured it would take me no more than
five minutes to strip them bare, after which Florence would be able
to give me a guided tour of the house, with the finale in a secluded
bedroom.

The two of us were still at that early stage in our relationship
where you need to touch each other all the time. Where as soon as
your fingers so much as brush against each other's skin, the other
parts of your body start saying they'd like to join in with this skin-
brushing business. It's probably not the best time to go and stay
with your mother-in-law.

And now the combination of glorious sun, thrusting vegetation
and Florence's exposed limbs (she'd found a bikini in the wardrobe) was making my whole lower body ache.

So I was gutted to learn that the courgettes I was supposed to
pick weren't in the little veg patch behind the house. They were a
ten-minute walk away across the lane and through the woods.
Worse, Florence wasn't allowed to come with me because she had
to help turn the morning's crop of cherries into a clafoutis, a sort of
mammoth fruit flan.

I was given an old straw hat that a donkey would have
refused for being too battered and a pair of gigantic wellies, and
told not to come back till I'd filled a laundry basket with
courgettes.

Just to be sure I knew what I was supposed to be doing, Brigitte came out of the kitchen and gave me a specimen.

"Voilà, this is what I want," she said.

"Yes, courgettes," I agreed, pointing intelligently at the courgette-shaped, courgette-sized courgette.

"Some city people mistake them for cucumbers."

"Not me, I am working five years in the food industry already."

"Ah, but I don't think you make tea out of courgettes," she said and, having put me firmly in my place, pirouetted back to her kitchen.

At this point, I must admit that a little matricide did spring to mind.

In fact it was fun playing the peasant for a couple of hours.

No matter where you are in the south of England, the city can always catch up with you in the shape of an off-road vehicle or a gang of mountain-biking yuppies. Not here. The vegetable garden was a hundred-yard-long, ten-yard-wide strip of cultivation in the middle of a medieval wilderness. On a gently sloping hillside, it was a sunlit clearing amidst huge, swaying chestnut trees. Even the rusting shell of an abandoned van looked hundreds of years old. It was one of those vintage French vans made out of corrugated iron, and now it was quietly biodegrading back into iron ore, with a sapling growing out of its back window and rotting wooden vegetable trays in place of its windscreen.

When I took a swig of water from the bottle I'd brought, my glugging was the only human sound in the world around me. The insects were humming, the birds were screeching, the treetops were swishing, and absolutely no one was driving cars at me. It wasn't as enjoyable as diving into the Med or on top of Florence, but spending an afternoon alone in the middle of France wasn't so bad after all.

Even though I was out here on my own, filling my basket with courgettes made me feel part of the family. Everyone had their task to do, and I was providing the vegetables. I hadn't felt this much at home in France in the whole ten months I'd been here, not even when I'd moved into Florence's apartment near the Père Lachaise cemetery, or when I'd first learned how to barge in front of someone to nab a Parisian café table. Now I was just like countless thousands of Parisians, enjoying a mild summer dose of peasant life at the family maison de campagne. It felt deeply satisfying.

This was the most productive kitchen garden I'd ever seen in my life—the courgette plants were hidden away amongst potatoes, tomatoes, green beans, aubergines, radishes, beetroot (I think), carrots, cucumbers, three sorts of lettuce, strawberries, raspberries, blackcurrants, a pear tree, and what looked like almonds. At the end of the vegetable patch there was also a small fig tree, with curled, springy branches, small unripe fruit and the phallic leaves we've all seen in paintings. The guy who first chose the fig leaf to camouflage his genitals got it exactly right—the long, central lobe of the leaf looks exactly like a hanging willy. Though he was a bit boastful about the size of his balls.

What I hadn't known about a fig tree is that when the sun is on its leaves, it smells delicious. The whole tree was giving off a glorious sweet fig smell that made you want to sit there and wait for a month until the fruit was ripe enough to eat.

The courgettes were surprisingly prickly, and annoyingly close to the ground. But whenever I got a backache I just went and raided the fruit plants.

This far south there were only a few kilos left on the raspberry bushes in early July, so I polished those off and then wandered down to the next row where there were several million strawberries. One thing was for sure—if I dropped dead from heat exhaustion, within a day my body would be sprouting fruit blossom.

When I staggered back into the garden with my full basket of courgettes, Florence was setting out glasses on a long teak table by the side of the house.

"The neighbours are coming for the apéritif," she explained.

"Think I'll have a quick shower," I said. "Can you, you know, show me where it is?" I accompanied the "you know" with an inquiring lift of the eyebrows, meaning, well, you know.

"I'll show you how it works," Brigitte said, arriving with an armful of alcohol bottles. "There is a knack."

I looked imploringly at Florence, but like a UN soldier without a mandate to intervene in a humanitarian crisis, she just shrugged and left me to my fate.

"Allez, Paul!" Brigitte had already got as far as the kitchen door. "They'll be here in ten minutes."

It was my first day at the kindergarten. Lesson one: this is a courgette. Lesson two: going to the bathroom.

Is it just me or does every shower unit in the world have a fiendish knack to it? Is this why we Brits preferred baths for so many centuries before we decided we didn't want to wash our hair in the sink any more?

With a bath, all you do is fill the damn thing. If the water's too hot, you add some cold. With someone else's shower, you need to be a kind of water DJ to get the mix right. And why is it always doubly difficult in a girlfriend's mum's bathroom?

"Turn on the water and let it run for two minutes," Brigitte explained, bending over the deep shower basin and pointing to the mixer tap. "It's a Butagaz water heater so you have to wait until the warm water arrives from the kitchen. D'accord?"

"D'accord." This is French for OK.

"Don't change the temperature, because otherwise after two minutes you'll freeze or get burned. D'accord?"

"D'accord."

"And don't turn it full on or it'll push the shower curtain out of the basin and wet the floor."

"D'accord." Very soon my ten-minute shower allocation was going to be used up and I'd have to meet the neighbours wearing a coat of sweaty dust.

"Put the shower curtain right inside the basin before turning on the water."

"D'accord."

"And don't put the plug in or you'll stain the tub."

I now found that my tongue refused to say "d'accord" any more. I nodded.

"And make sure you turn the water right off when you've finished."

I tried to nod but my head would only move a millimetre. My whole body was going on strike.

"But don't turn the tap too far or it'll get stuck."

All I could do was move my eyes up and down in agreement.

"And stay on the bathmat to dry yourself off, otherwise you'll leave wet footprints on the floor."

That was it. One more instruction and my head would fall off.

"D'accord?" she asked.

"Towel?" I managed to squeak.

"Use the big blue one. And hang it out on the washing line after you've finished otherwise it will rot. D'accord?"

I smiled, not only to show that I'd understood but also at the idea of hanging myself with the washing line and escaping from this maternal French version of boot camp.

4

T HE SHOWER DID its relaxing trick, and I was feeling at
peace with the world when I emerged into the garden
quarter of an hour later.

"Ah!"

I was greeted with a loud collective sigh of pleasure, as if I was
the guest who was bringing the only bottle.

"This is Pol," Brigitte announced, doing the usual French thing
of making me sound as if I was related to a Khmer Rouge dictator.

"Bonsoir," I said.

Sitting around the table were Florence's mum, brother and
nephew, Florence herself, and two suntanned old people who were
smiling broadly and toasting me with enormous tumblers of Pernod.

They were introduced as Henri and Ginette, lifelong owners of
the next farm down the road. I assumed they were husband and
wife, but they looked so similar that they might have been brother
and sister as well. It didn't seem polite to ask. They had the
carefree faces of aged children, and gnarled hands that bore the
scars of doing every menial job a small farm can throw at you. I
wondered if they fancied taking over from me at tomorrow's
cesspit-digging session.

"What are you drinking?" Michel asked.

Henri and Ginette gave an expectant "Eh oui?"

The foreigner's drinking habits were suddenly the most exciting
thing happening this side of the English Channel.

It was a difficult choice because I didn't recognize half the bottles. What were Suze and Banyuls, for example? I thought I'd risk it and go native.

"I'll try a Suze."

This got a bigger laugh than most of the jokes I'd told that year. Even little Simon joined in the hilarity.

"It is mostly a drink for the women," Florence told me, in English.

"Bon yool?" I attempted, and got another laugh, for pronunciation this time.

"Ban-yil-ss," Michel corrected me, and poured me half a pint of what turned out to be a port-like fortified wine.

Still, this choice seemed to satisfy everyone, and they all raised their glasses when I wished them good health. We clinked glasses, looking our clinking partner firmly in the eye as we did so. This eye contact is very important in France. They say that if you don't do it, then your sex life will be terrible for the next ten years. Even Henri and Ginette made eye contact, so there was clearly life in the old dogs yet.

The table was an obstacle course of apéritif nibbles—olives, pretzels, crisps, peanuts, and a plate of radishes that you ate with a knob of butter. I dug in. It felt like a long time since I'd gobbled that last kilo of strawberries.

The neighbours smiled at me with benign indifference as Brigitte explained that Florence and I were setting up an English tea room in Paris. I got the impression she might as well have said it was going to be a massage parlour on Jupiter. Paris? English? Tea room?

"The *Parisiens*, they like English tea?" old Henri asked. He pronounced it "Parisiangs."

"We hope so," I said, and got another big laugh. There was obviously a major joke shortage out here in the country.

"We get the Parisiangs here sometimes," Ginette said, as if it was a kind of diarrhoea.

"They rent old Yvonne's house," Henri added, provoking a discussion about what old Yvonne had died of (cancer, a heart attack or her homemade hooch?), which of her sons now owned her house, who had originally built it, when its roof had last been repaired, who'd repaired it, where he'd bought the slate to repair it, which slate mines had been the last to close in the region, and how to clean moss off slate (Brigitte looked at me meaningfully during that part of the conversation).

Henri concluded the debate with: "They complain because there's not one of those wash-things. What do you call them?"

"Lave-vaisselles," Brigitte said. Dishwashers.

"Oui. The Parisiangs have to have their lavevaisselle."

"We've just bought one," Ginette said, not contradicting him, just informing us of this piece of news.

"Yes, but we live here," her husband replied.

"Ah, oui!" Everyone agreed with this logic and chatted on, getting news about distant relatives who had died or gone to live in the city, trees that had been cut down, septic tanks that had been fitted, which vegetables were being eaten by pests this year, when in the last two decades there had been the most slugs, and whether old Yvonne put slugs in her hooch.

I sat there contentedly, watching the open, uncritical faces explore the farthest corners of small talk and enjoying the fact that I was so far from home but accepted as part of the community.

The world went orange then pink as the sun died and the alcohol reached my eyeballs. By eight o'clock I was full up and completely drunk.

"On passe à table," Brigitte announced. Dinner time? All I wanted was the chance to get some rest before my hangover.

Henri and Ginette went home—people were invited for drinks but not for dinner, it seemed. The rest of us filed indoors and squashed our knees against the table as we consumed vast quantities of roast pork, green beans, courgettes, lettuce, cheese, fresh strawberries and cherry clafoutis, washed down with enough coarse red wine to knock out a rugby team.

At ten o'clock it was pitch black outside, and the choice seemed to be between vegging out in front of the TV or going to bed. I knew which I preferred.

"I'll wash up," Brigitte said, then spoiled it by adding, "Henri and Ginette are waiting for you, Paul."

"They're waiting for me? What for?" Oh no, I thought, not the old "you're not sleeping with my daughter under my roof until you get married" trick. I'd come up against the problem with a lay preacher's daughter in Dundee once, but not in France, surely?

"Their field," Brigitte said.

"Their field?" So I was going to sleep outdoors?

"Come." Florence pulled me up out of my chair. I felt as if my weight had tripled in the last few hours, although I was pleased to note that the food seemed to have soaked up most of the alcohol.

Florence led me down the dark lane towards the silhouette of a farmhouse.

Apart from the moths fluttering in the beam of her torch, we were the only things moving in the universe. This was darkness like I'd never known it before. Even the light in Henri and Ginette's window looked like a distant star.

Feeling my fingertips on Florence's bare shoulder, I suddenly remembered that it had been almost twenty-four hours since we last went to bed in her apartment near the Père Lachaise cemetery—and a whole day of abstinence was a record for us back then.

"Why don't we stop for a few minutes?" I asked, trying my best not to beg. "No one will see us."

"Non, imbécile. They are waiting for us. Come."

She sped up, and my bloated limbs only just managed to keep pace.

When we opened Henri's gate, the old guy emerged instantly and turned on some kind of fog lamp that sent out a long, straight shaft of white light past Florence and me and into the lane.

"Did you eat well?" he asked.

"Oui, et vous?"

"Très bien. He was good, my pig, non?"

He explained that we'd just eaten some of last year's pet porker. Germain, his name was, and apparently he'd been like a family friend until Henri stabbed him and hung him up in the front garden to bleed out.

Henri led us further down the lane into the inky silence. The nocturnal ramble was very refreshing, and by the feel of my bare legs, it was also pretty enjoyable for the local mosquitoes. Though I still had no idea what we were doing out here.

After a hundred metres or so, Henri stopped and swung the beam of his lamp out into the night.

"Voilà," he said.

All I could see was overgrown grass and the spooky shadows of a couple of fruit trees.

"Voilà?"

"Voila."

"This is the field Henri told you about," Florence added helpfully.

"It's a beautiful field," I said.

"There are a few vipers at this time of year, but the chickens scare them away," Henri said. "They're sleeping now"—he mimed a snoozing chicken in case I hadn't understood—"but you can come and see them tomorrow."

"Tomorrow? Excellent," I said. Seemed I wasn't going to sleep out in the open after all, which was a relief. But no one had explained yet why I had to be shown this hectare of herbe in the middle of the night.

Oh God no, I thought, don't tell me that somewhere between two glasses of Banyuls I'd offered to mow this lot?

No, much more likely, Brigitte had offered my services. The French think we Brits are all experts with lawns, after all.

She was definitely asking to get murdered.

"Shoot," Florence said. She wasn't giving me permission to fire a gun at her mother, she was putting a finger to her lips and saying the French word for "sshh"—"chut."

We were back at the house, where everything was quiet apart from the muffled sound of the TV coming from the living room.

She took my hand and led me towards the bedroom. It was exactly like every man's dream—the beautiful French girl pulls you into her boudoir. You can just make out the large bed against the wall. Silently, you both shed your clothes and snuggle down between the cool sheets. Your lips seek out hers, and somewhere in the blackness they finally meet for a long, lingering kiss.

The only thing that isn't in the dream—well, not in my version, anyway—is a French boy's voice saying: "I can't sleep. Can I come into your bed, Florence?"

Yes, we were sharing a room with the brat.

"No, Simon, why aren't you asleep?" Florence hissed.

She stroked me apologetically on the cheek and turned away. The bed gave a loud creak. I rolled over on to my back to sulk in peace, and then, to my surprise, rolled straight back against Florence. I tried a second time. No, nothing doing—I was back in the middle again. There was something uncanny going on, and it couldn't all be down to the fact that I'd gained four tons in weight since lunchtime.

It turned out that the bed springs were totally knackered and had as much bounce as a deflated basketball. No matter how much we tried to stay apart, we rolled together again like drunks in a hammock. This would have been very pleasant (I didn't really want to roll away from Florence at all), but the bed was so spineless that my backside was about two feet lower than my feet and my head. I was lying down and sitting up at the same time.

"Let me guess, Florence," I whispered. "This was your great-grand-père's bed, wasn't it?"

"Oui," she replied. "He died in it. Goodnight."

5

WHEN I WOKE up next morning I was alone, face down, with my head on the pillow, my toes hanging off the end of the bed and my groin almost touching the floorboards. Intense lumbago was the first thing I felt, followed by gloom as I remembered that my misshapen back muscles were due to spend the day digging a cesspit or mowing a snake-infested field.

It took me ten minutes to straighten my spine and get back into my T-shirt and shorts, which were starting to smell distinctly rustic.

As soon as I was decent, I went to join the breakfast noises in the kitchen. And immediately regretted ever waking up.

Brigitte was walking around barefoot in a long pink cotton nightdress that made her look like an upright pig. It wasn't exactly see-through but it was thin with age and clung to her nipples, buttocks and a coral-like outcrop of pubic hair in a way that made me wish I was chronically short-sighted.

Even worse, Florence was wearing a floor-length, horizontally-striped green-and-yellow velvet dressing gown that would have made number two in a Least Sexy Garments Ever Worn by Womankind chart, after incontinence pants. She still had a young head, hands and feet, but the rest of her was an old-age pensioner on walkabout at the nursing home.

Holy shit, I thought, this is what rural isolation does for you.

Little Simon was sitting at the table, knees up to his chin, eating a squidgy-looking Nutella sandwich.

I'd read an article about French food which said that this chocolate-and-hazlenut spread is the glue that holds France together. Almost every kid in the country has Nutella for breakfast. Teenagers and jobless graduates turn to it with a spoon at times of stress. I'm sure it's the single reason why no one in France talks about nut allergy. Hazelnuts are in their blood. While I was still working for a French food company, a colleague brought her son in to see me. He was nineteen, a big lad with rower's shoulders who'd been offered a place at Oxford. He spoke great English and I could tell he'd fit in really well at university. And the one question about England that he was desperate to ask me was: "Can you buy Nutella?"

Simon gave me a chocolatey smirk and hummed along with the radio, where a voiceless French chanteuse couldn't understand why nobody loved her. Probably because she won't stop singing, I thought.

"Bonjour," I groaned.

Florence waddled over in her scary dressing gown, and I made sure I kissed her without touching the hideous velvet.

"Did your great-grandmother die in that?" I asked, not too loudly in case it was her mum's.

She frowned, raised her eyebrows at me as if I was forgetting something, then mimed kissing on both cheeks.

Oh God no, I just managed not to say, they kiss each other every morning.

I went and got Nutella smeared on my face, then edged over towards the sink, where Brigitte was scrubbing out one of last night's pans that she'd left to soak. Her buttocks were bouncing around in the nightdress like two bald men trying to escape from a tent.

"Bonjour, Brigitte."

"Ah, bonjour, Pol!" She turned, swiped me with her right breast, and gave me two loud, wet kisses. Her universal love was back, it seemed. "Did you sleep well?"

"Yes, very well." I didn't know how to say "for someone with a broken back."

"What do you drink in the morning? Coffee, chocolate, herbal tea . . ."

"We haven't got any herbal tea, Maman," Florence said mercifully.

"Ah yes, put it on the list . . . No, Paul, I know what you drink—tea." She pronounced the last word as if it was the star prize in a TV game show.

"No, thanks, I'd like some coffee please," I said.

"You don't drink tea in the morning?"

"No, coffee."

"I thought all Englishmen had tea in the morning."

"I prefer coffee."

"We've got some *thé Eengleesh brek-fass*."

"I'd like some coffee, please."

"If you're sure you don't want tea."

"I'm sure. Coffee, please."

Now that we were clear on that point, I gave my vertebrae another nasty surprise by wrenching them sideways to sit at the table. It was covered with packets of cereal, powdered chocolate and teabags, a plate of biscottes (miniature slices of dried white bread), a plastic bottle of sterilized milk, and an immense, round loaf, half of which had been roughly cut into thick slices. At one end of the table there was a cluster of bowls and cutlery.

In Paris I was usually a coffee-only man at breakfast, and grabbed a croissant at the boulangerie on my way to work, but today I thought I'd better get some starch inside me as early as possible.

I filled a white china bowl with cornflakes, on to which Brigitte poured black coffee.

A Corrézien way of saving time in the morning, I thought. Disgusting but undeniably clever. Why have your coffee and cereal separately when you can mush them together?

"Oh, what is he doing?" Brigitte laughed. "Look at him."

Simon screeched and almost fell off his chair, and Florence came over to join in the fun.

"Do you put cornflakes in your coffee in England?" Brigitte asked.

"No, it was you who . . ."

"Oh là la. Do you want some English marmalade in there, too?"

Brigitte chortled at my imbecility and took the bowl away. I turned to Florence for support, but she was arm in arm with Simon as they forced the last dregs of laughter out of their lungs.

"I hope you're better at digging than eating cornflakes," Brigitte said as she emptied my bowl into the slop bin by the window.

Of course, I should have remembered. Lots of French families have their morning drink in a bowl. My ex-girlfriend Alexa the photographer used to do that. Why French porcelain manufacturers don't bother putting a handle on all their drinking receptacles, I don't know.

"Are there any clean clothes in the house?" I asked Florence.

"Ah oui." She went off to the wardrobe in her mum's room and returned with a grey T-shirt and the most unpleasant pair of trousers I'd ever seen in my life. They had an elasticated waist and were made out of a blue-and-orange check material decorated with fist-sized red flowers. The design (if it was a design and not an industrial accident) seemed to have been conceived by an LSD flashback victim for use in homes for the colour blind.

Florence picked up on my lack of enthusiasm.

"They're African," she said.

"So is the Ebola virus," I replied. "Are they your brother's?"

"No. Oh, and are you going to take a shower?"

"I had thought about it, yes."

"Well, Maman says,"—at this, Brigitte's buttocks seemed to prick up their ears—"can you make sure you dry yourself off completely on the bathmat, because you left a wet mark on the floor."

"Of course I left a fucking wet mark on the fucking floor. It's a fucking bathroom, every fucking body leaves fucking wet marks on the fucking floor of their fucking bathroom," I wanted to say, but stifled the outburst with an attempt at drinking coffee from the large bowl that Brigitte had just given me. The hot liquid spilled over the sides of the bowl, slopped down my chin and burnt my fingertips.

"Do you want a straw?" Simon asked.

And to think that just the day before I'd been a fully fledged French peasant. Now I was the English bumpkin again, the outsider who couldn't even master basic skills like eating breakfast.

The problem is, and this sounds really obvious, that when you move to a foreign country you're a long way from home. What I mean is, you're a long way from your mates and your family. You're forced to fit in with everyone else. You don't have the comfort of knowing that later on, down the pub, you can tell everyone "and then she poured coffee on my cornflakes" and get some sympathy.

Of course, the situation is even more extreme if you have a Parisian partner. It's not so bad meeting their friends (though, like I said, you never know how many of them are exes), but the family is a different matter altogether. You're like a dog that has been adopted by another household, only to find that in the new family sofas are not for sitting on, bones are supposed to be eaten not buried, and everyone laughs when you start licking your backside. What's wrong with licking my backside? you think. Everyone does it where I come from.

6

I WAS LOOKING forward to getting outdoors and venting my frustrations on the land. Brigitte came down to explain to me how to hold the long-handled spade and how to fill up a wheelbarrow. I accepted her advice with averted eyes, because the strengthening sunlight was shining through her nightdress and showing me outlines I really didn't want to see.

I then jumped into the metre-deep hole and sank six inches into the clinging clay.

"Oh, and it's very muddy in there. Be careful not to get stuck," Brigitte said and left me to it, shaking her head.

Florence came for a giggle. She had every reason to. Along with my donkey hat and wellies, I was now wearing ugly trousers that were so huge I had to roll up the waist to stop them falling down, and a T-shirt that had been torn off just below the chest by someone who was determined to show off their six-pack. I looked like an eighties pop star who's fallen on hard times and had to get a summer job shovelling shit.

Florence, on the other hand, was looking totally gorgeous in bikini top and pareo, her long black hair bunched up on top of her head. If I'd been able to lift either of my feet I'd have scrambled up out of my hole and carried her into the barn, earth floor or no earth floor.

"I've got to help prepare lunch," she said. "I'll bring you a drink at ten."

"Ten? What time is it now?"

"Eight thirty."

"Holy shit, I must have got up at dawn."

In fact it was Michel who brought out a large glass of strawberry goo.

He was wearing faded blue boxer shorts and unmatching wellies—one green, one brown, both left feet. At least I wasn't the only one in comedy clothes.

"Wow, be cool, man," he said in English, with a Franco-American accent. "Don't dig so fast. We've got all the summer to finish."

"All the summer?" No way was I getting trapped here that long.

"Yeah, they will bring the new fosse septique in autumn." He walked down the plank that led into the shallower end of the hole and strolled over to scrape his cheek against my face. Men kissed men in the morning in this family, it seemed. Whether they'd shaved or not. Yuk.

Michel took over from me for a while and explained why his mother was acting the way she was.

"When she's in the town she's lost, man. It's a major trip for her to get a haircut. She loses her credit card two times a year. But here in the country, she has decided that she knows it all. Her plants die, and she's in a permanent panic that the house will fall on her head, but she feels in control and she tells herself she's a farm girl. That's why Papa refuses to come down here. Well, it's one reason."

"He never comes here?" I could understand why, but I was surprised.

"No. The people here accept us kids because they know us since we were babies. But a real Indian? No way. They are not racist, really, they just never see a guy with dark skin who's not, you know, emptying the . . . poubelles?"

"Bins. Garbage."

"The garbage men, right. And Papa has got this real complex about his class. He's a businessman, he says, not a garbage man."

"What sort of business is he in?" I'd never met Florence's dad. When we'd gone to pick up his car, he'd been away in India.

"He imports tissues."

"He's a Kleenex importer?" Good plan, I thought, in such a hypochondriac country. At my old office in Paris, they even sold packets of hankies alongside the chocolate bars in the food machines.

"No, *tissus*. You know, like, cotton. To make shirts and shit."

"Oh, fabrics."

"Yeah. He says he flies first-class to Bombay, but the peasants think that he's a garbage man. Also, he has a problem . . ."

Michel's voice trailed off tantalizingly.

"Problem?"

He stopped digging and grinned. "You know old Ginette?" He was whispering now, as if his mum was eavesdropping from behind the barn. Which she might well have been.

"Ginette? You mean old Henri's . . ." I didn't know whether to say wife or sister. Or both.

"Yeah. One night, Papa drank too much wine and chased her through the fields. Henri fired his gun to try and scare him, and he killed a cow. It was a big scandal in the village."

I could imagine it was, in a place where they could spend half an hour discussing slugs.

"And did your dad—you know—with Ginette?"

Michel laughed and began his leisurely digging again. "No, he came home, he went to bed, and next day he remembered nothing. Finally he paid for the cow just to stop the scandal."

"Wow." I gazed down through the trees towards Henri and Ginette's peaceful farm, the scene of such animal passion.

"So Maman comes here alone in the vacation and plays the expert, but, I mean, I spend much more time here than she does."

"You live out here?" It was hard to keep a note of incredulity out of my voice.

"No, I move around depending on my work. When I have no work, often I come here."

"What kind of work do you do?"

"I'm an electrician."

"An electrician and you have no work? Everyone needs electricians."

He laughed. "I'm an electrician in the movie business. So I have to wait very much between shoots. Especially because I like to work with American crews and they don't come here so often."

"But can't you get non-movie work between shoots? You know, fixing electrical problems in houses?"

He laughed again, as if this was the most surreal suggestion he'd ever heard in his life.

"Tell me about your salon de thé," he said.

As he dug, I stretched out in the grass and gave him the long, slow director's cut of my story. Out here, you had time to get into real detail.

I told him how I'd been headhunted by a Parisian company, got lumbered with a set of French colleagues who included my boss's mistress and a Hungarian-speaking walrus, and then been fired because I didn't fit in with the political ambitions of my boss Jean-Marie, the world's most charming hypocrite. He had won his local elections and was now rumoured, so I heard on the radio, to be a candidate in his party's next leadership contest.

"Vous parlez politique, c'est bien!"

A red-faced man with a beige check shirt and grey rocker's quiff was smiling down into our mudhole. A young Golden Retriever was panting happily at his side.

"Ah, Monsieur Ribout!" Michel dropped the shovel and held up his wrist to shake, as French men do when their hands are dirty.

Michel introduced Monsieur Ribout as the mayor of the village, and I went over to get my wrist shaken too.

"Ah, les Anglais," Ribout said. "You've invaded the Dordogne and now you're coming here, eh? You hope to go back to the days when your King Henri Huit wanted to possess all of France?"

My old boss Jean-Marie would have declaimed this anti-British sentiment with fire in his eyes and one hand holding open the ballot box, but Monsieur Ribout was smiling down at me as if my job in the English invasion was to bring free fruit cake for the locals.

"It is true," I said. "We British all want to live in France."

"Yes, but why is it that you all go to the Dordogne?"

"I don't know." It is puzzling why Brits have always congregated in that one département in western France. Apparently in the prehistoric cave paintings there, amongst the mammoths and the woolly rhinos, you can make out sketches of white-kneed *Homo sapiens*. These are prehistoric Brits, visiting the caves with a view to renovating them and renting out a side passage for bed and breakfast.

"Allez, les garçons, it is time for the apéro," Brigitte called out. It was always time for the apéro.

Michel and I washed our hands and joined the mayor, the ladies and little Simon at the teak table on the shady side of the house.

The usual bottles were there, but this time I stuck to beer. My change over from Banyuls naturally inspired a long conversation about national drinking habits, which ended in a general agreement that France's excellent wines and spirits produced the healthiest alcoholics in Europe.

"Ah yes! In women and wine, we are unbeatable." Monsieur Ribout emptied his glass of pastis and held it out for a refill. "But the women in this family prefer exotic men, eh? Eh?"

Brigitte and Florence blushed. "We Frenchmen have no chance with these women, eh?" He pinched Brigitte's cheek, and I imagined the two of them as teenagers in the village, playing hide-and-seek in Brigitte's knickers.

"That's why, since my wife died, I have to be content with my bitch here." He patted his Retriever pup on the nose and gave it a cheese biscuit. "Though she's English too, isn't she, eh? A Retriever, eh? What do you think of her, Pol? Should I marry her, eh?"

Out here in the country it might well have been a serious question.

"That depends," I said. "Can she cook?"

Before the mayor had a chance to tell me the pup's recipe for bone bourguignon, old Henri turned up to ask if I was coming down to his field. Luckily I didn't need to look for an excuse to say no.

"I'm taking Pol for a drive around the area," Monsieur Ribout said.

"Après la sieste," Brigitte decreed.

A siesta? Yes. Things were looking up. I pressed my unpleasantly trousered leg against Florence's thigh. She reached down and squeezed my knee.

Lunch was leftovers of last night's pig, with more beans, more courgettes, more lettuce, more strawberries and the second half of the giant clafoutis. We had coffee outside on the apéro table, and I managed to get ten seconds alone with Florence to ask where the siesta was going to happen.

In our bedroom, was the answer, and Simon usually siesta'd with his grand-mère.

I had to walk quickly to the bedroom, facing all available walls, in order to hide my delight about this good news.

After such a long period of chastity, I was pretty keen to get straight down to business, but I remembered my manners. French women appreciate old-fashioned courtesy in a man. They still like to have doors opened for them, to be given a red rose at the restaurant, to orgasm first. Old-school stuff.

So I pretended to wait patiently, sinking ever deeper into the mattress, as Florence closed the shutters and opened the windows, and then coyly removed her bikini top and her pareo to reveal that she had been wandering around knickerless. A chaste but knickerless French girl. It seemed such a sinful waste, like leaving a bowl of fresh raspberries to warm and ferment in the sun.

At last she rolled down into bed beside me, and we tried to find a position where we could press our bodies together in all the right places without rupturing any ligaments.

"Oh, one thing," she said as I was about to launch into a passionate kiss. "Maman says you don't have to dig any more."

The mention of "maman" reduced my passion levels, but not by much.

"Thank God for that. This is supposed to be a holiday, after all."

"She says you haven't been digging in the right place."

"What? It's a hole, there is only one place to dig. In the hole."

"She says Michel can finish the hole."

"But we were digging together, so he must have been digging in the wrong place, too." Why I was wasting time defending my spadecraft when I could have been enjoying some foreplay I have no idea, but something compelled me to do it.

Florence did a horizontal shrug.

"She never criticizes Michel. He's her little angel. Oh, he's driving me and Maman to the supermarket this afternoon, and we have fixed a rendezvous to go to the garage and get our luggage."

"At last, I'll have some of my own clothes. Whose are these clothes you gave me, anyway? Your dad's?"

Florence's laugh made the bed bounce. "No, Papa's as small as Maman."

"So who do they belong to, then? Simon's dad?"

"If you really want to know, it was an ex-boyfriend of mine." I thought I heard a tiny, defensive note of guilt. A twinge of jealousy stirred in my chest. And lower down, too.

"And when you split up he got all the CDs and you kept all his clothes? You were screwed."

"No." She put a hand up to my mouth as if to end the conversation, but like an idiot I wasn't finished.

"Everyone remembers this giant ex-boyfriend really well. That's why Simon was going on about me being small, isn't it?"

"Yes, he was physically . . . imposing."

"Imposing? What was he—a judo champion?"

Lying next to your naked girlfriend when you're dying to make love is not a good time or place for a fit of jealousy. And for some reason this particular fit was getting worse with every idea that popped into my head.

"It wasn't Nicolas the architect, was it?" I demanded.

"No."

"He's an ex of yours, though, isn't he?"

"Yes."

"Is he also a good architect?"

"Yes." Then, less decisively, "I think so."

"Florence, for Christ's sake."

My chances of making love were shrinking with every second. I took a handful of Florence's left buttock and decided to make peace.

"Let's stop talking about your family, your ex-boyfriends and our business worries,"—my libido didn't like that little speech, either—"and concentrate on more pleasant things."

"Mmm," Florence hummed her agreement and slipped a cool hand between my thighs.

"Allez, Florence!" Brigitte's voice was accompanied by a loud knocking on the door. "We have to go now."

"Now?" Florence sounded as surprised as I was suicidal.

"Yes, you know the hypermarket shuts early today. Départ dans deux minutes."

"Two minutes," I whispered to Florence. In my present state of terminal frustration it sounded like a whole night-time.

"Thirty seconds would be enough for you, eh?" she teased, and managed somehow to roll uphill out of the bed before I could prove her right.

I think France has abolished the "crime passionnel" law, but I'm sure any judge in the country would have ruled that there was sufficient provocation for bludgeoning Brigitte to death with a blunt courgette.

7

THERE WASN'T MUCH point staying in bed alone and waiting for my backbone to set at a right angle, so I got up and wandered around the empty house. Except for our bedroom, the rooms were all laid out in a chain. You walked from the kitchen into the lounge, from there into Brigitte's bedroom (where I kept my eyes shut to avoid catching sight of anything that might give me flashbacks later), and then into a hall with three doors off it—one to the bathroom, one to Michel's room, another to the garden. So basically, if I wanted to go to the bathroom, I had to go via the garden or through Brigitte's room. It was as impractical as the floor-level dinner table.

I went back into the living room and settled on the sofa, an immense pseudo-rustic creation with over-ornate wooden arms and rough, tasselled cushions.

The Tour de France was on TV. I'm sure that watching the whole race would teach you more about the French than a three-year degree course.

I've never understood the thrill of televised cycle races, but every summer the French go nuts for "Le Tour." They criticize cricket for being boring because it can last five days. But here's a race (so no ball, no goals, just endless slog) that lasts three bloody weeks. Days and days of watching unnaturally thin men in Lycra pedalling up and down mountains. A commentator giving the population size and local specialities of every town they pass through. Here's Grenouille-les-Bains, home to three thousand souls, famous in the region for its disused slate quarry and spectacular floods.

But the crowds were loving it, and every kilometre of roadside verge seemed to be covered with spectators, some of whom had set up camp. They waved at the cameras for their five seconds of fame. In one of the helicopter shots I saw a huge painting on the road surface. A massive white phallus with the inscription "Je t'aime, Sophie." The route was announced months in advance, so you were sure to get your graffiti on TV if you timed it right. The commentator wasn't fazed at all by the giant—and very detailed—penis. He just made a comment on how romantic the locals were and they cut to the next scene of sunburnt men on bikes unwrapping protein bars.

I was almost sorry when the mayor rapped on the kitchen door and called out, "'Ello, eez somm-body?" in deliberate cod-English.

He'd dressed up in a pink shirt and grey suit trousers, and had either bathed in or drunk a whole bottle of cologne. He put my torn-off T-shirt, grotesque trousers and smelly shoveller's armpits to shame, but it didn't seem to bother him.

"Viens, viens, we will go for a tour," he said in his heavy accent.

The engine was running in his flash Citroën, and the air-conditioning was on ice-cold, which was a blessing, because the sun was at its highest and trying to roast every piece of vegetable matter in sight. And there was a lot of vegetable matter about. Whole hillsides of neatly pruned, angular apple trees, their fruit golfball-sized and growing. High, old-fashioned hedgerow, dividing fields of grass and cereals that followed the contours of small valleys rising up either side of bullrush-lined streams.

There were no humans, though. We saw their farms—little clusters of buildings like Brigitte's place, with a few outbuildings and the occasional chicken pen or duckpond. But no people. All asleep, I guessed. Or watching the Tour de France.

"Where are we going?" I asked.

"To town. I have to say two words to the curé."

We passed a concrete-walled cemetery, then pulled into the square next to a squat stone church and a school bus stop.

"You wait over there," Monsieur Ribout told me. On the other side of the square was the Mairie, like a tiny two-roomed classical château, and a simple war memorial with a stone First World War soldier standing at ease as if waiting his turn to go and get shot. Apparently there's only one village in the whole of France that lost nobody in the trenches.

But Monsieur Ribout wasn't telling me to go and pay my respects to the dead. Well, not exactly. He was pointing at the nondescript glass-fronted building in one corner of the square, marked Café de la Mairie.

Back then, I didn't understand something very important about sitting in a café in a non-touristy part of rural France. The people aren't necessarily unfriendly. It's just that they're so unused to strangers that they don't notice you. Or if they do see you, they don't know what to do with you. The barman knows what every one of his customers drinks at any time of the day, so the arrival of a non-regular doesn't compute. Why is there someone sitting in Marcel's seat when Marcel's been dead for three years?

I wished everyone a friendly "bonjour" and made eye contact with all the men who looked my way. The customers were all men, their ages ranging between thirty and death. There were about ten of them, and at least half had moustaches. The air was full of smoke, beer and Tour de France commentary, an ambience that was being wafted lazily about by a ceiling fan.

Several of the men replied to my greeting, but the only one I really wanted to talk to didn't react. The barman was taking a slug from a glass of beer and listening to the twangy patois of an old guy sitting at the bar.

Oh well, I thought, they'll know Monsieur Ribout. He'll get us served.

The local paper was lying on the table, and I deciphered the front-page report about all the accidents on the region's roads. No mention of my crash, but then it wasn't in the same league as a Vel Satis clocked at two hundred kph on the autoroute, and a wine lorry that had skidded out of control and caused sixty kilometres of jams as people stopped to help themselves to free bottles of Côtes du Rhône. The perfect wine for the thirsty driver, it seemed.

"Salut, Pierre!"

There was a chorus of hellos as Monsieur Ribout strode into the café carrying a plastic bag full of cucumbers.

"What? You haven't served my English friend yet?" he said, dumping the cucumbers on my table and going to shake every-one's hand. He harangued them all for being unsociable, and the younger men came over to shake hands and say bonjour. The older ones seemed to be stitched in place on their bar stools.

"Viens, viens," Ribout called, and I went to stand at the bar like a real man. He explained who I was, which elicited a lot of nods and aahs.

"Didn't you use to be taller?" one of the men asked.

"Yes," I said, "before the operation."

"No, but didn't Brigitte's girl have—" the questioner went on.

"And your wife, doesn't she have a lover who's two metres tall?" Ribout interrupted.

Laughs, backslaps and insinuations killed off any more talk about Florence's ex.

Minutes before, I'd been sitting alone and ignored, and now we were getting offers from all the men to go and have a drink at their place.

"No, not now," Ribout said, downing his coffee. "We've got some visits to make back at the village."

We shook hands all round and left, with Monsieur Ribout promising to go for an apéro at everyone's house within the next week. One sure way of making a fortune out here, I thought—set up a liver-transplant clinic.

For the next two hours, Ribout drove me around to say hello to practically every farmer within three miles of Brigitte's place. There were oldies whose kids had gone to work in the city—meaning Limoges, Tulle or Brive. There were younger couples whose kids were planning to work in the city. It was rural depopulation before my very eyes.

I sat at tables in a dozen kitchens and ate strawberry tart, strawberry cake, strawberry mousse, strawberries in red wine or just plain strawberries. The downside to eating seasonal food is that you eat nothing else for the whole damn season.

I drank wine and cherry eau de vie. I was welcomed everywhere with smiling curiosity and presents of strawberries and courgettes. The bag of cucumbers was for me, too, a gift from the curé.

I was shown around fascinating barns and enticing septic tanks. I was offered the chance to shoot at rabbits—"they won't run away," dig up moles—"you only need a hundred skins to make a waistcoat," and watch TV—"we can get three channels here, really clearly, too."

By five o'clock I was drunk, overflowing with strawberries and dizzy from such a concentrated dose of country life.

"We'd best go home for the apéro," the mayor announced.

We were standing at the top of a hill, in a gaggle of houses near the centre of the village, and somehow I managed to scrape together enough energy to have a constructive thought. Up here, my phone might actually work, whereas Brigitte's place was down in a basin, hidden from every phone mast in France. Trust her arrière-grand-père not to foresee the coming of the mobile phone.

"Can I just see if I've got any messages?" I asked the mayor.

"Mais off course," he said in his fake English, and went to sit in his car.

I hooked up to the outside world. It was almost a surprise to discover that there still was one. There were three messages, including a text from my ex-girlfriend Alexa.

We'd been together for the whole of the previous winter, and I'd been certain that she was The One—great to be with, buzzing with crazy ideas, and pretty damn good to look at, too. But I'd fucked up, and we hadn't been in touch for months, not since we split up for the second time. The first time had been because I slept with someone else by mistake (it can happen), and the second was after I made a bad joke about a politician (it can't happen enough). Now it seemed kind of stupid. How can you end a relationship over something so unrelated to your relationship? It seems reasonable to end it because you've slept with someone else, because you realize you have nothing to say to someone, or even because your girlfriend makes you dress up in her ex-boyfriend's clothes, but not because of politics. But then Alexa was a serious girl.

The message she'd left was only half political. It seemed she was lightening up. "Well done," she wrote in her fluent English, "I heard u left ur job when u discovrd ur boss was fascist." This wasn't quite true, but I wasn't going to deny such a flattering interpretation of my getting fired. "Where ru now?" she asked. "Starting salons de tea? In Fr or Eng? I am in Eng."

Maybe it was because Florence was pissing me off with her exes, but I chose the "appeler" (call) option.

"'Allo?"

I made a "just one more minute" gesture to Monsieur Ribout.

"Alexa, hi, it's Paul. I just got your message."

"Paul? Hi. Where are you?"

"Standing on a hill in Corrèze."

"Corrèze?"

"Yes."

"What are you doing in Corrèze?" As if no one would ever dream of going there.

"Trying to digest about five tons of strawberries."

"Ah, yes, you and your digestion. I remember the effects of your Christmas pudding. A great example of the noisy English digestion."

"It wasn't the pudding, it was the French custard. there weren't enough lumps. It's the lumps that help us digest our Christmas pudding."

"Remind me not to come for Christmas lunch at your salons de thé. Are you starting them?"

I told her about the September opening, she told me her news— she was in England visiting her mum who'd now gone to live over there.

"You remember, she was in Moscow with the Ukrainian DVD man?"

"What, and now she's found an English DVD pirate?"

"No, he has come to live in England. It is safer. He is buying a football team."

"A football team? Which one?"

"I don't know. Newcastle something."

"Newcastle United? Holy shit, that's one of the biggest clubs in England. Are you sure he's not dabbling in second-hand plutonium?"

"Maybe. I will tell him you want to know."

A car horn broke the spell. I was enjoying myself after all the smalltalk with the farmers. Jokes were back on the menu for Alexa and me, it seemed.

"What's that? Your girlfriend is getting impatient?" she asked.

I turned to see old Ribout miming "time for a drink" through the windscreen.

"No, it's the mayor of the village. We're late for his Pernod. I'd better go."

"OK, bye."

"Bye, Alexa. It was good—"

But she'd gone.

"Who was that? Un ami anglais?" Ribout asked.

"Yes, he's an old English friend," I replied, wondering why I lied. It must be the sexual frustration, I told myself. My genes were trying to cast their net more widely. But they were just being stupid. I wasn't seriously going to start fantasizing about an ex-girlfriend, was I, any more than I would fantasize about Brigitte.

"What's wrong?" the mayor asked as I clenched my eyes shut and tried to pound the image of Brigitte's nightdress out of my head with both fists.

When we got back to the house, I was reunited with another old friend—my bag. At last, I could feel almost human again and not like some half-sized apparition from Florence's past. I changed into some clothes of my own—loose things, so that I'd have room for another gargantuan dinner.

We had terrine of calf's head, followed by cold pork and the usual landslide of annoyingly abundant green vegetables. I struggled gamely through the meal until it came to the strawberries, when I really could not force another one of the shiny, red bastards down my throat.

While everyone was clearing the table I suggested, at a volume so low that bats would have had problems picking it up, that maybe Florence would like to come for a quick stroll in the dark.

Brigitte must have had her Batgirl costume on under her kaftan because she declared that it was our turn to wash up, after which Florence had to read Simon a story.

I sloshed soapy water about for the required time then went and passed out in bed. At least in my dreams I stood a fair chance of getting laid.

8

THE NEXT DAY, Monday, turned out to be the last full day of our country vacances.

It was yet another gloriously sunny morning, I noticed as soon as I woke up around six. That perfect, pollution-free blue sky was one thing you could never get fed up with.

After breakfast, during which Florence passed on the news that I'd let water get down the back of the sink last night while washing up, which was probably turning the foundations of the house to cold porridge as she spoke, I said that I was off to have a shower. I put a meaningful hand on Florence's knee (she'd given in to my pleading and sworn never to wear the velvet dressing gown again), and let her know that this was an invitation. The only way to avoid being disturbed, I reasoned, was to lock ourselves in the bathroom. If anyone did knock, I'd just tell them that my poor English digestion was confused by all this fresh food and needed half an hour of uninterrupted concentration.

Florence reached down to rub my hand and it looked as if we were game on.

So as I showered, I was feeling decidedly happy at the prospect of us soaping each other down and then finding some way of making love in the bathroom—lay some towels out on the floor? I sit on the loo, she sits on me? The possibilities were endless and all equally enticing.

I let the water massage the top of my head while I pictured

various scenes from a hardcore porn film entitled *Amour dans la Salle de Bains*. When Florence finally snuck in, I was, let's say, fully geared up to play the male lead in the movie.

"Lock the door and come on in," I whispered. I pulled back the curtain to let her see how pleased I was to see her.

And there was Brigitte, a toothbrush in her hand and a strangled squeak in her mouth.

From the look on her face, you'd think she'd never had a man open a shower curtain and point an erect penis at her.

From the time it took for her to look away, you'd think she was afraid it would never happen again.

I found Florence standing by the barn in her bikini. She was holding a broken, rusty knife. Was this it? I wondered. Was I being offered the honourable way out? Hack off the offending member and let's say no more about it.

She gave me an "oo-err" look and I gathered that words had been said between mother and daughter.

"What did she tell . . ." I began, but Florence silenced me with a frown. Maternal ears were on red alert, it seemed.

"You're not picking courgettes today," she said.

"No?"

"No, you've been picking them too small."

This was the last straw—or courgette. Digging in the wrong place, showering incorrectly, and now this?

"But surely it's best to kill the bloody things before they grow too big," I said. "This place is suffering from a courgette plague. Pretty soon the whole département will be taken over by courgettes. They'll block all the rivers and smother the apple trees. Courgettes, cucumbers and lettuces. Why is it that you plant the only vegetables in the world that you can't freeze?"

Florence shrugged. The problem of controlling a courgette population explosion came a poor second to keeping her mum happy, which was fair enough, I suppose.

"You're scraping the moss off the roof," she said. "There's a ladder in the barn."

"Any particular scraping technique I'm supposed to use? Forehand? Backhand? Underarm? Tell me now, because I'm bound to do it wrong otherwise."

"Paul . . ."

"Meanwhile you can call your friend Nicolas and make sure they're starting work this morning, right?"

"Hey, a bit less aggression, please," she whispered. "It's not my fault you exhibited yourself to my mother. This situation is not easy for me, you know."

She was looking annoyed but apologetic. Maybe there was a chance of a consolation shag coming my way soon, I thought.

I was just hauling the antique, half-rotten ladder out of the barn when a high-pitched voice started calling "Monsieur" behind me.

I turned to see two gendarmes—one approximately two metres tall, the other half his size—standing by the gate. They were both approaching retirement age, and both were in immediate danger of weight-induced diabetes. There was probably a sweepstakes going round the gendarme station as to which would be the first to burst his trousers.

Florence and I arrived at the gate at the same time, with Brigitte looking on from the kitchen door.

The gendarmes saluted.

"Monsieur Wess?" the little one said in his strange high voice, mistaking one of Florence's breasts for an Englishman to judge by the direction he was looking in.

"Oui, c'est moi."

"Did you make a complaint against a driver for leaving the scene of an accident?" Now he was under the impression that Florence's navel was the plaintiff.

"Yes. Did you find him?"

"Ah." He looked pained, apparently because he'd just noticed Florence's bare legs. "The gendarmes in Montpellier found the person who corresponded to the number you gave, but, ah." He stared apologetically at Florence's crotch. "He said he wasn't at the scene of the accident."

"What?" I said this so loudly that he finally tore his eyes away from Florence. "But we saw him."

"He says you are making an error."

"Mais c'est ridicule!" Florence looked as if she was about to thump one of the policemen.

"Calmez-vous, Madame," the short guy said, though he was obviously hoping she'd need some physical restraint.

"But did you check that he has a red 4WD? Because if he does, then that proves we are right," I said. Pretty devastatingly, I thought. "All you have to do is take some paint from our car and see if it . . ." I couldn't remember the word for match. "Corresponds," I said. The French use that word a lot. "See if it corresponds with his car. And if it does, then our complaint . . . corresponds."

"Mais quel enfoiré!" Florence wasn't having any of this reasoned debate. "It's my father's car. It was brand new. This enfoiré crashed into us on a roundabout and you're not going to do anything?"

"Madame, Madame." The squat one held his hands out as if to ward off an attack by Florence's chest.

"Do you know how many accidents there were this weekend?"

the taller gendarme asked, looking as exhausted as if he'd had to write the report on every one of them.

"I don't care how many accidents there were!" Florence shouted. "This enfoiré crashed into us and he's going to pay for the damage."

I really must look up that word enfoiré, I thought. It seemed very fashionable. I knew it meant idiot, but I didn't know what sort.

"Have you seen our car?" I asked. The gendarmes shook their heads. "Because if you can tell your colleagues in Montpellier, yes, there is red paint on our car, and if you can show that the number of his car . . . corresponds to a red car, we are not making an error. N'est-ce pas?"

I could tell that this sentence had been too long. They wouldn't have time before retirement to think through that much logic.

"Do you know Pierre Ribout?" Florence demanded.

This had a lot more effect than my logic.

"Pierre, oui, bien sûr!" The mayor's name seemed to evoke happy memories of many an apéro gone by.

"Because he is a very good friend of our family," Florence said.

Which gave me an idea.

"Come and have a drink," I said. "It is much too hot to talk in the sun."

There didn't seem to be any rules about not drinking on duty, because these two settled in at the apéro table and saw off almost a whole bottle of wine while Florence and Brigitte lied to them about how Monsieur Ribout had seen our car and noted the particular redness of the dent.

I could sense the gendarmes' resistance weakening as the wine settled into their ample bellies, and I broached the subject of going to the garage to look at our car for themselves.

"Will you promise to go?" I asked, my glass raised as if for a toast. I wasn't used to drinking at nine in the morning, so I was tipsy to say the least. "Vous mettez votre main sur votre coeur et vous promettez?" Will you put your hand on your heart and promise?

At this the two gendarmes exchanged an anxious glance, emptied their glasses and stood up. Florence was staring at me open-mouthed. Brigitte was hyperventilating. I wondered whether it might be treasonable to make gendarmes swear an oath.

"Mesdames, Monsieur." The small one nodded, backed out of the garden and squeezed himself into the car. The tall one followed him, holding his képi in place with one hand and his crotch in place with the other. Weird.

"Are you mad?" Florence asked me when they'd driven off.

"What do you mean? All I said was . . ." and I repeated it, in French, putting my hand over my heart this time, to stress my meaning.

"Oh, Paul."

Well it wasn't my fault, was it? It's the way we Brits say things. We call a car a cah, a bar a bah. We don't pronounce our r's. So it's not my fault if when we say "cœur" it sounds as if we're saying "queue." And you can't blame me if "queue" is a rude word for penis.

Surely the gendarmes ought to have known that I'd never tell them to "put your hands on your dicks and swear." Did they think I was some English Mafioso who'd castrate them if they didn't go and look at the red paint marks on our car?

Well, yes, they obviously did.

Then it struck me. Why has no one ever mentioned it before?

All those English tourists asking directions in Paris: "Excusez-moi, Madame, where is the cathedral of the sacred dick?"

Brigitte had to go and lie down to get this second helping of male genitalia out of her nervous system, and there ensued a short row between Florence and myself about whether I'd permanently screwed up our chances of getting the bad driver to pay damages, during which I learned a new word. Not a swear-word, exactly, though Florence was using a few of those. I discovered that French drivers are so bad that they have a special word for them. The normal word for driver is "chauffeur." A bad driver is a "chauffard." Bad driving is such an institution that it's made it into the dictionary.

I ended this row with some simple retaliation. If I was screwing up some things, maybe she was screwing up others.

"Did you call Nicolas?" I asked.

Florence blushed and her whole body swerved away from me as if to avoid the question.

"Oui."

"Well, is he at the tea room? Has work started?"

She suddenly seemed excessively interested in a small lizard crawling up the wall of the house.

"Pas tout à fait," she finally admitted.

"Not completely? They haven't *completely* started? What does that mean? It's like saying the baby's not completely born. I mean, has it popped out of mummy's tummy or hasn't it?"

There ensued yet another short row. This one was about the possible motivations for choosing an architect. Top of my list: he or she is a good architect. Down there at number fifty (in my view at least): I used to shag him.

This time it was Florence who got in with a killer question.

"But didn't you tell me that your motivation for coming to work in France was to see women's lingerie?"

"Well, yes, but I haven't been seeing much of that in the past two or three days," I huffed.

"No, because I haven't been wearing any." She hooked a long finger in the top of my shorts. "And I won't be wearing any tonight. And little Simon is going to stay with my uncle in Brive."

Florence certainly knew how to end a row in style.

As the sun climbed higher and began to bite into my arms and legs, I shaved off half the barn's moss moustache, scraping away with the knife until every mast molecule of green was gone from the smooth grey surface of the slate. Some of the tiles had been replaced with asbestos, I noticed. I didn't scrape those, and prepared a little French speech in my head in case Brigitte complained. I'm sorry, Brigitte, but your ancestors have already destroyed my knees and my spine—I'm not giving them my lungs as well.

Michel woke up just before midday apéro time. He scraped his increasingly unshaven cheeks against my face and gave me a hand clearing away the clumps of moss littering the lawn at the foot of the barn wall. I knew the word for asbestos—"amiante"—from when I'd tried to buy a country cottage the previous winter, so I explained about the toxic roof.

"Boh," he puffed, as if I was scared of pricking my fingers on a courgette plant. He climbed the ladder and started hacking away at the soft grey tiles. The knife sent mossy pellets and asbestos flakes raining down into his face, but it didn't seem to bother him.

Had no one told the French about this stuff? I wondered. But then the tiles were stamped with the name of a French manufacturer, so I guessed not. It'd be bad for the economy to slag off a local poison.

Apéro time went surprisingly well. Brigitte was bubbly and talkative, as if the wet-flasher incident had never happened. Monsieur Ribout came over, dog in tow, for a quick drink and announced that there was going to be a party at the Salle des Fêtes that evening, and we were invited. Especially me.

"Pourquoi moi?" I asked.

"Ah!" Big surprise, it seemed. I just hoped I wasn't going to be asked to judge the courgette-of-the-year competition.

After a lunch of neighbour's pig and unfreezable vegetables, I offered to make coffee for everyone.

"We'll have it outside," Florence said, and went into the garden with Michel and Simon.

"No coffee for me," Brigitte said. "I'll have tisane." Herbal tea. "I'm going to lie down. Can you bring it to my room?"

Oh no, I thought. Will this be her chance for revenge? The naked siesta?

The French love their herbal tea. Not strawberry tea or cranberry or any of those sweet concoctions that we Brits go in for. The French drink infusions made out of different sorts of shrubbery. Some of it's not bad, if you like boiled twig. Personally, though, I'd rather endure a bout of gastro-enteritis than have to drink camomile.

At first I couldn't find any herbal stuff amongst the packets of tea and coffee, then I remembered. They'd gone to buy some more from the hypermarket. It was probably a test, I thought. Will Paul have to come and ask for help? No, he won't.

I found the big cupboard where Brigitte stored her recent

shopping and there, right at the front, was a transparent glass jar with a flowery label saying "Verveine." Verveine is verbena, though I have no idea what verbena is. A type of shrub, that's for sure. Inside the jar were some extraordinarily complicated muslin sachets, like frilly little testicles. Must be very high-quality shrub, I thought.

I made the coffee and carried it outside while the verveine brewed. When the tisane was a sickly green colour, I poured some out into a thin china cup (why couldn't they use these at breakfast? I wondered) and psyched myself up for a lightning delivery mission. Into Brigitte's bedroom, cup on bedside table, out of there. Don't even look at the bed.

And it went perfectly to plan. I saw out of the corner of my eye that Brigitte was lying on her bed in her kaftan du jour, reading. Phew, no nude nap. She didn't even have time to look up before I was out through the doorway and back in the lounge.

I joined Florence and the others in the garden and had just enjoyed my first sip of coffee when the scream erupted from the house.

We all stopped in mid-sip or stir and looked at each other. Had we heard correctly?

The second scream confirmed that we had. Florence and Simon leaped indoors. Michel and I followed on cautiously, in case it was strictly a women's problem.

Brigitte's bed was empty. The only signs that she'd been there recently were her discarded book and the upturned china cup. From the bathroom we could hear gagging sounds and choked half-sentences of female conversation. A tap was running.

Florence came out of the bathroom frowning. She picked up the cup from the bed and sniffed it.

"What did you give Maman to drink?"

"Verveine."

"Show me."

I did.

"Imbécile," she moaned when she saw the packet.

"What?"

"These are for the bath."

"What?"

"They've got soap in them. They're bath crystals parfumés à la verveine. Didn't you read the ingredients?"

"Read the ingredients? Of course not. I don't read the ingredients on tea and coffee packets. It said verveine on the label. How was I supposed to know you bathe in the same stuff you drink? We Brits don't drink soap."

"Oh, Paul! Maman drank almost the whole cup in one go. She thinks you tried to poison her."

"Oh merde."

Michel, Florence and Simon all looked at me solemnly, trying to work out whether I was a bad tisane-maker or a particularly inefficient killer.

Luckily for me, it was Michel who laughed first. Poor Florence had to go back to the bathroom and help her mum to puke up the soapy water. We three boys were able to go outside and roll about on the lawn, howling up at the pure blue sky.

9

I APOLOGIZED, of course, and took it like a man when a distinctly pale Brigitte asked whether the customers in my tea room were going to get similar treatment.

As penitence, I spent the afternoon with Michel taking it in turns to scrape the toxic and non-toxic roof tiles. (Yes, who was trying to poison whom round here?)

Brigitte didn't emerge for the apéro or dinner (for which I subversively cooked pasta), and Florence said she oughtn't to be left alone.

"I can't come to the Salle des Fêtes with you. I have to stay with Maman."

"You'll come with me, won't you, Michel?" I begged.

"Ah non, ça m'emmerde." This kind of thing bores him, literally "shits him up." It's like "faire chier". The French seem to have real psychological hangovers from their toilet training.

All this meant that I was alone as I wandered up the hill in the purple dusk. Huge mosquitoes tried to head-butt me to the ground and siphon off my blood, but I swatted them out of the way and plodded doggedly onwards and upwards, heading for the pool of halogen light around the Salle des Fêtes in the centre of the village.

The Salle looked as if it had been a gift from Soviet Russia in about 1970. It was modernist and proud of it, with glass walls jutting out of the ground at various angles, like the trajectory of plutonium particles in the first milliseconds after a nuclear explosion.

The main hall covered an area about the size of three or four tennis courts, but because of the angular design there seemed to be only about ten square feet in the centre where you could actually organize a fête. Through the windows I could see that this area was taken up with a long plywood trestle table covered in bottles.

I recognized all the faces I could see—they were the people Monsieur Ribout had taken me to visit. The only names I could remember were Henri and Ginette.

As soon as I walked through the double doors I was greeted with another of their aah's. This one started out with one voice and grew as other people saw what the aahing was about and joined in.

How come they're all so pleased to see me? I wondered. Surely it wasn't because they'd heard about my murder attempt on Brigitte?

"Pol!" Ribout got up and took me by the arm. His dog was snapping at his heels. The two of them shepherded me over to the table and I went all round shaking hands. The women shook my hands, too, presumably because I was too young and foreign to kiss. I was the youngest by at least thirty years.

It was swelteringly hot in this abstract goldfish bowl—the sun had been heating the air since early May, and now at least ten people were replacing the oxygen with smoke. No one else seemed to be sweating, though. The men looked very comfortable in their Sunday-best shirtsleeves, and a couple of the women were even wearing light cardigans. I was in T-shirt, jeans and flip-flops, but feeling that everything except the flip-flops was extraneous.

We raised glasses of warm red wine and toasted the Queen and the memory of Princess Diana (or "Leddy Dee" as they called her).

I had a few conversations along the lines of "I expect it's not as hot as this in England" and "so you live in Paris, do you?" while

Monsieur Ribout looked on benevolently, as if I was a stray puppy that was putting on a good display of tail-wagging and was about to find itself a new home, just like his Retriever had done.

When he finally joined in the conversation, everyone stopped talking and listened.

"Do you see that house across the road? That used to be the café," he said. "And the commune" (the village) "has just bought it. We're going to open it as a café again. We've got the licence."

There were nods of approval, and someone reminisced about the last owner, who, if I understood correctly, had hanged himself in the back garden.

"And we have a little shop that's open in the mornings. But we have the tabac licence so we're going to find someone who'll open it all day."

"And Sunday mornings," a woman at the end of the table chipped in.

"And Sunday mornings," Ribout confirmed.

I drank a sip of congratulations, and felt it instantly shoot out of my pores as sweat.

"We have a Dutchman living in the village, but he doesn't try to integrate. He comes in summer, and at Easter, sometimes at Christmas, but he drives here in his camping car and he brings everything with him. We see him unload his cans of beer, his packets of cheese."

"And his PQ," someone added, and got a big laugh. PQ was toilet roll, I knew. Short for papier cul, arse paper.

"But the English aren't like that," Ribout went on. "There are some English families over in Tulle, and they live in their houses most of the year. And they buy local cheese and wine."

"And PQ," the same man added, and got a bigger laugh.

"They integrate," Ribout said. "This is why the Dordogne still has its markets. The English even send their children to the local school."

A circle of smiling faces seemed to suggest that the healthy state of the Dordogne's economy was all thanks to me.

"So we are happy that you have decided to come here. You are the first, but as soon as there is one English person in the village, others will come. We know this."

The faces were still smiling at me, but my expression of goodwill to all men had faded ever so slightly. What was Ribout saying here?

"We are sure that you will find what you are looking for in one of the houses you have visited."

"Or fields," Henri said, raising his glass to me.

"Yes," Ribout said, "if you prefer to construct, I can guarantee that you will have no problem with the building permission, if you see what I mean . . ." Chuckles all round. "The same goes if you wish to renovate to your taste in the English style, it will be no problem. And of course it is so much cheaper here than in the Dordogne."

They were all looking expectantly at me. I'm sure my half-smile was stuck to my face like a pickled anchovy, just hanging there waiting to fall off and reveal the grimace of horror beneath.

Strangely, my first thought was not, How could they think I'd want to spend the rest of my life in this place? Because I could see the upside of living in a village where the biggest sources of stress were Who shall I have the apéro with today? and What the hell am I going to do with five tons of unfreezeable fruit and vegetables?

No, my first thought was, I'll kill that Brigitte. She set me up, inviting her neighbours round to sell me their field and then getting the mayor to take me on an estate agent's tour of the region.

But immediately afterwards—and this is where the horror kicked in—came the thought, Florence. That first evening, Henri and Ginette must have thought, bingo, un Anglais, and improvised from there. Otherwise they'd have taken me down to the field in the daytime, wouldn't they? You don't sell a house or (I supposed) a field when all you can see is its current population of moths and mosquitoes.

Florence must have known what was going on when she walked me down that lane. And when I went off for the afternoon to be force-fed strawberries by every farmer who ever voted for Ribout. And she must have known what was going to happen tonight. I doubted very much whether every boyfriend she'd brought chez Maman had got a civic reception like this one.

She also knew that I'd tried—and failed spectacularly—to buy a house in the country the previous year.

This was the biggest case I'd ever known, and I have known a few, of dropping your boyfriend in the merde.

"Merci, merci," I mumbled, clinging desperately on to that anchovy of a smile. I took a big gulp of wine, and let Ribout refill my glass. "I am very . . . touched. Your words . . ." I couldn't think of a verb to finish the sentence. "Your words really . . . correspond."

Everyone nodded happily. Maybe it meant something after all.

"But I must return to the house now," I said. "Brigitte is a little bit ill." Thank God I poisoned her, I thought. What a brilliant excuse.

"Oh no!" So they hadn't heard about the verveine incident yet.

"Yes, a mystery illness. We don't know what it is."

I stood, grinning as if the dentist was trying to photograph my new dentures, and shook everyone's hand farewell.

*　　*　　*

Outside in the warm but smokeless air, I poked at my phone, speed-dialling Alexa. At that moment she just seemed like the most sensible, and most neutral, person I knew. The only person who would understand what was going on.

"You are stuck in Corrèze?" she asked, and I could hear the amusement in her voice.

"Oh yes." I headed out of sight of the Salle des Fêtes and told her everything. Not just the house-buying stuff but the wet marks in the bathroom, my inability to pick the correct size of courgettes or dig the right sort of hole, and the attempted poisoning.

I was halfway down the hill by the time I'd finished, and I stopped walking so as not to lose the signal.

"It is simple," Alexa said. "Both my parents have been in therapy since before Sigmund Freud" (she pronounced it "frod") "invented therapy. So I know. Liquid is sexuality. The wet marks in the bathroom, even the herbal tea, it is a sexual exchange."

"Exchange? No way."

"Yes. She herself is the house, the bathroom floor. And the courgettes are phallic, of course." She wasn't joking either. "The digging? It is sex, that's for sure."

"No, it was just digging a hole, Alexa. With a spade, not my—"

"A big, hard spade?"

I thought back to the shovel's long, straight handle. My God, if it had been painted pink it couldn't have been any clearer.

"And she said I wasn't digging in the *right place*. Oh no."

"Oh, yes, she wants you to dig with your spade somewhere else. Like between her legs."

"Alexa, stop, please."

"I'm sorry, it is very clear to me."

"OK, OK. But it's all over now, she doesn't want me to dig any more. She's got me cleaning moss off the barn roof. So she's calmed down, right?"

Alexa thought about this. "How do you clean this roof?"

"With a knife."

"Hmm. She is probably fantasizing that you are shaving her pubic hairs."

"Oh God save me."

"What?"

"Now she wants me to hose it down."

"Yes, you see, it is so clear. She wants you to shave her and then spray her with your hose. Or maybe, when your courgettes are big enough for her . . ."

"No, please, Alexa, stop! This is all bullshit. They're just random household tasks. Picking vegetables, digging in the garden, cleaning a roof. Totally normal country stuff." Though I had to admit that wandering around in a see-through nightdress and accidentally-on-purpose getting a faceful of my dongler were not quite so normal. "But now that I've tried to poison her, she'll take it as a kind of subconscious message, won't she? Leave me alone or I'll kill you?"

"Yes, don't worry, I expect it will stop now."

"Thank God for that."

"And apart from this, everything is going well?" Alexa laughed. "Oh, poor Paul." She sounded almost nostalgic.

"Yeah, yeah, what about you?"

"I'm coming back to Paris in two or three weeks from now," she said. "I will work on a film."

"You're making films now as well as taking photos?"

"Trying. This is a—how do you say—work experience? On a real feature film."

"Wow."

"They're filming some scenes in Paris and I will be an assistant. You could come along one day. But I don't suppose you'll be in Paris?"

"I don't know. What if they won't let me leave this place?" She laughed as if I was joking.

When I got back to the house, things were in uproar. All the lights were on, and the front and back doors were wide open. Florence and Michel were running about with cloths and mops.

"What is it?" I asked.

"It's Maman," Florence said. She was wet and soapy from the knees down. "She got up to turn on the washing machine and forgot to put the hose in the shower basin. The machine has just pumped ninety litres of soapy water over the bathroom floor. It has gone down into the cellar, too, and soaked all the vegetables you picked."

"Ninety litres of warm soapy liquid? Out of a hose? All over my courgettes?" Brigitte had gone into Freudian meltdown.

That was it, I decided—as soon as the water was mopped up, we were getting out of the house. Out of the village. Out of Corrèze. Somewhere where there were no spades, no mossy roofs and no courgettes. Definitely no courgettes.

2

Can You Be Arsed?

1

THE FRENCH ARE pretty shameless about telling politically incorrect jokes. There are lots of gags about the people from Auvergne being stingy, the Swiss talking slowly, and the Belgians being of less than French intelligence.

Take, for example, the one about a Belgian who falls down a lift shaft. As he falls, he thinks (in his guttural Belgian accent), hey, this isn't too bad. It doesn't hurt at all. No, still doesn't hurt. Still doesn't hurt. Still doesn't hurt. Ouch.

OK, not exactly hilarious, but I was laughing inside because I'd turned into that Belgian.

I was heading for a collision with the Earth at a hundred mph, and I was feeling great. This was going to be the tenth, twentieth time, and I just kept coming back for more.

I was speeding up now, two hundred mph at the very least, with my feet in the air and my head full of noise. I was thinking, falling out of a plane without a parachute would be a fantastic experience if you could enjoy the freedom of flying without worrying about what was going to happen when you hit the ground.

Things got bumpy, then dark, and the world flipped over on to its back. I felt my neck about to snap, and then whoosh, everything was normal again and I was lying on my stomach, grinning breathlessly towards my topless girlfriend.

That last wave had been bigger than the others, and it had

wrenched the bodyboard out of my hands and somersaulted me over. Time for a rest, perhaps.

I picked up my board, tipped my head to the right and left to empty my ears, and walked up the sand towards Florence. She was lying stretched out on an immense orange bath towel, her eyes closed, meditating (I hoped) on how good it was to have put a few hundred kilometres between us and her mother.

We were on the île de Ré, a thirty-kilometre ribbon of an island off La Rochelle. On the map it looks a bit like a scrawny chicken leg with a long, curved foot at its western end. Actually it's not really an island at all, because now—after much environmental wrangling— an immense suspension bridge has hooked it to the mainland.

We'd only been here a couple of days but I had already come to the conclusion that Ré contained everything you could possibly want from life. Unless you were an Arctic explorer, trainspotter or rhino hunter, I suppose.

For a start, the small town where we were staying had a daily market selling local seafood and enough melons, nectarines and apricots to help me forget that courgettes and strawberries even existed. There was a great stall selling bright and breezy island wines that lifted your spirits without hammering them back down again too violently. It also stocked a yeasty beer from the micro-brewery in the centre of the island, and if I didn't fancy drinking it at home, there were plenty of bars and cafés where the other customers were just as anonymous as I was.

The breakers on the Atlantic side of the island were big enough for a belly-first amateur like me to get some white-knuckle thrills, but not so huge that they attracted the clever bastards who try to disembowel you with their stand-up surfboards if you dare to go for "their" wave.

In early July, it was also a sock-free zone. I find that when my toes are on the loose, the rest of me feels that much freer to wiggle and enjoy itself too.

And then there was Florence, liberated at last from maternal inhibitions.

Florence was the perfect girl to go on holiday with (I thought back then)—not only was she shaped as if the bikini had been invented especially for her, she also had an almost inexhaustible capacity for enjoying sex, or at least for faking it very convincingly. There are girls who do that "Oh, don't worry about me, you enjoy yourself" thing that makes me feel totally inadequate. Not Florence. She was definitely not the woman Madonna had in mind when she wrote "Like A Virgin." She was more like the girl in "Do It To Me One More Time."

We were staying in her dad's seaside holiday home, which had three bedrooms and even more beds, plus a couple of sofas and a jumbo bathtub, all of which had seen action in the short time we'd been there.

And as I stood over her on the beach and let two droplets of seawater drip from my hair into her golden navel, I couldn't wait to get back to the house and start again.

It's a stupid guy's trick, I know, waking your girlfriend up by splashing her with cold water. But it's irresistible. She squeals and writhes, her stomach muscles tighten, making the flesh rise up around her belly button and her breasts swell and jiggle. Then, if you're lucky, she smiles welcomingly up at you and you just want to kneel down and kiss that smile hello.

"Isn't it about time for me to rub some more sun cream all over you?" I asked.

"But I haven't been in the water."

"Well why don't I rub it all off then rub some more in? You can't be too careful about protecting yourself against sunburn."

"No, but I must protect myself against your sandy hands."

Oh well, no rush, I thought, and crashed out on the bath towel beside her. We weren't one of those couples who do separate beach towels.

"You're all wet, Paul, go on your own towel!"

Spoke too soon.

We were lying on a long, white beach on the north-west coast of the island, up on the chicken's foot. It wasn't a developed beach at all—the only way you could buy something to eat or drink was from the student shoving a trailerload of refreshments back and forth along the sand. About a mile away, near the old lighthouse, there were a couple of massive Nazi blockhouses that had tumbled off the dunes and on to the beach, but on the stretch where we were lying there was nothing but sea, sand and sunbathers. It was as if all of human history had been devoted to beach holidays. What a great place the world would be if that was true, I thought.

Even though my mind was taken up with such noble sentiments, it was impossible to ignore the fact that a lot of guys were committing Florence's naked breasts to memory. But as long as they stopped short of photography (I did lean over and block the view of one guy who was pretending that he had to point his phone towards Florence to get a signal) I honestly didn't mind. Mainly because I was free to get my fill of all the other fine specimens of sun-roasted femininity around. This bit of the beach was like a photo shoot for a swimwear catalogue for which the bikini tops hadn't been delivered. And we were on the fringe of a fifty-yard section where none of the swimwear had turned up at all. There, the beach towels were populated by middle-aged all-over tans, shaving rash, and tattoos in places I would have preferred not to know about.

I couldn't look at the women without being reminded of

Brigitte. And why, I wondered, when the guys got up to swim, did they all feel obliged to spend several seconds gazing down at the fleshy little bundles hanging between their legs? Their looks of self-satisfaction suggested that the tourist office really ought to mention their genitalia in its list of the island's architectural highlights.

Not being a regular at nudist beaches, there was something about the male body I hadn't noticed before. Something they don't show you in naughty films, either.

"Look at him," I said to Florence. "Over there on the right, the guy with the paunch and the hairy nipples."

"Yes?"

"He's got big puffy balls and a small dongler."

"Dong-leurre?"

"Yes, his todger, you know, his *queue*."

"Ah yes." She lay back down again, totally unmoved by my breakthrough in human physiology.

"It's not so much a pair of walnuts and a chipolata as two kiwis and a button mushroom. Don't you think that's weird?"

"Honestly, Paul, it is not because a man's zizi is small when it is in repose that it is not big when it gets excited." She sounded protective, almost as if she wanted the guy to hear. "You know, quite often a man has what looks like a small queue, but when he is dans le feu de l'action you get a very pleasant surprise."

"OK, OK, I get the message, thanks." There are some things about a woman you don't want to know, like how extensive a study she's done of the excited zizi.

"You have a complex?" she asked, opening one mocking eye.

"No, should I?"

"Ah, les hommes." She closed her eyes again, the better to philosophize. "You all have something to offer, you know. And the best men are the ones that know what they have to offer, and who offer it generously. Without wanting to make you feel arrogant, mon chéri, you are a spontaneously generous boy."

My mood gave a little jump at this, as did my surfer shorts.

"But with other men," she went on, "sometimes you have to reassure them that they can be generous and show them how. I remember one man, his zizi was much smaller than yours, but he . . ."

It's a basic rule of life, I guess. As basic as the one about not stepping into a lift shaft without checking whether there's a lift there first. Don't comment on other guys' zizis or you may be heading for a fall.

2

LIKE ANY GUY, as soon as I get on a bike I start suffering from sex problems. Chromosome problems, to be precise. I personally don't want to pedal as fast as I can—it's my male chromosomes that are craving for speed.

Now they were urging me to leave Florence behind as she cycled slowly back to the house. They wanted me to charge off and explore side trails, go on ahead then double back to meet her, or at the very least zig-zag along no-handed.

As it turned out, though, I was pedalling as fast as I could, and I would still have lost a race against a one-legged lobster. This was because a stone shed round the back of Florence's dad's house was home to four of the oldest, rustiest bikes known to man. The frames, wheels, chains and handlebars were flaky brown; even the tyres were rusty, and I'd always thought that was a scientific impossibility.

They'd been there when he bought the house, apparently, and Florence insisted that we should use them, even though they transformed what would have been a six-kilometre jaunt along the flat, well-tended cycle lanes into a clanking, squeaking battle between two lumps of old iron and our vulnerable legs.

Admittedly, there's something sexy about a beautiful girl on an old bike—it's the contrast, like serving a hot dessert with ice cream. But there's nothing at all sexy about having your coccyx fractured by a bone-hard saddle and non-existent suspension.

Every crack in the cycle path vibrated up through my pelvis and threatened to dislodge teeth.

Getting back to the house on that rusty bike was only a bit more painful than our meandering trek across France to get to the île de Ré.

The morning after Brigitte flooded her bathroom, I'd got Michel to drive us into Brive, where we'd caught a local train across the Dordogne. The *train régional*, a tiny TGV, was so new that people would get on and say "Oh, pardon" because they thought they were in first class. None of the other passengers crossing the Dordogne in comfort were English-speakers, by the way, which goes to show how much we've lost the habit of taking the train because of the dire state of our own railways.

The smooth, air-conditioned part of the journey ended when we got to Bordeaux. A main-line train was waiting for us (the French railways are very polite like that—they wait for connecting trains to arrive), but we hadn't reserved a seat on it. And this twenty-carriage monster was crammed with people who'd booked well ahead for their migration up the west coast from Biarritz to Nantes. If it hadn't been for the holiday smiles and the beachwear, you'd have thought the whole of southwest France was on the run from a Spanish invasion. Eight-seat compartments were full of picnicking, chattering, card-playing families whose suitcases were blocking corridors or balanced precariously on luggage racks threatening to give snoozing grandad a violent wake-up call.

Florence and I battled our way through two carriages, crawling over people and bags like spiders on a coal heap, before giving up and plonking ourselves outside a first-class toilet. Here, we were disturbed every one or two minutes by disapproving passengers who suspected that we weren't of the required class to be in their carriage, and finally by a ticket collector who said we had to pay a supplement for standing outside such a privileged toilet.

I paid up, but only on condition that he found us a seat, which he did. One seat, which I gallantly gave to Florence while I returned to play concierge outside the executive washroom.

We got off the train at La Rochelle, and went to stuff our bags into the baggage compartment of a stiflingly hot coach. But after half an hour in a traffic jam to get across the bridge to the island, suddenly we were in a holiday zone and it felt right to be sweating in a sunbaked bus. We were driving through villages of low, white houses with sunburn-coloured roof tiles. The people wandering about were half-undressed and totally unhurried, clearly on their way to or from the beach. Florence took off her T-shirt to reveal her bikini top, and I was now sitting next to a beach babe.

Signs by the roadside promised cheap bike hire and fresh seafood, or pointed the way to campsites, hotels and holiday villages. Even the posters for the itinerant circus, with its garish clown and lost-looking elephant, managed to give off a holiday buzz.

Everyone was staring intently out of the windows now, taking in each little detail of the place they'd be staying in for the coming fortnight. Or, knowing the French, for the next month or two.

I say "everyone," but a select group of our fellow travellers did maintain a studied indifference to the holiday scenery. Our bus was the shuttle for the daughters of the island's rich summer residents. They all had golden ponytails, tight sleeveless tops and logo'd sunglasses, and were permanently hooked up to their phones or MP3 players. At pretty well every stop on the island, one or two of the girls got off, to be met by a leather-skinned parent in torn shorts and a car with a Paris region registration number, or by a barechested, barefoot big brother in his Mini Moke.

Florence and I were heading almost to the far end of the island, to the wonderfully named little port of Ars, which was pronounced just as rudely as I hoped. I'd insisted on buying the bus tickets myself, purely for the thrill of getting on and asking the driver, "Do you go as far as arse?" There are English cities where that would get you killed. And I was looking forward to my next Paris dinner party, when the conversation would turn to holidays and I'd be able to tell a girl, "I love arse."

All in all, a great place to buy a holiday home, if only for the postcards you could send to all your friends.

Now, for the second day running, we were on the boneshaking bike ride from the surfing beach back to Ars.

Clanking across the île de Ré was made even more difficult by a sidewind that was trying to use my bodyboard as a sail to blow me into the ditches. The cycle path ran beside ripening vineyards and irrigation ditches that carried seawater to and from the salt marshes. Between hedges and clumps of trees you could see small piles of white salt that had been raked up by the sauniers, or salt-collectors. Apparently they flood their chess-board fields and then block off the flow, letting the water evaporate away in the sun until they can rake up the crust of salt that is left behind.

A young guy, naked except for a wide-brimmed straw hat and a pair of washed-out, rust-coloured shorts, stopped raking as we passed and waved to Florence. I was in too much pain to wonder who he was.

The worst thing was that my suffering was entirely unnecessary. A minute's walk from the house there was a cycle shop where I could have hired a brand-new machine with a saddle that would have caressed the parts that were currently getting bruised and chafed. But Florence refused to even consider changing for something more practical.

"It's OK for you, you have a little more padding in the saddle area," I argued. "Not too much padding, of course, and very picturesque padding . . ."

"No, Paul. My family has always used these bikes and I don't see why we should change just because you're not used to cycling. Your bottom will soon acclimatize."

"If it doesn't fall off first."

"We are not changing." And that was final.

I could have ignored her and hired myself a bike, but when you're a guest in someone's house, in someone's country, you try to avoid snubbing them. At least until the pain gets unbearable.

However, her attitude made me start to think that there was a basic difference between our outlooks on life. I was under the impression that my opinion was occasionally worth taking into account. Florence didn't seem to agree.

Of course I'd asked her why she hadn't warned me about Henri's field, and why she hadn't mentioned that the party at the Salle des Fêtes was probably supposed to end in a game of bingo with my bank account as first prize.

She just shrugged it off. Did it matter, she said, what a bunch of old farmers thought? She knew I had no intention of buying a house or a field there, so what was the point of worrying me?

It might have saved me some embarrassment if I'd known why everyone was plying me with drink and strawberries, I said.

And it might have saved her some embarrassment, she countered, if I hadn't made her mum puke up all over the bathroom floor.

Stalemate.

*   *   *

At last, after a good half-hour of pedalling, with my buttocks clenched to stop the narrow saddle from trying to get too intimate with my colon, we hit the bike jam that meant we were nearing Ars.

It was a typical Parisian traffic jam, adapted for two-wheelers and transported five hundred kilometres across country. Mountain bikes, boneshakers and Tour de France imitators had to get in line as we rolled wheel to wheel along the last few hundred yards of the cycle path and then clogged up the road that ran past the quayside restaurants and the (ahem) rent-a-bike shop.

Five minutes later, we turned into the lane where Florence's dad had bought his house. It was cute, like most of the houses in the town. A two-storey, terraced fisherman's cottage with grey-blue shutters and a tiny courtyard where a passion-fruit plant grew like a vine up a stone wall. We stowed the bikes in the shed, and I decided it was time to face up to the fact that nobody was going to answer my silent prayers that the old tetanus traps would crumble to dust during the night.

"I'm sorry, Florence. Tomorrow morning I'm going to rent us some decent bikes."

She tutted. "You do not understand, do you, Paul? You have not noticed the difference between the bikes we ride and the bikes that other people ride."

"Yes, I have noticed that difference. Theirs go in a straight line and don't clank like medieval windmills. That's what I'm saying. I want to be the same as everyone else. I want to belong."

"Ah, no. We are the ones that belong. I will show you tonight when we go out for dinner. Now stop arguing about bicycles and come and help me get all the sand and sun cream off my body."

"OK." There are, after all, some things in life that are more important than bicycles.

3

I T WAS EARLY EVENING. The sun was still out and glinting off the low rooftops of Ars.

Florence and I were strolling hand-in-hand along a flowery lane that was just yards from the town centre but silent and deserted. High garden walls were draped with creeping clematis and plants that I didn't know the names of. Fig and apple trees hung out into the lane.

Florence was giving me a French sociology lesson.

"You see? Bright-green paint looks good here, doesn't it?" She tapped on the glossy window shutters of a newly renovated house.

"Yes, it kind of livens up the grey of the stone."

"Hmm, but is very nouveau. And that one, oh!" She pointed across the street. "White shutters are totally ignorant. Did they not want to pay for coloured paint? Do they think they are in Paris? These are much better." She paused to pick a tiny flake of dull green paint off an ancient, peeling shutter. "This green is acceptable, as long as it's faded like this. But none of these are really the correct colour."

"No?"

"No, no one in this street has it. The correct colour is the one my father has used. That grey-blue, that is the real colour for windows and doors on the île de Ré."

"And people really care about this stuff?"

"Oh, yes, come and look at some people."

Time for a bit of anthropology.

The main drag from the town centre to the marina was busy with cars, bikes and pedestrians. It was a one-way street, but cyclists were ignoring the traffic signs and going against the flow. Again, just like Paris.

We stopped on a street corner and Florence pointed out a man to me. A tall guy, about fifty, unshaven, slightly unkempt, with an air of salt incrustation, was wandering along like a round-the-world yachtsman who's mislaid his catamaran.

"I will bet you that his shutters are exactly the right colour."

"Is he a fisherman?" I asked.

"Huh, no. He is almost certainly from Paris, or maybe La Rochelle. A summer resident. Look at his watch, his shoes, the sunglasses on the string hanging around his neck. You see, he shows discreet signs of wealth so no one thinks he really is a drunken old shrimp fisherman. But when he goes to the market, he will talk to the fishmonger as if they had caught the fish together. It is all snobbery. And look at this guy."

A handsome teenager was passing on a rickety old bike. His loose white shirt and old Levis were creased and stained, making him look as if he'd spent the last six months living on the beach, rolling up at night in blankets of dried seaweed.

"Rich kid," Florence snorted. "He will have a rusty car, too, probably even a rusty surfboard."

There were so many levels of inverted snobbery going on that I started to get dizzy. Here was Florence, a Parisian who looked down on people because their bikes and window shutters were too nouveau riche, looking down on people because they were doing exactly the same thing as her. Why didn't she just give up and get herself a decent bike?

There was nothing rusty and rickety about Florence this

evening. She'd left her old bike at home and was looking stunning, her golden skin oiled and aromatic, with a Lycra top and white trousers that left no one within fifty yards in any doubt that she was sporting top-class lingerie. Her bra straps were out, and the T of her thong arched up out of her waistband as if it was trying to tell the trousers to get the hell out of there. Her hair was loose and brushing the curve of her naked shoulders, her navel was at its most navelsome, the tiny bulge of her lower belly was achingly kissable.

We had an apéro at a café in the church square, then headed towards the quay. I clutched Florence's hand, mainly so that no one would try to kidnap her.

"No," she said, "you are just accompanying me. When you go to dinner, you do not try to look like a fisherman any more. You must display me, show me as if I was the first prize in the game show of life. The Kama Sutra game show. You have won me, and at the end of the evening you will be taking me home and enjoying every possible pleasure of my body."

"Well that's true, isn't it?" I hoped.

"Probably. But you do not look proud enough of this fact."

"OK." I didn't really know what the correct protocol was for displaying your girlfriend like a sex toy, but Florence seemed to be happy with the way that I placed one arm on her waist and held her hand in the other, as if accompanying her in a Jane Austen-type dance.

At first sight, the restaurant was a bit disappointing for two people who'd just won the Kama Sutra game show. It was a large, pale-blue shed next to a semi-abandoned garage that had an old mechanical rake dumped on its forecourt, presumably some kind of salt-gathering implement.

The interior was a combination of white wood, fishing nets and dried flowers that would normally have sent me running to fetch the style police. Even so, three groups of casually chic diners were already queuing just inside the entrance, trying to get a table. A beautiful young waitress with a pierced belly button was frowning a refusal.

We'd reserved, though, and she took us out into the garden, to a small table set against an olive tree. If we'd had a jar of brine with us, and a few months to spare, we could have pickled our own apéritif nibbles while we waited to order.

Another young girl, a friendly but witheringly cool brunette, came out with a menu written on a blackboard. She perched it on a chair next to our table and left us to cogitate. As she turned away she revealed a plunging backline and a snake tattoo that spiralled up from her skirt. If the food was as tasty as the staff, we were in for a treat.

A man at a nearby table stopped the waitress as she walked by. He was a slightly younger version of the rich-but-lost fisherman we'd seen earlier, dressed up in a Lacoste pullover and polo shirt.

"We'll have a bottle of our usual wine," he said.

"Which is?" the girl drawled. Ouch.

Dinner was tasty as well as tasteful. We each had a whole roasted sea bass, or bar de ligne, the "de ligne" meaning that it had been caught with hook and line and not in a drift net. This place was popular because it was good, I realized, not just because someone had decided that it was fashionable.

But Florence managed to spoil my dessert (a strangely named but delicious "soupe de pêches"—cold "peach soup") by telling me that "Papa" was arriving next day.

"Here?" I asked.

"Yes, here. It is his house."

Though it had been more fun while it was just our house. And it meant that we'd have to go round changing the sheets on the extra beds we'd rumpled.

"He says he's very impatient to meet you," she said.

"Oh yes?" Call me a coward, but I wasn't particularly impatient to meet the guy whose car I'd helped to crash.

NEXT MORNING I was up before Florence was awake, and decided to sort out the most pressing (literally) of my problems.

"You should have come here on Saturday afternoon or Sunday morning," the oily-handed bike-rental guy told me.

"I wasn't on the island. I was in Corrèze."

"Ah." He sympathized deeply with anyone who'd been in Corrèze. "This is all I have left."

He nodded his headbanded surfer hairdo towards a top-of-the-range mountain bike with enough gears to get me up Everest backwards.

Ré is a totally flat island. An averagely tall heron could see right across without wearing high heels. So all I really needed was two gears—one to get started, one for cruising. The machine he was offering me was so hi-tech I was looking for the remote control.

This was an emergency, though, so I paid a week's hire—approximately what it would have cost to buy a normal bike outright—and went for a test ride around the half-asleep town. Compared to one of Florence's bikes it was like riding on a cushion of warm air. It took only two or three presses on the pedals to propel me to the church square.

Opposite Ars's black-and-white steeple there was a large café terrace, filling up with people who'd just been to buy their newspapers at a shop called Ars Presse, which sounded to me like an illegal wrestling move. Next to the newsagent was the post office, a grand, grey-shuttered old building that was just about to open.

As the church bell started to strike nine, the postmistress ambled out of her house, crossed the square and unlocked the large shutter barring the main door. This revealed a sticker on the glass entrance—"accès Internet." I quickly padlocked my bike and nipped inside, the first customer of the day.

"We're not open yet," the postmistress told me. She smiled warmly, the expression of a woman who is very glad indeed not to have been put in charge of a post office in the industrial northeast.

"I just want to read my emails."

"Ah." She pointed at a green iMac by the window. "Do you know how to turn it on?"

"Yes."

"OK, go ahead. Can you open the shutter, please?"

"Of course." I pushed back the heavy shutters, turned on the computer and inserted my phone card in the slot. Nothing happened.

"You need a special card," the postmistress informed me. She was now behind the counter. "I can sell you one." She held up a plastic package.

In the few seconds it took for me to walk to the counter and complete the transaction, a thirty-something guy with sunglasses perched on top of his head strode in, saw what was happening and made a beeline for the computer.

If I hadn't had almost a year of practice dealing with French queues, I might have groaned and resigned myself to second place. But I was at the peak of Parisian fitness, and stepped sharply in front of him.

"I was already here." I sat down and inserted my card before he had time to object.

"But . . ."

"He was already here." The postmistress backed me up.

The guy grumbled unhappily and slumped down on a chair against the wall behind me. I could feel his every impatient breath on my neck as I logged on.

My list of emails included one from my American poet friend Jake, and one from Alexa. Hmm.

I decided to save that one. I often keep the most intriguing email in the list till last. If there'd been one from the architect Nicolas with the subject field saying "We've started work on the tea room," I'd have opened it straight away. But Alexa? Something made me want to savour her.

There were two or three emails about the tea room, all boring workaday stuff. Creating a company had been surprisingly simple, but ever since that day I'd been receiving an endless stream of letters and emails from various social-security offices, health-insurance companies and small business organizations, all wanting me to pay them a couple of hundred euros to go away and leave me in peace. This was all Florence's department—accounts—I decided, and flagged them for follow-up.

"Will you be finished soon?" The loser of the race to read emails was leaning over my shoulder.

"Two more to read," I told him, as if it was any of his business.

I read Alexa's next. The guy had spoilt the idea of leaving her till last.

She had attached a file. I heard the guy behind me groan as I clicked on it and the aged computer opened a tell-tale blank window for the download. It wasn't my fault that the post office didn't have broadband, I thought, but I hoped Alexa hadn't sent any images. Even though I was now as good as a Parisian at pushing in, I still had my British guilt complex about making people wait for me.

She'd sent an article on the interpretation of dreams about water. It reminded me of the first email she ever sent me, which included a text by some guru about how joy and sorrow were inextricably linked. And when she gave me the elbow, she'd quoted the know-it-all guru again, saying she thought I was only capable of sorrow, not joy. It was a self-fulfilling prophecy, wasn't it? Of course I wasn't going to feel joyful about getting dumped.

This essay on wet dreams brought back too many nightmarish memories of Correzian shower curtains and orgasming washing machines, so I clicked back into the email.

"What a joy to read that I'm not the only person to be sexually harassed by water," I told her. "And talking of sexual harassment, how are you getting on with Newcastle men? Having bilingual problems?"

This had been another of her theories—that people of different linguistic origin couldn't be happy together because they would never truly communicate. Again she'd proved herself right by dumping me.

As I hit send, something made me hope she'd say she wasn't getting the chance to have bilingual problems with an English guy, although I had absolutely no right to think that. I was with Florence, wasn't I?

"So this is your last email," my shadow asked me, or informed me, when I opened Jake's message. I ignored him.

Jake was his usual self. Ever since I'd met him the previous autumn, his English had been withering away like a virus under attack from French antibodies. It took me all my knowledge of French to decipher what he was trying to say.

"I'm enchaining with a new part of my poesie project," he'd

written. He was carrying on with his poetry project. This was his ambition to sleep with a woman of every nationality living in Paris and write a poem about each encounter. Last I'd heard, he'd been trying to decide whether a girl from a Bosnian Serb refugee family would do for both Bosnia and Serbia. Could an ethnicity count as a nationality and vice versa? If not, he was going to spend the rest of his life chasing after exiles from hill tribes in Thailand. "But now I have decided to edit myself in line." He was going to self-publish on the Net. "Have you other ideas for titles? If not I'll rest with mine." He'd originally intended to get the poems printed, and I'd suggested (not seriously, of course) the title "Around the World in Eighty Lays." Well at least it was better than his (totally serious) proposal, which had been to change the first "o" in "Controversy" to a "u." Oh yes.

I'd asked him if he could imagine anyone going into a bookshop and ordering that.

If they were too prudish to ask for it, they didn't deserve to read it, he'd replied (or Franglais words to that effect). Fine, I said, but that won't help you pay your printing bills.

Now he was writing to tell me that he thought his title was perfect for an on-line publication because everyone who typed the c-word into a search engine would automatically access his poems. As if it was poems they were searching for.

"Go for it, Jake," I replied. "But I can't promise you a link from my café's Web site."

I was about to sign out when I saw that Alexa had replied. She was online.

"I thought that was your last email?"

I turned to face the guy.

"If you are impatient, buy a computer," I told him. "Or come before nine o'clock to wait. I am waiting fifteen minutes here before the post office was opening." When dealing with an impatient Frenchman, always go for the big lie, and don't worry if he doesn't believe you. He already hates you for making him wait.

"You did not buy this computer." He'd taken the sunglasses off and was waving them at me as if he wished they were an empty wine bottle.

"No, but I pay to use it, and I have—" I pretended to check the counter ticking away at the bottom of the screen "—forty-five minutes if I want them. So if you will permit me . . ."

French has so many ways to say "fuck you" politely.

Alexa had sent another attachment. This time it was a biggie, but my self-righteous outrage stopped me caring how long it took to download.

I soon wished I hadn't bothered, though. The photo that slowly materialized was of Alexa and a guy. Hunky, blond, pleased with himself, one arm draped over Alexa's shoulder.

She was looking more beautiful than ever. Her hair, a darker blond than the guy's, was cut short and spiky. The nose I used to nibble on was doing its cute crinkling thing as she smiled. Her eyes were looking deep into mine, but I knew they weren't really seeing me. Her smile was for someone else.

"Yes, she is beautiful but she already has a boyfriend," sunglass man chipped in.

"Please leave me in peace for forty-five minutes."

"You are not staying on that long. You promised to stop."

"C'est cela, oui," I replied. An only-just-polite way of saying "fuck you."

"Here are my bilingual problems," Alexa had written. "No, not bilingual. Sacha is Ukrainian, and English is his third language after Russian and Ukrainian, and it's my second language. So in fact we have quintilingual problems. Is that a word?"

Frankly, who cared.

Then it hit me. Ukrainian? So this was her mum's boyfriend's son? That was incest, wasn't it? At the very least it sounded every bit as screwed up as my problems with Brigitte.

"Just don't get your tongues tangled up in all those languages," was all I could think of in reply. And what a gross image it conjured up, their tongues entwined like two mating snails.

I got away from the computer as fast as I could and went to unpadlock the bike.

Next confrontation of the morning—revealing my new luxury mode of transport to Florence.

5

F LORENCE WAS ALONE, eating coffee and biscottes in the courtyard, draped along a teak lounger as if she was advertising garden furniture. The sun had burnt away the morning haze, but Florence wasn't topless, as she had been for our first breakfasts here. Dad's influence was making itself felt before he'd even arrived.

She was in her bikini-top-and-pareo combination, one long, smooth leg uncovered and getting some rays. I felt a few seconds of guilt, or maybe stupidity, about my recent fit of jealousy over Alexa. Florence was all flesh and blood, not a load of pixels standing next to a Ukrainian.

"I got myself a bike," I told her.

"Where is it?"

"I left it outside."

"Ah, you don't dare show me?"

"Dare?"

I went and untethered my new mount from its lamppost.

Its arrival in the tiny garden was a bit like an aircraft carrier pulling into a farmyard, so I excused Florence her outburst of shocked laughter. "Oh, Paul, take it back, it is ridiculous."

"Maybe, but it's efficient."

"I will pretend you are not with me."

"I know, it's not what I wanted, either, but look at this." I plunged a finger into the padding on the saddle.

"It would massage your bum almost as well as my fingers."

"Does it vibrate?" she asked.

As usual, our disagreement ended in the bedroom, then in the bathroom, then in the bedroom again.

"So when's your dad arriving?" I asked an hour or so later, lying spreadeagled on the bed, no part of my body capable of movement except for my lips and vocal cords. I was addressing Florence's rear end as she chose some panties from the small pile in her open suitcase. One of her buttocks still had my finger marks on it. Or were they her finger marks, I wondered idly.

"This afternoon."

"Great, time to go to the beach before he gets here."

"I don't want to."

"You don't want to go to the beach?"

"No, these are my holidays too. I do not want to work so hard every day. Not on cycling, anyway." She flicked a pair of flowery panties at my leg. Well, "pair" was a grand description for such a tiny piece of clothing. A pantie singular was more like it.

"If you let me get you a decent bike, it wouldn't be like work at all."

"I don't want to do anything this morning. I just want to lie in the courtyard, read, do nothing."

I mulled this over while she chose a T-shirt and another pareo and laid them out on the bed, ready to put on after her shower. Just lying about all day struck me as a waste of a good beach, especially as we were going to be marooned in Paris for several months once the café was up and running. If it ever was.

"You'll have time to give notre ami Nicolas a call this morning, then, won't you?"

"Later, Paul. I didn't even finish my breakfast, remember?"

"OK, I'll call him now, before I go to the beach. It's, what, ten thirty? The workmen should have been at it for two hours already."

"OK, you call." She went into the shower room. Not her problem.

I really didn't understand how someone who was so active and communicative in bed could be so passive about everything else. I wasn't complaining about the sex, of course. I just thought that it might be nice if she showed the same sense of teamwork in the other parts of our relationship.

Still, it's very hard to feel aggrieved at someone who has just done certain things to your tingling body, so I swallowed my pride and picked up the phone.

I was lying on the bed naked, as if to taunt Nicolas about who was sleeping with Florence these days. Petty, I know, but you need all the help you can get when dealing with French architects.

"They will start Monday at the latest," he assured me, after needing to be reminded who I was. "How is Florence?" He clearly thought that we'd said all we needed to about boring stuff like work.

"How is *Florence*?" I switched to English, which he understood very well. "Is that all you have to say? What I want to know is, how is the *tea room*? How is it ever going to be finished on time? That's what you should be saying to yourself. How is it zat ah am all-raidy four days late and ah aven't e-venn start-edd yet?" The fake French accent was going to piss him off majorly, but so what?

His self-love won through. "T'inquiète pas, Paul, pas de panique," he crooned, telling me not to worry with the all-chums-together "tu" form.

"But I *am* worried, Nicolas." I was back to pure, crisp English vowels now. I was the matron at the posh private school explaining why failing to wash behind his ears would get him sent to hell. "I am worried, and so should you be. Because if the tea room opens late, I will be paying you late. Very late. OK, mon ami?"

6

"BONJOUR, MONSIEUR BOURBON." I shook the proffered hand and did my best to look as if I was worthy of having sex with his daughter in his holiday home. I'd put on a clean T-shirt and my best swimming shorts. "Bonjour, Paul." He pronounced my name correctly, which I appreciated. So few French people bothered.

He was a very good-looking man for his age, a kind of veteran Bollywood film star. He had perfect skin, much darker than Florence, and looked as if someone had just spent hours shaving his chin and cheeks to total smoothness. Unlike his son, he wasn't balding, and his thick black hair was cut in a mid-nineties Hugh Grant. Artily floppy. He was fifty-something but dressed twenty years younger, in impeccably faded jeans and a loose, plum-coloured shirt that covered his affluent little paunch. He was sockless in sailing sneakers. An instantly recognizable rusty-bike rider, although he'd just arrived in a La Rochelle taxi.

"I've heard a lot about you." He shook my hand warmly. "Especially your talents with herbal tea."

"Oh oui, I'm very sorry." I tried to look guilt-stricken.

"Oh, don't worry about that." He chortled, as if it was the kind of thing that happened all the time to Brigitte, which it probably was.

"And I'm terribly sorry about the car."

His laugh died as if it had been hit by a Korean off-road vehicle.

"The car?"

Oh shit, he didn't know.

"Florence?" both of us asked.

She gave an "uh" of irritation and reeled off a brief explanation of how it happened, which, to my mind, didn't make it clear enough that I was completely blameless.

"You demolished my car?" His dark-brown skin had turned red around the chinline.

"No, a man crashed in me. To me. With me." I defended myself in my best approximation of lawyer's French.

"So his insurance is paying for the repairs?"

"Well . . ." If I'd known I was going to have to make this speech, I'd have prepared a short Powerpoint presentation to put my case. But my look of discomfort might as well have said, "No, mate, you're paying."

My new father-in-law put his well-manicured hands on his hips and let his fury out. Coming from the volcanic island of La Réunion, he really knew how to blow his top. Everyone from the post office to the surfing beach must have heard what he thought of me and Florence—our ingratitude, incompetence, lack of respect, lack of manners, lack of driving skills, lack of anything that might raise us above the level of baby chimpanzees.

Then abruptly, Papa stopped yelling and clomped upstairs to throw luggage and furniture around.

"Don't worry," Florence whispered, after we had observed a minute's silence for the passing of our peaceful holiday. "He will calm down very quickly. He always shouts like that, but if you don't contradict him, he forgets all about it in a few minutes."

"I don't think he'll forget about his car getting wrecked. Didn't you tell him?"

"Noh," she replied, a "non" with an in-built puff of indifference. Here was that infuriating passivity again.

"What, it was like me with Henri's field? You didn't think it was worth mentioning?"

"Oh, Paul, please, don't start."

She was right, I suddenly realized. There was no point starting. Because she wasn't really interested in what I was going to say. The crashed car was a long way away, in the past and in Corrèze, and as far as she was concerned it could stay there. I was rapidly coming to the conclusion that she was incapable of facing up to problems.

She was going to be in for quite a shock at the café, I thought. If we didn't get things back on schedule, our problems weren't just going to bawl us out as her dad had done, they were going to march right up and punch us in the teeth.

7

A S FLORENCE HAD predicted, the volcano was soon dormant again.

Monsieur Bourbon had phoned the garagiste, got the full story, schmoozed with the local gendarmes, and was feeling refreshed and full of bonhomie by evening. He said I could call him Charles, and "tutoyer" him.

By way of apology, I paid for dinner at the chic shed. He was very gracious. He even suggested that we all go on to a bar by the quayside for a drink.

"There is going to be a show, I think. Singing and dancing."

"Great," I said diplomatically.

"I am too tired, I want to go home." Florence yawned to prove it.

Was this real tiredness, I wondered, or just parent fatigue? And if it was parent fatigue, why couldn't she try to include me in on it, too?

"OK, Paul and I will go to the bar," Charles said.

He went for a pee, and as Florence and I stood outside in the cool ocean breeze, I begged her to come along just for one drink. Nothing doing.

"Just try to stop him drinking too much," she said. "He gets a little bizarre when he's drunk."

"So that's why you're so tired all of a sudden? You don't want to play nursemaid for your dad—you want me to do it for you?"

"Oui," she admitted shamelessly. "You can do this little thing for me, can't you?" She pressed her wonderful body against me and gave me an irresistibly doe-eyed kiss.

But how, I wondered, was I supposed to stop her dad drinking? I can't stop *myself* drinking.

Soon, Charles and I were sitting outside a big, touristy restaurant opposite the marina, in a corner of the terrace where the tables had been cleared of cutlery and were open for drinking again.

A brisk young waiter arrived, tanned and sure of himself after two or three weeks of his summer job.

"Messieurs, qu'est-ce que je vous sers?" He had the waiter's patter off to a tee.

"Fizzy water?" I suggested.

Charles looked at me as if I'd suddenly come down with mad-cow disease. "Deux ballons de blanc," he said. Two glasses of white wine.

"Petit, moyen, grand?" the waiter asked.

I almost laughed. I didn't realize the waiters tried to rip off French tourists too.

Charles flushed lava red.

"I haven't seen you in the twenty years or so that I have been coming to my holiday home in Ars. You're new this season, aren't you?" There was a bead of sweat on Charles's upper lip.

"Oui." The waiter was shifting from one foot to the other.

"And has the French language changed since you started working here?"

"Monsieur?"

" 'Un ballon' is the word for a normal-sized glass of wine, n'est-ce pas? So how can you ask if we want a big one? It would be like asking if I wanted a big litre of beer. Don't you agree, young man?"

The waiter was old enough to know that it was not worth arguing. He asked us what type of wine we wanted, and left.

"Huh, his parents rent a house for one month a year and they think they own the island," Charles said. Meaning, presumably, that he was a *real* islander because he'd actually bought his holiday home.

"And you know how much they pay to rent one of these little cottages?" Charles turned his nose up at the people sitting around us, some of whom hadn't noticed how dark it was and were still wearing their sunglasses.

I didn't know, and he told me. I was shocked.

"Yes, it's true," he said. "And these days, if they want to buy a decent place here, one that isn't just a prefabricated cube in an infestation of identical cubes, oh là là!" Again, he told me the price. "You could buy all the farms in Corrèze for that," he exaggerated slightly. "Or three houses on the mainland, just a few kilometres away. But they have decided that this place is chic, so they pay."

The drinks, with a small bowl of shrimps and a couple of toothpicks (probably dipped in curare) as an apology, arrived.

"But it is a very beautiful island," I said. I had noticed that some of the people at nearby tables were taking offence at Charles's loud lecture on current trends in real estate. It is, after all, not polite to talk about money in France.

"Oh, yes, it is a beautiful island. Green, fertile." His hand gripped my leg, as if I was the source of the fertility. "Sunny, sexy," he went on. "But when I bought my house, almost no one wanted to come here. There were just a few rich Parisians who came here because it was so inaccessible. Before the bridge, you had to queue for days for a car space on the little ferry. So the Parisians all kept rusty old 2CVs on the island. The most dangerous cars in Europe. The sea used to rot them away like sugar in coffee and you didn't know when one of them was going to fall to pieces until the wheels dropped off. A bit like you with my car, huh? Cheers!" he said in English, and his hand slapped my thigh.

"Cheers. And I'm really sorry about votre voiture."

"It will be OK. And call me 'tu.' Hey, le petit!" He beckoned to the waiter. "What was I saying? Oh yes, those snobs with their rusty old 2CVs. Hah!" He was oblivious to the fact that several of the tables around us had fallen grimly silent.

I tried the fizzy-water ploy one more time, with no more success than before, and then gave up. What was a holiday in France for, if not to sit outdoors drinking wine while the yachts in the marina pinged their mast cables at you like so many clinking glasses?

Each drink seemed to open up a new Pandora's Box of provocation.

"We're all immigrants," was Charles's taunt when he started the third or fourth ballon. "We're all immigrants on this island." He let the people at the other tables know who he was talking about. "But I'm probably more of a local than any of them. One of my ancestors, a White Frenchman, oh yes, sailed from La Rochelle to La Réunion before the revolution. And I bet no one has a first name as French as mine!"

"Charles is very French, yes," I agreed.

"Oh no, Charles is not my real name. Not my full name. My first names are Charlemagne Napoléon Vercingétorix." He had a bit of trouble pronouncing the last one, which I'd never heard of anyway.

"Ver . . . ?"

"It is the name of a Gaul. The king who resisted the Romans. I am Astérix's Indian brother!"

He coughed up a throatful of wine and convinced one couple nearby that it was time to go home.

"And you know why my birth certificate calls me Napoléon and all that?" he asked.

"Because your father couldn't spell Charles?"

"No. Because of the marvellous French law that decides what children should be called. When you go to the town hall to register your baby's name, the person at the counter—l'employé au guichet—can reject it. Don't forget that l'employé au guichet is the most powerful person in France. Any guichet. Vive le guichet!"

I raised my glass in a toast. I'd met some of these people when trying to get my resident's permit. I'd experienced how one person's mood could determine your entire future.

"And the employé au guichet decided that the name my father wanted was not French enough. It was an Indian name, Rajiv, like the son of the architect of Indian independence. 'C'est pas français, ça,' she decided, and so my father said Charlemagne, Napoléon, Vercingétorix as a joke, and she wrote them all down and stamped the paper and voilà. She had transformed me from a future Indian president into two French kings and an emperor. Vive le roi!"

He drained his glass and started to bellow some kind of royalist song that might well have got us chucked out if a fisherman hadn't distracted everyone by exploding.

8

O VER ON A STAGE by the harbour, a man in a ruddy canvas smock and blue peaked cap was tapping his feet and howling a sea shanty. The microphone was amplifying every consonant into an explosive distress flare. This was bad enough, but then his three chums joined in and started scaring every shrimp on the west coast out of French territorial waters.

Charles was either too drunk or deaf to care. He stood up.

"Let's dance!"

King Charlemagne wasn't going to be argued with, and dragged me to my feet.

Fortunately we weren't the only people to get up. We went to join a small group of local-costumed folk dancers who were performing jigs that seemed to consist of a massive amount of effort for no result, a sort of outdoor show of shared constipation.

I've been to Scottish ceilidhs where you heave your partner off their feet, or twirl each other round till the centrifugal force makes your underpants fall down. Here, though, people were gazing at their tip-tapping feet and flapping their arms with the restrained energy of a parrot that's afraid of flying.

Charles knew all the steps, and got admiring nods from some of the ladies in their black dirndl-type dresses as he did a loose, Bollywood version of their jigging, with an emphasis on suggestive movement of the eyebrows. He selected a grey-haired, spinsterly folk dancer and seemed to perform a fisherman's fertility dance in her honour, with him as the trawler and her as the shoal of sea bass. It confirmed what Michel had told me about the incident with Ginette, the old farmer's wife. When he got pissed, Charles seemed to get the hots for the aging folksy type.

For the moment, his current victim was continuing her bobbing jig unperturbed except for the occasional worried glance at Charles's gyrating groin. Meanwhile, I jogged on the spot and wished that the giant pink moon would come crashing down and end the party early.

"Did you see her?" Charles asked me when the jig was over and I'd managed to unclamp his fingers from the hem of the old dirndl's petticoat. "Not bad, eh? Do you think I should ask for her phone number?"

"No," I said, "I think you should come home with me now."

"Not yet, look!" Charles was pointing to the stage, where an old guy in tight jeans began yodelling a deafening French version of the da-doo-ron-ron song.

At this point we had to join in with the French crowd's jiving, which might have been fun if I'd had one of the cool young girls as a partner instead of Charles. I thought it best to keep hold of him, to stop him jiving off in search of some other unsuspecting pensioner.

It was only after he'd fallen over while attempting to twirl himself above my head that I managed to drag him away from the dance floor.

"Where are you taking me?" he demanded.

"Home?" I suggested.

"No, it's much too early," he shouted. "Let's go for a drink!" His legs wandered off in different directions as if they couldn't decide which bar to go to.

I grabbed him to stop him falling over again. If he collapsed now, I would have to go and get the singing fishermen to carry him home.

"Oh, you are angry with me because of the woman," he said, looking hurt. "You must not be angry with me. It is not my fault. You have seen Brigitte, so you understand why we are not sexually active any more."

Not sexually active? That explained Brigitte's courgette fixation and the flooded bathroom.

I began to tug Charles away from the quayside, mainly so that the people around us wouldn't have to share the gruesome details of his inactive sex life.

"We used to be active," he yelled above the music. "Very. She had beautiful breasts. Like hers. Bonsoir Madame!" I pulled him out of range of his new lady love, who was in fact an obese man in a pink T-shirt. "She was very good at oral sex, too," Charles foghorned. "With her tongue, she used to-oo—"

His last word was extended into a shocked gasp of pain as he collided with a concrete pillar.

Now that I'd shut him up, I was able to seize him under one armpit and frogmarch him down the lane to the house in relative peace.

"Here we are." I opened the latch gate to our courtyard and heaved him through.

Suddenly Charles was fully conscious again.

"Bonne nuit, Paul, bonne nuit. Don't worry about the dancer woman. We will have better luck tomorrow night, eh?" He tapped me on the cheek and went meekly indoors, humming along with the song being ritually slaughtered down at the quayside.

It was midnight. I was somehow too exhausted to go to bed. Time, I thought, for a moonlit bike ride.

Only trouble was, my state-of-the-art bike didn't come with lights. How is it, I wondered, that technology can make such huge leaps backwards as well as forwards? Haven't mountain-bike designers heard of lights? And mudguards? When I was a kid I could go cycling after the rain and not end up looking as if I'd shat my trousers.

There was nothing else for it but to take one of the old killer machines. I spun their wheels and found that one of them had rusted but workable dynamo lights. Pausing only to strap one of the cushions from the lounger on to the saddle with a bungee elastic, I headed out into the noisy moonlight.

The cycle paths were empty and spooky, and it took me at least twenty minutes to ride out of range of the music at the marina. When I stopped beside an inky-dark pool in the salt marshes, I could hear the rustle of reeds, the plop of a jumping fish, the sudden screech of a bird or animal—the hunter or the hunted, I didn't know. I looked back towards the illuminated steeple and the strings of lights over the marina, and smelt the salt in the air. And suddenly I had to phone Alexa.

Why was I calling, though? Especially so late. When it's not your actual girlfriend you have to have an excuse.

I could mention that I'd just been doing the French jive, which she'd once tried to teach me, but that'd only remind us both of the first time we broke up, when I ended a drunken evening of dancing by going off to use a condom in another girl's bed. I could ask with false indifference about the exact nature of her relationship with the guy in the photo. No, not cool.

Or I could just say that I wanted to talk to her.

That was the scariest excuse of all. Because it was true. No, half true. It wasn't so much that I fancied an idle chat with her. I had to tell her about my worries and doubts. My stay on the paradise island was getting just as flaky as my disastrous exploits in Corrèze. Was there something about me and French holidays that didn't mix? I wanted to know what she'd say, because I respected her opinion.

And I wanted to talk about her stuff, too, her film course, her plans. I liked sharing her energy. I liked the way she giggled when she made fun of herself, or of me.

And when you came right down to it, I simply liked hearing her voice.

Shit. The moon and the wine have got to you, I told myself. I speed-dialled her number before I had time to chicken out.

My phone shone bright in the darkness, hooking itself up to her satellite.

"Hello?"

"Hi, it's Paul."

"What? Who?"

"Alexa?"

"Yes, I can't hear you. Shut up, people, will you!"

In the background there was a happy babble of voices. She was out on the town somewhere.

"It's Paul."

"Paul, hi! What are you doing?"

A loud male voice rode over the wave of background noise. I couldn't make out what he said.

"Shut up, will you?" she shouted. The words were angry but her voice was laughing. "Hey, Paul, we were online at the same time. Isn't that funny?"

"Yeah, but I was in a post office, I couldn't—"

"What? I can't hear you."

"I said I was in a post office . . ."

"What? It's very noisy here. We're in the pub."

"Yeah, so I hear. It's OK, it wasn't urgent. I'll call you some other time."

I got on my bike and cycled out of the marsh as fast as I could without risking a broken neck. It was a combination of that "we" and the pub. I felt excluded, alone.

But you're just being stupid, I told myself as I pedalled. You're here on a superb island, with an incredibly sexy woman, setting up a new life in France. As an old English girlfriend of mine, Ruth, would have said, stop whingeing and start bingeing.

9

FLORENCE WAS ON the floor doing her Pilates, a cross between yoga and aerobics. Weirdly, seeing her doing it naked was only marginally more sexy than watching a girl get a bikini wax. It took all the mystery out of her body.

"Good morning," I said from the bed.

"Bonjour. How was your evening?" Florence was flexing an arm like someone banging on a door in slow motion.

"Great. We danced."

"Yes, he adores to dance, Papa." She lay on her back and kicked a tensed leg upwards. I decided I didn't want to see any more and concentrated my attention on the soothingly blank white ceiling.

"He likes dancing with old ladies, that's for sure."

"Oh. Did he drink a lot?"

"Twice as much as me."

"You didn't stop him, then?"

"No, I didn't. And it was lucky Michel warned me that your dad gets a bit amorous when he's had a few."

"He told you that?" As if Michel should have kept the warning to himself.

"Yes, he did. Thank God. It was just one more thing that you might have told me yourself, Florence." I sat up and caught a eyeful of her crotch as she stretched her thighs.

"I did."

"No, you didn't. You said he got a little bizarre when he drinks. I mean, who doesn't? But anyway, from now on, if he wants to go out and get drunk, he can do it, I'm not going to stop him. Or we'll all go out together, and we can both stop him chatting up old folk-dancers. OK?"

"OK." Florence thrust her rear end at me and carried on Pilating.

This whole non-communicative relationship thing really didn't bother her at all.

For the next three or four days, it was almost as if we were on separate vacations. I'd cycle off to catch the incoming tide while Florence would use up half the world's supply of sunblock relaxing in the courtyard, and her dad hit the tennis courts.

In the evenings, we'd meet up for dinner with Papa, on whom we tried some subtle sobriety control. Florence kept his water glass full of Badoit, and I made sure we never needed a second bottle of wine. This way, he showed no signs of wanting to go off and get in some exercise with the local pensioners.

A couple of times, Florence and I went on to a club. The first time it was quite an exotic experience watching sixteen-year-olds dry-humping each other while a DJ whooped "Shake eet, shake eet, yé!" over the beat of bad French R'n'B. A second visit was one too many.

I made one early-morning trip to the post office to read my emails.

Alexa had replied, but she hadn't picked up on my intense curiosity about The Hunk, and just made some joke about Ukrainians being a lot like us Anglo-Saxons. All mad about football and alcohol, she said. She mentioned again that she was going to be working on a film shoot, and said she'd let me know about an exhibition of her photos that was going to happen in Paris soon. There was one of me she'd like me to see, she said. I couldn't remember her ever taking my photo, though. She must have taken one while I was asleep. I just hoped I hadn't been drooling.

I'd now been on the island for just over a week.

I was cycling home from the beach at the end of an afternoon workout in the waves when I felt an unusual vibration in my backside. No, I thought, I wasn't using my phone as a suppository. It had to be a problem with the bike.

It was. A puncture. The tyre was totally flat.

How the hell could that happen, I moaned, with these inch-thick tractor wheels?

I hadn't heard a pop or felt a sudden loss of pressure, so I figured it had to be a slow puncture. I just had to pump it with enough air to last the short journey to the hire place, and I'd be OK.

Which was when I noticed the bigger problem. The bike had a frame made of jet-fuselage aluminium, handlebars designed by a team of physiotherapists, brakes that could stop a train, but no bloody pump.

And what's more, the valve was so damn new and complicated that no one who cycled past me had a pump that would do more than hiss vainly when it tried to give the kiss of life to my tyre. The worst thing was when a snooty woman on a rusty medieval Raleigh gave me a lecture about how I ought to have stuck with good old English technology rather than trying to show off with this Formula One contraption.

"Now you will have to walk all the way home with your piece

of modern art," she said, and trundled off in a haughty trail of rust flakes.

As it turned out, though, she was wrong.

I'd walked only a couple of hundred yards when I saw a car driving along the road beside the cycle path. It was a large green people-carrier with a taxi sign on the roof rack.

A miracle that was not to be ignored.

I leaped down from the path and stood in the middle of the road, waving my arms in the universal gesture for "If you don't stop I'll leave bloodstains all over your windscreen." The driver, a hardy-looking old guy with a freckled tan on his bald head, leaned out of his window. "Do you want Ars?" he asked.

"Ah oui," I said, the voice of a man in desperate need of Ars.

"Because I'm not going any further."

"That's perfect. I rented this bike in Ars and I must repair it. I am punctured."

We loaded the bike in the back and took off.

"You're English," he said.

"Yes."

"You made a mistake." As if it would have been advisable to be born French.

"Really?"

"Yes, you said, Je suis crevé."

"Yes."

"That means I am very tired."

"Ah yes?"

"You should have said, J'ai crevé. That means there is a hole in my tyre. Enfoiré!"

This last word was not an expression of disgust at my misuse of French, but an insult directed at a teenager who'd just done a

BMX jump off the cycle track and across the road right in front of us.

"Crever also means to die. He was nearly crevé, uh?"

We enjoyed the joke together.

"Beautiful bike," he said, nodding over his shoulder towards my useless machine.

"You like it? It is too complicated."

"I have one like that. I ride it along here through the forest every morning when I am not working. And I often ride it from my house to my boat, out in the main channel there." He pointed away to the north of Ars, where the channel to the marina met the sea. He explained that at low tide the channel was only inches deep, and he kept his boat near the sea so he would only have a few yards to push it through the mud. That way he could go fishing whenever he wanted.

"You are a fisherman?" I asked, with a little too much incredulity. He looked nothing like the jigging accordion players I'd seen. He was a thoroughly modern man in a T-shirt with a bamboo motif. No sign of a fisherman's smock or oilskins.

"In the winter. In the summer I'm usually a taxi driver."

"You live here all year?"

"Oh yes. All year."

"And you have a mountain bike, not one of these old rusty things that people use here?"

"Ha!" He laughed loudly, a bellow that almost punctured his windscreen. "No, every two or three years I get a new mountain bike at the end of the season, when they sell off the hire bikes cheap."

A beautiful irony, I thought. Such a shame my hi-tech bike wasn't equipped with a dictaphone so that I could prove to Florence that she was grating her pelvic bone for nothing. The real islanders were just as fond of soft saddles and well-oiled pedals as I was.

"So where do people get these rusty old bikes?" I asked. "Does someone import them from India or Africa?"

He did his bellow again. "Not a bad idea. You'd make some money from the Parisians, eh?"

"Or maybe you can leave last year's hire bikes in the rain," I suggested. "They rust, and then you sell them for a big price?"

"We will tell the boys at the hire shop, eh? They will start a new business. Ha!"

Just before we reached the town, he pulled off the road into one of the lanes running towards the sea-salt pools. A large white ibis flew away in terror as the big car bumped along the track.

"Come," he said, "we'll have a drink."

"And my bike?"

"Oh, the hire shop is open late. Come."

He pulled up amongst several newish cars parked outside a long, white wooden hut. It had been built next to an oyster pool that a gushing tidal gate was filling up with greenish-brown water.

Nailed above the door of the hut was a sign, "Amical des anciens pêcheurs." The ex-fishermen's association.

Inside, things smelled of tar, dried shrimp and stale beer. But apart from a pile of newly repaired lobster pots it looked like a normal café. An old wooden bar with a coffee machine, beer pumps and bottles of wine and spirits. Ashtrays on each of the five or six vinyl-topped tables, three groups of men talking, drinking and smoking, their voices echoing off the unpainted walls. They were rugged outdoor types, pretty healthy-looking for their age, all except one old man who looked about a thousand years old, with wafer-thin skin over his cheekbones and long salty eyebrows. He was sitting at a large table, letting the smoke from his cigarette drift up to form a cloud over a photo of a fleet of large trawlers heading out to sea. A reminder of the days when the waters around here were full of tuna.

"Salut, Albert," one of the smokers called as we walked in.

Albert, my saviour, walked around the room shaking hands and introducing me as "an Englishman I found at the side of the road."

"What's your name, son?" one of the guys asked, a small man with a face deeply creased by the sun. He called me tu.

"Pol," I told him. I thought it'd save time.

"You want a drink, Pol?"

"Yes, a beer, s'il vous plaît, and one for my friend Albert."

"Ah non, pas de bière," Albert objected. "Get out the Pineau."

I'd had this before. It was Pineau de Charentes, the local fortified wine. Pretty strong stuff, a cross between wine and cognac.

The creased-faces guy got up and poured out two glasses of white Pineau on ice. We all sat around the largest table and clinked glasses, looking each other carefully in the eye.

"To mountain bikes!" Albert proposed the toast.

He explained how he'd picked me up, and told them what I'd said about rusty bikes. This led on to a long discussion about who the "real" islanders were. Some of the fishermen had originally come from the mainland, but they lived here all the year round, which, they said, made them real Rétais.

"And you were happy when the bridge was built?" I asked them.

"Ho! Yes," Albert said. The ancient sailor smiled in agreement. "We were delighted, absolutely delighted, eh?" The others all nodded. "It was no wonder all the young people were leaving. You imagine, a pregnant woman in winter with complications, she had to wait for the weather to be good enough to take her to hospital in La Rochelle by helicopter, eh?"

"And the kids left anyway," another guy chipped in. "If they stayed at school after fifteen, they had to go to the mainland, and they stayed there."

"Anyway," Albert went on, "it was only the Parisians who said that the bridge would spoil the character of the island. They just wanted it peaceful for the month of August. And now they are secretly glad because they can bring their Ronge Rovair to the door of their holiday home, which has multiplied in price by ten."

"And so have ours," the ancient guy said.

This provoked laughs, fresh drinks, and stories about people who'd sold their old fishnet sheds to be turned into holiday homes. It was the exact opposite of poor old Corrèze.

"We wouldn't leave, though, eh?" Albert asked them. "No, the weather here is too good for old bones. It's a micro-climate. It never freezes here."

"Like England," I said. "It's always hot there." The French love jokes about English weather. There's nothing that makes you more popular than joking about our reputation for 365 days of rain and fog, even though the southeast of England is drier than some parts of southern France.

The gag earned me yet another drink. I began to wonder who was paying for this. And whether Albert had left the taxi on the metre. But Pineau doesn't let you think morose thoughts for long.

"Hey, hey!" Albert had had an idea. "Do you play baby foot?" This is the French name for table football.

"Yes," I said. Like jiving, it's an essential social skill in France.

"OK, let's get the table out."

Suddenly chairs were being pushed out of the way, and a couple of men went into a room behind the bar and returned carrying a baby foot table.

Soon we were set up for a tournament. Pairs were formed. I was in a multinational team with Albert.

"We will be the most fair-play team," he said. "We have an Englishman."

He explained to me that when you play table football "properly," without spinning the players, it is called "jouer à l'anglaise."

"You say we English are fair-play," I said. "But that's only a polite way of saying we always lose."

More laughs, more drinks, table football, more drinks.

Soon the sun was going down across the marshes. I thought I heard the church bell strike. Was that six or seven? Or ten?

10

I T'S TRUE THAT you always know when a drunk man is trying to get indoors quietly. I say "man" because I've never heard a drunken woman trying to get indoors quietly. Either I've lived a sheltered life or they really are better at being quiet when they're drunk.

Anyway, when I'm drunk I'm physically incapable of coming home quietly. If I decided to open the door and lie on the hall carpet till the morning paper dropped on my head, maybe I'd have a chance of slipping in without waking up the whole household.

But if you factor in getting dropped off by a loud group of equally drunk fishermen, trying to squeeze through the garden gate with a mountain bike that has suddenly turned into a giant octopus, failing to locate the lock on the house door, crashing about in the shed in search of some source of light, remembering that the door is never locked anyway and having a fit of the giggles, tripping over the staircase that someone has inconsiderately placed in the middle of the hall, then taking off a pair of sandals at the top of the stairs and discreetly dropping them down to the ground floor like two hand grenades, well, you can be sure that the next morning will start off with a few rounds of recrimination.

What's more, I am one of those people that the world has treated unkindly. Maybe I didn't eat enough bacon when I was a kid. Because something about my body, perhaps the lack of a decent layer of fat around the kidneys or liver, means that I occasionally get hit by a hangover as destructive as a tank.

It fires heat-seeking missiles into my head, torches my mouth with its flamethrower, and rolls back and forward over my stomach for a whole day. I lie there wishing for death or at the very least a gallon of morphine milkshake. No, not a milkshake. No milk and no shaking. Just let me lie still until time drags me back to life and relative painlessness again.

But Florence could not have known this, because at dawn the next morning she was haranguing me mercilessly, emphasizing her various points about my being a drunken lout by tapping on the mattress and making the bed buck like a rodeo horse. She was probably using words, but they felt like needles in my ears.

I tried to apologize. My tongue didn't seem to be working, though, and she didn't accept "subby" as an answer.

"Where were you?" she repeated for the fifth time. "We tried calling you from the restaurant but you weren't answering your phone."

"Fish," I groaned. Not very helpful, I know.

"Fish?"

"Bike, taxi, fish, baby foot."

"Uh?"

"Lobster pots," I added, filling in some of the finer details for her.

"Paul, what are you talking about?"

"Pineau," I concluded, with the accent on the "oh."

"What happened?" Was she stupid or what? Hadn't I already explained?

"I die," I said, in French.

"What?"

"No, I am very tired."

"Uh?"

"Tyre, bike, fff?"

"Ah, tu as crevé?"

"Yes." For someone under attack from a female bucking bronco, I was almost happy. At last things had been cleared up.

"But how did that cause you to arrive here completely drunk at midnight?" And we were off on another round of bed rodeo.

"Coffee?" I managed to beg after being bounced halfway across Wyoming. "Lots? Please?"

"When you have explained where you were."

"Where was I?" The mere prospect of coffee seemed to have got my brain in focus. "Where were *you*? If you'd been with me, you would have been with me."

Well, maybe focus wasn't the right word. It was my blurred way of saying that we weren't actually spending much of our holiday together these days.

"You two, will you please be quiet?"

A grumpy Indian man with ruffled hair and dark-red silk pyjamas had materialized in the doorframe.

"Yes, sorry." I agreed with him. There was too much noise going on.

"It's bad enough having to share my holiday home with two people who treat it like a free hotel, but I don't appreciate getting woken up in the middle of the night by a gang of men singing 'God Save the Queen' in terrible French accents, and then having to listen to one of them trying to demolish my house."

"Yes, sorry," I repeated.

His eruption over, he calmed down and left me in peace. He was so much easier to manage than Brigitte. Or Florence, for that matter.

* * *

Next time I was conscious of anything, there was a huge white cup looming up beside my head.

Coffee, yes.

My numbed brain willed the nearest arm to move in the direction of the bedside table, and fingers made contact with drinking receptacle.

The cup was cool. The coffee must have been there quite a while. No matter. A starving man does not ask for his first hunk of bread to be lightly toasted.

The only trouble with trying to drink coffee while lying face down, though, is that the human mouth is not located on the side of the skull.

Holding the cup tantalizingly near my mouth, I lifted my head a painful few inches off the pillow and managed to tip half the coffee in one ear. Oh well, some of it would eventually dribble into my mouth, I reasoned, or soak through my eardrum into my nervous system.

"Paul! Are you listening to me or not?"

I looked beyond the cup towards the source of sound. It was true, during my attempt at drinking coffee I had noticed someone speaking rather loudly, but it had seemed of secondary importance in comparison with my need for caffeine.

Standing next to the bed was Florence, looking a little blurred, I thought. Maybe she was coming down with something.

"Yes?"

"Go downstairs now!"

"Why?"

"Your friends have brought you a present."

"Friends?"

"The fishermen."

"No." Whatever they'd brought, even if it was a brace of

the finest lobsters ever caught on the Atlantic coast, it could wait.

"Come now." Florence was pulling me towards the terrifying cliff at the edge of the bed.

"No, please. I'm punctured. I just want to puncture."

"Paul!"

This was a murderous hiss, like a cobra just before it bites you in the jugular. Something told me that it might be better to go downstairs after all.

The stairs were much steeper than I remembered, and the walls seemed to have trouble staying vertical, but I made it down to the hall, where the floor tiles were deliciously cool beneath my feet. I wanted to lie on them.

"Paul. Outside."

Florence was pointing into the courtyard, but the light out there was much too fierce for me to see anything. I wondered if the fishermen had brought me the lamp from the lighthouse and forgotten to turn it off.

"Go on, go out and look."

After some violent blinking, I finally managed to drag the contents of the courtyard into view.

"Ah, they've had babies," was my first thought."

Arranged in a neat row against the door of the shed were at least seven rusty bikes. Some were missing wheels, saddles or handle-bars, all the tyres were deflated and rotten, most of the chains were brown and hanging off, but they were still recognizable as bikes, or ex-bikes.

"Why?" I asked philosophically.

"I came back from the boulangerie and found some men filling the courtyard. Your friend Albert said they'd looked in their gardens and boathouses, and their friends' gardens and boathouses, and brought you all the old bikes they could find. I told them to get the hell out but they refused to take them away again. He said they were for you."

"Me?"

"Apparently you're going into business? Selling rusty old bikes to the tourists?"

"Me?"

"Yes."

"No."

"What is this bordel?" Papa, dressed in tennis gear, was standing at the door and gaping at his new collection of fishermen's rust.

Florence gestured at me to explain.

"I punctured," I said, pleased with myself at getting it right for once.

King Charlemagne flew into a Napoleonic fury. Didn't I think he had enough problems coping with maniacs in his job without being followed on holiday by them? After trying to poison his wife, was I hoping to kill him with a heart attack? Was I planning to take delivery of a dozen crashed cars as well, to replace the new one I'd demolished?

His ranting only stopped when a blue minibus with red and white stripes on its roofrack pulled up outside the gate.

We all stared as a gendarme with one of those French moustache-less beards got out of the minibus and put on his black képi. He saluted.

"Monsieur Bourbon?" he asked.

"Oui," Charlemagne confessed warily.

"You are the owner of a Renault Vel Satis?"

"Oui."

"I have a complaint against you."

Florence and her dad both looked expectantly at me, as if this was going to be my fault. Which it wasn't at all. Well, not entirely.

As the gendarme explained it, the owner of a red Korean 4WD, finding himself unjustly accused of causing an accident, had finally decided to break his silence about the true circumstances of the crash. He now felt morally obliged to reveal that the Vel Satis had been travelling at an illegal speed, which explained why he had been unable to avoid the regrettable collision at the roundabout, about which he now wished to make a formal complaint, backed by his insurance company, which was refusing to accept liability.

This was not all. Monsieur had no doubt heard, the gendarme went on, of the case of a Vel Satis reported travelling at some two hundred kilometres per hour on the autoroute near Brive that same day, allegedly because of a manufacturing fault in its accelerator. Although the reports all described a car of a different colour to Monsieur Bourbon's, the gendarmerie was now forced to investigate the theory that it had in fact been the same Vel Satis in the two cases. The witnesses of the speeding incident were all being traced so that they could be tested for colour-blindness.

By the time this little speech was over, Charlemagne's face had turned a red so deep that even the most colour-blind of accident witnesses would have picked it up. His volcano was going to blow and take the whole town with it.

He opened his mouth and let the lava flow. I didn't attempt to contradict him, I waited for the eruption to die down, but this turned out to be his Krakatoa. I was his Pompeii.

"I'm sorry," he said, when his outburst had turned from a general rage into a more focussed bollocking. "There is too much bordel here. You must leave my house." He was using the singular "tu" form, so it was only me who was being banished.

"But Papa . . ." Florence pleaded.

"That is my final word," Charles snapped.

"It's OK, Florence," I said. "You stay. I'll go. I ought to get back to Paris and see what your friend Nicolas is up to."

I turned and walked unsteadily indoors.

Before we'd started drinking, Albert had given me a business card with his mobile number on it in case of emergencies. Ars Taxi, it said. A pretty apt name for the vehicle that was going to get my ass off the island.

3

Don't Get Merde, Get Even

1

I ARRIVED BACK in Paris on July 14th, Bastille Day.
Jet fighters were spinning trails of coloured smoke across
the skyline. The whole neighbourhood around the Champs-
Elysées was festooned with red, white and blue, and flooded with
soldiers, police and flag-waving tourists waiting for the parade. I
hung around to see what all the fuss was about, but quickly came
away again. To me, a parade of tanks through a city centre isn't a
celebration, it's a threat.

Why didn't they have a parade of wine-makers, foot-ballers and
lingerie designers? I wondered. That's what France should be
proud of.

I was just as disillusioned with what I found at the tea room—four
bare walls, showing no sign that a builder had even crossed the
threshold while I'd been away.

I didn't blame the builders, though. French builders are exactly
like their counterparts all over the world. They're all in the global
conspiracy. From Tunbridge Wells to Turkmenistan, they use the
same techniques—Taking a Deposit Then Buggering Off for a
Month, Leaving the Water Disconnected the Whole Weekend,
Making Sure Pipes Are Inaccessible So That the Tiniest Leak
Means You Have To Smash Every Tile in Your New Bathroom.
The usual stuff.

So I had no complaints about my builders—they were as

unreliable as I'd expected. My beef was with Nicolas. I thought it was his job to disbelieve the builders' promises and threaten them with bankruptcy until they got the job done. But Florence's suave exshagmate was under the impression that all he had to do was print out some drawings and then pocket a whopping ten per cent of the various workmen's estimates as his fee.

I decided to take advantage of the only good thing about having a girlfriend who used to sleep with your architect—namely that if the architect won't answer your own phone calls, you can get the girl to pass on the message that if said architect isn't at the site at eight-thirty the next morning, then he's fired.

It worked like a dream.

Not a particularly pleasant dream, but a dream, anyway.

At eight the next morning, I went in and started chiselling at a ridiculous purple-tile mosaic that ran around two of the walls. Strictly speaking, it was the builders' job, but it was great for getting frustrations out of my system—about Florence's dad, Florence's passivity, and of course Florence's ex-boyfriend. Yes, I was thinking a lot about Florence as I hammered away at that wall.

It was ten to nine when Nicolas finally poked the tip of his refined nose through the open door. I'd expected him to be late— for people like him, punctuality is a sign of weakness.

You'd have thought he had never set eyes on a naked brick in his life. When he saw the mess I was making, he recoiled as if he was about to get mugged.

"Bonjour," he called out from the doorway.

"Bonjour, Nicolas, nice to see you at last."

Despite the humidity, he was wearing a pale linen jacket over his crisp white shirt. He looked as though he never exerted himself enough to feel the heat. Why he'd chosen to associate himself with a business as physical as construction I don't know. I got the impression he'd have preferred to be an orchestral conductor if it wasn't for all that tiresome baton-waving they had to do. When he'd shown us his first sketch for the layout of the basement area, he'd swept his hands over the page as if it was a symphony rather than the plans for a toilet. Today, though, he looked more like one of the île de Ré herons I'd seen out on the marshes—long white neck; immense, stick-thin legs; slow, studied movements.

I didn't bother holding out my hand to shake. It was obvious that his fingers never touched anything that hadn't recently been wiped with a moist towelette.

As he'd done on the phone, he tried to make out that we were social acquaintances meeting up for a chat about the holidays.

"Yes, yes, Florence is very well and she is probably in bed dreaming about me," I assured him. "But I am not very well. I am not happy. We are two weeks late and nothing is happening. Where are the builders?"

"Ah, builders," Nicolas moaned. His expression suggested that his whole life was being made a misery by this incomprehensible "builder" phenomenon that had suddenly struck the nation.

"Yes, the builders. Where are they?"

Nicolas shrugged.

"Can you call and ask why they are not here?"

"I know why they are not here," he said. "They are finishing another job."

I am not at all the violent type, but I was beginning to wish I wasn't holding a hammer, because pretty soon there was going to be a large dent in Nicolas's elegant skull.

"Of course they are finishing another job, Nicolas. Builders are always finishing another job. But it is your job to bring them here to my job. That is why I will pay you." I was very careful to use the future tense here, to imply that payment was nowhere near the present. I gave him a second to chew on the implied threat. As soon as he opened his mouth to reply, I interrupted. "Call them now. Tell them that if they don't start tomorrow, they are fired."

I might as well have touched Nicolas's linen jacket with an oil-soaked rag. He almost wet himself.

"I can't do that! We will never find other builders."

"I know that, they know that, but we're in France, Nicolas. If you don't get angry, nothing happens. So please get angry. It is your job."

And to be fair, he gave a good performance. He cajoled, he threatened, and finally settled into a rant about his "chiant"—literally, shittingly annoying—"client"—who was saying he'd call the whole job off if it didn't start tomorrow. As he called me "chiant," he glanced apologetically at me, but I could tell it was the most sincere word in the whole conversation.

Frankly, I didn't give a shit. A year of living in Paris was the perfect preparation for this—I no longer gave a damn if people hated me, as long as they did what I wanted.

And miraculously, at eight the next morning, a large white van drew up and disgorged its load of builders and tools.

The workmen were a bunch of Poles, four guys called Fred, Pavel, Stan and Stefan, who didn't have more than fifty words of French between them. But I didn't care, because their chisel-scarred hands and muscle-bound backs looked as if they possessed all the skills necessary to fit out a tea room.

They were quite impressed that I was there to meet them—being awake and at a building site at eight on a July morning was about as un-Parisian as you could get. But they were not so keen when they saw that I wasn't going to bugger off and leave them to it. I knew that the only way to get anything done was to turn up every day and stay there, asking anyone who stepped towards the exit where they thought they were going while the tea room was still unfinished.

"We make much noise, much merde," the gang leader, Pavel, warned me in his gruff voice. He was only about thirty-five, but his voice was as croaky as a retired sergeant major's.

"Good," I said. "More noise, more merde, that means more progress. I must open the tea room on the first of September."

"First September?" Pavel translated this joke for his friends. The other three men, their skin the same shade of plaster-grey, threw back their heads and laughed.

"I am serious," I told them. "It is in the contract with Nicolas, the architect."

"Ha, contract," Pavel grunted. "I tell you something about contract."

He did, too, and as soon as I'd understood the full implications of what he'd told me, I started dialling Nicolas's number and rehearsing a volley of French insults to yell at him. But then something made me hit the red button and kill the call. No, I decided, much better to work out a way to get even with the bastard. As the French say, revenge is a dish best eaten cold.

Nicolas didn't put in another appearance until the builders were a week into the job. They had got to the end of the dusty demolition stage; and were now embarking on the filling-every-square-millimetre-of-floor-space-with-crap-(and-more-dust) stage.

The wannabe tea room was littered with heaps of tiles, an igloo of plaster slabs, a half-assembled steel food counter, and a lone toilet that sat invitingly and vulnerably at the top of the stairs leading down to the basement, where the atmosphere was one-third oxygen, one-third brick dust, and the rest Polish swear words.

I was half dead from the boredom and noise, but quietly content—things were coming on fast, and I'd had time to work out what to do about my scumbag architect.

It was a typically sweaty July Monday morning. Every weekend, Paris had been getting emptier of Parisians, and now it felt like an end-of-season beach resort. The dowdy clothing store next to the café was trying to sell off its overpriced swimwear before the last posh Parisians left town. The recruitment agency on the other side was advertising nothing but temporary replacements in its window.

As usual, Nicolas didn't think it was necessary to cross the threshold of the building site he was supposed to be supervising. So my architect and I were standing outside the recruitment agency, beneath a sickly poplar tree. Even in the shade it was hot and humid, and the car pollution drifting over from the ever-busy Champs-Elysées was hanging in the air like cheap perfume.

I gave Nicolas the good news first, congratulating him on his choice of workmen. This, at least, he'd got exactly right. Not only were they skilled at demolition, they'd even done a refresher course in how to answer a mobile phone while pushing a wheel-barrowload of cement bags across a crowded pavement. I didn't want to alienate any of my future clientèle by crippling them in an industrial accident before they'd had a chance to sample their first cup of real English tea.

"C'est bien, c'est bien." Nicolas shot a paternal look at an approaching Pole, which morphed into a microgrimace of distaste when Pavel got within sweat-smelling distance.

"But there's something I need to discuss with you, Nicolas," I said.

"Oui?" He frowned seductively, showing off the crease in his noble forehead to a passing tourist woman.

"It's our contract."

"Oui?"

"I think there is an error."

"Error? Ho!" This seemed to him to be as credible as a Frenchman agreeing to drink Californian wine.

"Come in and I'll show you." I'd brought most of the tea room's paperwork along with me, safely stashed in a thick plastic bag. A rubbish bag, actually, one of the last batch I'd bought to protect my shoes before I learned how to avoid stepping in Paris's dog merde every day.

"Why don't you bring it out?" Nicolas tucked his long clean hair behind his ears and waited for me to obey.

When I returned with my plastic bag, he was on the phone. He said an earnest "oui, oui, OK" before folding his sleek little Nokia away.

"I am sorry, Paul, I must go to an urgent site," he said.

Oh, you are so crap, I thought. Even builders rarely use that one any more. The riposte is so obvious.

"*This* is an urgent site, Nicolas."

"I'm sorry, I really must go. Ciao."

And suddenly his legs were the fastest-moving things in the neighbourhood.

I let him go—he was only postponing the inevitable.

"You not tell him, no?" Pavel said. He had been standing in the doorway to watch our exchange.

"No, not yet."

"When you tell him?"

"Next time. If he doesn't run away again."

We turned to laugh at the spider-like figure disappearing over the Tarmac horizon.

"OK, boss. Now we go to buy some things," Pavel said.

"You're going?"

"Yes."

"Not all of you?"

"Yes. We buy heavy things. Then is lunch. We return two o'clock. OK, boss?"

They were in their van before I could object. Oh well, I thought. It'll give me a chance to do some dusting.

My phone rang about an hour later.

It was Florence. We had been speaking most days since I left Ré, though I got the impression that my news didn't exactly enthrall her. I understood why—when you're lounging in a garden by the Atlantic, it must be difficult to identify with someone who's excited because four Poles have just delivered a stainless-steel sink unit.

Today, though, there was one thing about the job that interested her a lot: the contract with Nicolas. Was there something wrong with it? she wanted to know. Notre ami l'architecte had obviously been trying to sound her out.

"Oh, it's just a problem with the dates," I lied. "You know we're very late." Something told me it was best not to reveal the truth.

"Yes, well, there is no need to be aggressive to him. It will all be OK. I know Nicolas very well."

Exactly, I thought, that's the bloody problem.

2

A MIRAGE ISN'T a hallucination, is it? It's when something real that is far away looks as if it's a lot nearer. The image of the oasis is projected over the horizon towards you by the hot, buckled atmosphere.

In my case I assumed that the fume-laden vapours hanging over the zinc rooftops of Paris were sending me visions. The oasis had been catapulted right to my doorway.

"I was just thinking about you," I said before I could stop myself.

She blushed.

"Hi," she said, leaning forward for a kiss, seeing how dirty I was, backing away, and then finally thinking what the hell and pressing her cheek to mine.

Yes, cheek, not lips. It was Alexa. And when she appeared in the doorway of the building site a couple of days after my meeting with Nicolas, it instantly struck me that she was number one of the list of people I'd have wanted to appear there. Except maybe a re-incarnation of John Lennon so he could sing me a few songs to make the days seem shorter. And sign a guitar for me to sell on eBay.

I came out of the tea room to get a good look at her. And good it certainly was.

She'd changed in the months since I'd last seen her. Her hair was a bit punkier—the English influence, I guessed. English women never leave their hair alone like French women do. It has to be "styled." It was cutely styled, though, with a hint of scarlet in there with the blond.

Her figure was still gorgeous, as was her apparent ignorance of its gorgeousness. Did she really not notice that the strap of her shoulder bag was thrusting her breasts out like the carseat headrest of my dreams?

And I'm pretty sure it was the first time I'd seen her wearing a skirt without tights. Now her legs were on public display, and they were a wonderful shade of . . . well, beige. People say that beige is a boring colour, but it was pretty damn interesting when applied to those legs. She could have been the cover girl on *Beige Is Beautiful* magazine.

"You've got legs," I told her.

She blushed again.

"You've seen them before, Paul. Or have you forgotten?"

"No, no. Of course not. I often dream . . . I mean . . ."

Thank Christ this conversation is in English, I thought, so no one else can understand it. Stan and Pavel were hovering near the door, pretending to be in deep discussion about a tub of tile cement.

"Your girlfriend, she isn't here?" Alexa asked, peering into the dust.

"No, she's not exactly the building-site type."

She looked me up and down. "And you are?"

And there was me thinking I looked rugged.

"Well, yeah, but I'm also the taking-you-for-a-cup-of-coffee type if you want."

"I have a better idea. I'm going to an exhibition. Why don't you come?"

"Is it your photos?"

"No." She laughed. "The new Monet show. At the Grand Palais. Haven't you been to see it?" The tone of her question implied that all species more highly evolved than shrimps had been to the exhibition, which made me some kind of whelk.

"No, I've been a little too busy to go to art shows."

"Well come with me now."

"What? Like this?" I slapped at the leg of my jeans and sent up a small geyser of plaster dust.

"Yes, everyone will think you are an artist. It is very chic to go to an exhibition in dirty clothes."

"I can't. The builders will all disappear."

She turned towards Stan and Pavel, and granted them a huge smile before addressing them in French through the cloud of their airborne lust. "Bonjour, Messieurs. Can I borrow Paul for a while?"

"Ah, oui," Pavel wheezed, already reaching for his van keys.

"We will be back in, say, an hour. Around four o'clock. You will still be here, won't you?" Her tone was totally innocent, which ironically made it sound as if she was just off to slip into lingerie and high heels.

"Oui," Pavel said. "We are here."

"Super." She turned back to me. "Et voilà."

Such a trusting girl.

We were only five minutes' walk from the Grand Palais, which is down near the bottom of the Champs-Elysées. As we strolled along the frying-pan-hot pavement I thought how different it was to parading through Ars with Florence. That had been an exhibition in itself. It was a show. With Alexa it just felt like two people chatting, one of whom had recently survived an accident at a flour mill.

"So you're living in Newcastle now, then?" I asked.

"Ha, no. I'm staying in London at the moment. My mum's partner, Yuri, manages his business from there. From his house in Notting Hill."

"Notting Hill, eh? Posh. And your Sacha bloke, he lives there too, does he?" Sacha was the grinning hunk in the photo she'd emailed me.

"Yes." She gazed evasively at the window of the Courrèges shop, a sixties retro-fest of white dresses displayed against a white wall under white neon. It was like looking into a cloud. "I want to take a photo," Alexa said, rummaging down into her bag and making her breasts wobble out of control. I felt that I ought to grab them and stabilize her body for her own good.

"But you won't see anything. It's all white."

"Exactly. Stand against the window."

"You want me in the photo too?"

Like I said, she never used to take photos of me when we were together, at least not while I was awake. Now she was smiling at me from behind her little silver digital camera, singing "White Light White Heat."

"How do you want me?"

"Just like you are. Hands in the pockets, looking at the camera. Yes." She checked the little screen at the back of the camera. "Perfect. Now if you want, we can go to a café and you can maybe wash some of the dust off before we go to the exhibition."

I stood and gaped. Had I heard her right?

"Wash off the dust?"

"Yes."

"Hang on. Five minutes ago you said it'd be cool for me to go there dirty."

"So?"

"So you only asked me to come for a walk so you could take that photo, didn't you?"

"No, of course not." She blushed, with embarrassment or annoyance, I didn't know which.

"All that bollocks about me looking like an artist. It was all . . . bollocks, wasn't it?"

Half of me was saying so bloody what. The other half couldn't resist confronting her.

"No. When I saw the shop window I thought it'd look good. Then I thought, maybe you don't like to be dirty like that."

"Honestly, Alexa. You're just like Florence. Letting me do weird stuff for your amusement."

"What are you talking about?" She was standing there with her hands on her hips, in self-defence attack mode.

"When I was in Corrèze, they dressed me up in stupid clothes, let me cover myself in muck, tried to sell me their fields. I felt like the family clown."

"Well, if you have problems with your girlfriend, that is not my problem, Paul. I am not your girlfriend, OK? I saw the white shop, you're covered with white dust, I said to myself, good photo. Et basta."

"Yeah, well it was just the way you said 'now maybe you can wash.'" I did a cruel impression of a female voice with a slight French accent. "It sounded so snobbish. Like, I really ought to clean up a bit so it doesn't look as though you hang out with homeless people."

Now Alexa was the one gaping.

"OK, Paul. Perhaps in place of 'maybe you can wash,'"—she pulled off a damn good imitation of my imitation—"I could say 'maybe you can bugger off'? That is a new expression I learned in England. Bugger off. Good, isn't it?"

And as if to prove it, she buggered off, taking her shapely skirt for an angry walk down the Avenue François Premier.

The street was named after Frank the First, my old boss Jean-Marie told me, a king who'd tried to make friends with Henry VIII and got told to bugger off. His name clearly did not bode well for Anglo-French relations.

"Alexa."

She half-turned. "Bugger off!"

As I watched her get ten, twenty, thirty yards away, I knew I'd never speak to her again. Her walk, which had been tense and staccato, gradually became more relaxed, her footsteps getting shorter and slower, as if her whole body was shaking off my memory.

Once she turned the corner she'd be gone for ever.

3

I DON'T KNOW who was to blame for the accident.

Morally, it had to be the scooter's fault. I mean, any accident between a pedestrian and a scooter that takes place on the pavement has to be the scooter's fault. The fact that in Paris scooters quite often use the pavements instead of the road is irrelevant.

Though I had to admit he wasn't actually riding along the pavement. He was just mounting it, to padlock his scooter to the base of one of the large table-tennis-bat-shaped tourist maps you see all over the city. He shouldn't have been listening to an iPod, though. That was plain dangerous. If he'd had his ears unplugged, he would have been aware of the dusty Englishman sprinting down the hill yelling "Stop!"

Now I was sure Alexa was a hallucination. Or an angel, staring down at me from heaven, backlit by the glare of the sun.

"Paul, are you OK?"

Her voice sounded real enough, anyway.

"I think so." I did a quick finger and toe-jiggling survey. Everything seemed to be there. And my vision was fine. I could see all four of Alexa's legs perfectly.

"Can you get up?" she asked, looking beautifully worried.

"No."

"No?"

"I mean, not yet. Can you take a photo?"

"A photo?"

"Yes, of me and the scooter. In case I want to sue this bastard."

She described the accident to me as she washed my grazed elbow with warm water out of a teapot. She was dabbing at it with a large cotton napkin.

We were at a café, where Alexa's looks had earned us instant grade-A service from the waiter. Two cold beers and a steaming first-aid kit.

"I turned and you were sort of flying. You had bumped the scooter and then you . . ." She did the sign basketball referees use to show that someone has walked with the ball.

"Somersaulted?"

"Yes. Between the man and the, you know, little window thing."

"The windscreen."

"Yes, and you turned over in the air, and boom, you came down on your feet and then you fell back like you were surprised that you were OK."

"Which I was. Surprised, I mean. Ouch."

The graze was painful but clean. I didn't know where I'd got it. Probably scraping my arm against the little blade of a windscreen. At least I hoped so. A graze from Paris's summer pavements, with the likelihood of *E. coli* germs crawling out of the sun-fermented dog merde, did not appeal.

Alexa took a deep draught of her beer.

"OK, shall we go to the exhibition now?" she asked.

"You mean you still want to go? With me, I mean?"

"Well, you were running after me to say sorry for being an imbecile, weren't you?"

"Yes."

"So let's go."

By all the laws governing the universe, from the creation of a new blood cell to the explosion of a supernova, I should have kissed her.

The waiter who was watching us from the bar, his empty tray still in his hand, seemed to be willing me to do it. Even the sparrow hopping forlornly about by the wheel of a Smart Car outside seemed to be chirruping "Go on, give her one."

Alexa was wiping the beer from her lips as if making way for a kiss. Or just spreading out the beer froth so I'd get an all-over tingle.

But I didn't kiss her.

Something told me that if she was really just wiping away the beer froth, and if the sparrow was only complaining that its feathers weren't air-conditioned, then I'd look a right dick-head when she asked what the hell I thought I was doing. She had a new boyfriend, I was with Florence. So kissing her just wasn't on.

Yes, I was being way too logical. It must have been concussion.

Alexa was looking at me with cruelly kissable concern. "The salon de thé is giving you stress, isn't it?"

"Yeah. The more tea cups you have, the more storms you can have in them. And I have to deal with them all by myself."

"When is she coming back to Paris to help?"

"As soon as the dust settles, I guess. As soon as the place is finished and ready to open." It was the only way I could explain things. Florence wasn't into chaos. She was an accountant, used to clean filing cabinets and neatly tallied figures. Once the tea room was working, and life had become more like one of her filing cabinets, she'd slot back in there. I guessed.

"Let's look at some paintings. They will take your mind off

your problems," Alexa said. "And now, with your wounded arm, people will think you are a performance artist."

The bad news was that there was a real anaconda of a queue snaking across the courtyard of the Grand Palais. Every pair of foreign shorts in Paris had decided to come and hang out in front of the museum.

The city knows all too well the pulling power of its Impressionists, so there'll always be at least one of them in some kind of show. Renoir's women, Manet's laundry bills. Any excuse. And there had to be at least two hundred people waiting in line to see Monet and some unknowns who were sharing the bill with him. Tourists of all types were guzzling water, rubbing on sunblock or simply broiling in the airless open courtyard. There were groups of well-equipped Americans with jungle-ready backpacks and hi-tech walking shoes. Trendy young Japanese couples, dressed for the Jean-Paul Gaultier cat-walk, apparently oblivious to the heat. English families with obese kids speed-licking enormous ice creams before they melted away down their sunburnt arms. And a dozen more tourist subspecies, all in front of Alexa and me.

It looked like a wasted journey.

"Come," Alexa said, and pulled me towards the entrance. "I am a friend of the museum." She held up some kind of pass.

"But I'm not."

"No, you are an artist. Come."

It worked, too. She gave the security guy at the entrance some blah, and he was too cool, and too fascinated by her body, to bother stopping us.

At the reception counter inside, things didn't go quite so smoothly.

"If he does not have a card from the Maison des Artistes or from the Ecole des Beaux Arts, he cannot enter without paying," the woman behind this particular counter said. She had straight black hair, square black glasses and a cold black soul. Or an airconditioned one, anyway. She had her own private little air-cooler on the floor behind her, blowing a pleasant breeze up her skirt.

"But he is an artist. He does not have *cards* on him. He is working," Alexa said.

I held up my elbow as proof that I suffered for my art.

The woman did a Parisian shrug of indifference, comfortably aware that all her job description called for was for her to perch on her stool getting her bum chilled until the museum closed.

"Can't you let him in? He is an English artist and I want to show him some French art."

Alexa didn't realize it, but the way she leaned forward over the counter to plead would have got us and every member of our extended families in for free if the woman had been of the right sexual persuasion.

"No. I need some identification." She was not going to budge.

Alexa gave a little squeak of despair. "But we will have to queue up for hours."

"Why?" the woman asked. "Just go and pay."

We looked over towards the windows where the visitors were paying. They were being let into the hall from the courtyard in small groups of three of four, and then going to stand in line at one of the ticket windows.

The black-haired woman was a genius. We simply crossed the hall, joined the shortest queue, and three minutes later I had my ticket. In a nation where queue-jumping is a sport, we'd just won Olympic gold.

The show itself was disappointing. One huge canvas on which

the half-blind old Monet had splodged what could have been lilies, bullet wounds or the results of an Impressionists' pie-throwing contest, plus a series of views of nineteenth-century France painted by people who thought that trees looked like cabbages.

The commentary explained that these were all "artists—gifted and less so—liberating themselves from the confines of the studio." It was a shame, I thought, that some of them hadn't liberated themselves from the confines of painting altogether.

As we walked around the exhibition, people stared at me, and then, seeing the girl I was with, smiled to themselves. It seemed that Alexa was right. Here, everyone assumed, was an artist and his muse. I did my best to look intellectual, sculpting the air from time to time as if I'd been inspired by one of the paintings. I got a few laughs from Alexa, and even got myself photographed by a complete stranger. An artist's life was fun, I decided.

By the time we reached the exit sign, I'd had enough artistic fun for one day, but Alexa dragged me back to the beginning of the exhibition again and flopped down on a bench in front of the Monet.

"What do you think?" she asked me.

Oh dear, time for intelligent comment.

"Well, I like Impressionist paintings. You know. The cafés, the picnics. It's happy art, isn't it?"

"Yes." Alexa smiled. Seemed I'd hit the right note. She turned back to the Monet and nodded. "It is joyful," she said.

"Right. It's so French."

"So you think we are all joyful?"

"No, I mean, it's all about lifestyle, isn't it?"

"Lifestyle?" Alexa broke off from her contemplation of the lilies or raspberry flans or whatever they were.

"Well yes. I remember when I was at school we went up to

London to see a big Impressionist exhibition. And apart from all the fleshy ladies, what I liked about it was, well, they had fun. They invented this way of getting paintings done quickly so they could spend more time knocking back absinthe."

"What?" This didn't seem to be exactly what Alexa had studied during her art course.

"Yes. I mean, who was the guy who did all the paintings of can-can dancers?"

"Toulouse-Lautrec?"

"Right. What a great excuse for hanging around in bars looking up women's skirts. And the guy who went to Tahiti . . ."

"Gauguin."

"Yes. He took it to the limit, didn't he? He just wanted to go and shag a lot of exotic women."

Alexa laughed dismissively. "Well, thank you, Paul, for this new interpretation of our art history. Monet invented Impressionism so he could go on more picnics."

"Don't get me wrong: respect where respect is due. Britain's greatest contribution to art recently has been sawing cows in half. If I really was an artist," (I lowered my voice so as not to disappoint my public), "I know why I'd go out into the country. A painting picnic would be much more fun than chainsawing the livestock. Don't you think?"

I hoped she did.

She was looking at me as if I was a painting too, to be examined for symbols and meaning, and she couldn't decide if I really was just a mass of pointless daubs.

"I think you're right," she finally said.

"You do?"

"Yes, Monet didn't go so far that he could sell his old bed as art, but he took the first step."

"He did?"

"Yes, lifestyle. It's all about lifestyle. You have given me a brilliant idea."

"I have?"

"Yes, for a series of photos. No!" She shouted the word, and people turned to see who was trying to rape her. "A film. A documentary. Yes!" She shouted the yes too, and the people looked over again to watch me take advantage of her sudden consent.

"A film?"

"Yes. It is brilliant."

And then she kissed me.

There is, apparently, a particular kind of kiss that a girl gives to a guy who's just inspired a documentary.

It lands smack on your lips. It's wet and passionate, as if you've just told her you love her. But it's non-sexual. For the girl, at least.

And it only lasts a second before life returns to normal.

Outside, the heat of the day was abating a degree or two as the streets sank into shade. We strolled up the hill, keeping a respectful six inches between us.

When we got back to the tea room, Alexa was genuinely surprised to see that the builders had not hung around.

"Oh, they are not here," she said.

"No, they often aren't. I'll have to call them and shout a bit so they turn up early tomorrow."

"OK, well . . ." She stood in front of me wondering how to say goodbye.

I put a hand chastely on her upper arm and pressed my cheeks to hers. "We'll have to meet up again so you can explain what this documentary is going to be about."

"Yes, yes. But I must go back to London tomorrow. It is Sacha's birthday. There will be a big party."

"Oh yeah? He's going to be eighteen, is he?" Miaow, I know.

"Ha, no. Twenty-one."

"Right." She was only twenty-three and already into toy boys. Brilliant.

"I will call you when I come back to Paris."

"I'd like that."

"Well . . ." She did that nodding-with-raised-eyebrows thing American actors do when they've run out of lines and the scene isn't over yet.

I put her out of her misery.

"It was good to see you, Alexa. Thanks for coming and taking my mind off my problems."

And filling it with new ones, I wanted to say.

4

T HE GOOD THING about being in work merde is that it doesn't give you time to think about all the other types of merde you might be tempted to get into.

Over the next couple of weeks, I was forced to concentrate all my energies on getting the tea room fitted out, and it paid off. Pavel and Co. were hammering and troweling things slowly into shape.

There were a few crises, like when they realized that Nicolas's plans for the toilet would have meant customers having to stand on the bowl to shut the door, but we sorted them out with common sense, which came a lot cheaper than Nicolas's expertise.

At the end of every day I got out the mop and cleaned up so my craftsmen could start with a fresh canvas the next morning. One evening, I noticed a weird smell in amongst the kitchen units behind my new stainless-steel counter. It took me half an hour of crawling around on the floor and jamming my whole upper body into the cupboards to locate the cause. And believe me, there's something about scooping up the remains of two-week-old builder's lunch with your bare fingers that reminds you why you used to enjoy having a cosy office job.

Like the one that Florence was giving up to come in on the tea room with me.

As the days went by, it became clearer and clearer to me that she didn't realize what she was letting herself in for. She was doing her usual thing of closing her eyes to problems.

I, on the other hand, before I'd served a single cup of tea, had come to realize all too well that I needed a business partner—if I needed one at all—who had their eyes wide open.

What you needed to make a small business survive, I now saw, was a desire to work twenty-four hours a day, seven days a week, and the ability to cram every detail of the business into your throbbing head. Managing the tea room was going to be like running a marathon while juggling ten plates of spaghetti. And what you really don't want when you're doing that is someone tweaking continually at your armpit hairs.

And in the evening, when I was trying to put in an order for plastic spoons on the Internet, Florence would say, "Oh, I'm fed up with this. Let's go out."

I'd be fed up with working late too, but I'd want to get it done before I relaxed. It was the only way to get to the stage where we could pay someone else to order the spoons.

I could see it all coming.

The honest half of me was saying, you've got to accept it. You and Florence were great for a holiday, but it ain't going to work no more.

The trouble was, though, that there was one major logistical problem with telling her it was all off between us—I was living rent-free in her apartment. If we split up, I'd be homeless. And last time I'd looked for a place of my own in Paris, it had been a total disaster. There was no way I had the time or energy to face up to that humiliation again.

So it seemed that I'd have to grin and bear it, even if that did make me a total hypocrite. I looked at myself in the mirror of my half-finished new toilet and tried out a guilt-free Parisian shrug: "Hypocrite, moi?" If I said it fast enough, it sounded like "Hit me."

This inbuilt masochism is the only explanation I can find for why I went to Florence's apartment, grabbed a few essentials, and came back to kip in the tea-room cellar.

Compared to the luxury of Florence's orgy-sized double bed, it was uncomfortable dossing down on a concrete floor, but I found that I slept better on an easy conscience than I had on her expensive mattress.

What was more, now that I was free of moral debts to Florence, I could spring the Nicolas trap.

Next morning, Pavel and I went into a huddle and sketched out the details in our ungrammatical but efficient French.

Pavel would call Nicolas and tell him they had an urgent problem with the toilet that they needed him to solve. He'd say I was away—paying a surprise visit to the île de Ré, for example—so they couldn't ask me. And as soon as Nicolas set foot in the building, I would pounce.

"Is good plan, is very good plan." Pavel's cruel chuckle summed up our feelings perfectly.

So it was with childlike glee that I sat on the downstairs toilet that same afternoon and waited for Pavel to guide Nicolas to his Paul-in-the-box. I had Nicolas's contract on my lap, alongside the estimates that Pavel had provided for the job. I read through them again, and yes, the heron-man fully deserved the kick in the tail feathers that he was about to get.

He was, of course, twenty minutes late for his meeting with Pavel, but at last I heard voices on the stairs.

"Oh, bonjour," I said, as Nicolas opened the door. His panicked eyes and nostrils flickered down towards my trouser level to check whether I was actually shitting.

"Is there a problem with the . . . ?" He stopped and frowned.

He'd already guessed that this was a trap. And a quick glance over his shoulder told him that there was no point trying to do his usual vanishing trick—Pavel and his mates were sitting on the stairs like the audience at a basement comedy show.

"No, no problem. I was just sitting here reading these."

I handed him the two documents to compare. He looked puzzled, which wasn't surprising, because he had to be baffled about how the hell I'd got my hands on one of them.

"I don't understand," he said. He shook his head as if the documents were an assertion that architects were mythical creatures, like abominable snowmen. Actually, part of me wished they were.

"This is your contract, with the estimate for the calculation of your ten per cent." I'd spent a good hour preparing the French sentences I needed for this little interview. The French for estimate is "devis," which seemed to be related to "deviner", meaning to guess. They're very honest about it. "And this second—much smaller—estimate is the one given to you by Pavel for the same work."

"He gave you his . . . ?"

"Yes, he says this is not the first time that you've done this. You see the difference?"

"Yes, but I . . ."

". . . am a thieving shit," I wanted to say, but I hadn't prepared that bit.

"I am sorry, Nicolas, but after seeing this, I have offered Pavel to make an accord. I will pay him his estimate, plus more if he finishes on time. To you I will pay enough for drawing the plans, and I will pay your administration charges for finding Pavel, for ordering some materials, et cetera, and nothing else."

"You—"

I held up a dusty hand that was close enough to his black jacket to convince him not to interrupt.

"You said to Florence that you were giving us a prix d'ami, but you are ripping us off." This was the verb "arnaquer," a very practical word taught to me by a totally impractical friend, Jake the American poet.

"I . . . You cannot do this. We have signed a contract." Even supercool Nicolas was looking overheated now.

"Your contract said the work would begin on this date." I prodded the relevant page. "It did not. Your contract said you would come to see the beginning of work. You did not. And your contract with me has an estimate for the work which is false. Also, this toilet was completely wrong. It was only thanks to Pavel and me that you were able to open the door and find me."

Nicolas stood there and fumed. I guessed that he would have punched me if the venue for our fight had been less dirty.

"Here," I said, holding out two more sheets of paper for him. "One is a new contract between us, with my new conditions. One is a letter that I will send to the Société des Architectes Français if you do not sign the new contract."

He didn't even acknowledge their existence.

"This is jealousy," he snorted. "You are just jealous that she was with me."

"Perhaps. I did not like the idea that you screwed Florence. But I like even less that you want to screw me as well."

He misinterpreted my grin. I was just pleased with myself for getting my French sentence right, but he must have thought I was gleefully imagining a three-some, because he raised his eyebrows as if to say "In your dreams, dustboy."

"You will pay me everything or you will have problems," he threatened, and stomped up the stairs past the grinning builders, his buttocks clenched defiantly in the pose of a man who knows his retreat is being watched by four Polish workmen.

They clenched even tighter when his audience burst into raucous laughter.

5

T HE BEST TIME to invade France is at noon on the first
Wednesday of any month. At midday on the dot, the air-
raid sirens all start howling, and the French totally ignore them.
An invading air force would have several minutes of unchallenged
invasion time before anyone realized it wasn't the monthly test run
and there really were bombers buzzing the Eiffel Tower.

The first Wednesday in August would be ideal. By then, Paris's
ruling classes have left the city. This includes government
ministers, who are ensconced in their holiday homes and have
all forgotten what politics is. One summer recently, France had a
killer heatwave that had old people dropping like flies—especially
those who'd been left alone in Paris by families going away—and
the few Parisian doctors and nurses who hadn't gone on holiday
were begging the Minister of Health to declare an emergency. His
reply was basically, well there's a nice breeze here at the seaside,
what are you moaning about?

Over two hundred years after the French Revolution, "Let
them eat cake" lives on. Let them buy Evian facial sprays.

On this first Wednesday in August, I felt as if the alarms were
sounding for me, too.

Not only was I bedding down on an inflatable mattress in a
building site, I had less than four weeks before I was supposed to
open. I still had no staff, no furniture and no menus—the French

printer kept sending back proofs with new spelling mistakes. Where did he get "hand sandwich" and "hot buttered stones" from?

What's more, after heroically bringing the tea room within sight of being finished, Pavel and his mates had buggered off. It seemed that our bonding over Nicolas hadn't been meaningful enough to stop them adopting the old builders' tactic of Leaving Everything Half-Finished So the Customer Is So Grateful When You Turn Up Again That He Doesn't Care If You Botch the Finishings.

It was a cruel example of completus interruptus.

The air in the streets could have steamed asparagus. And inside the goldfish bowl of the not-yet-air-conditioned tea room it was just as bad. The guys had finished the wiring downstairs but had left upstairs decorated with garlands of hanging cables, so I couldn't even plug in a fan in the main part of the shop, where I was working.

Then in walked Michel, Florence's brother, as carefree as ever, perfectly equipped for the heat with his baggy Indian shirt and loose drawstring trousers. He looked around and nodded his admiration.

"You have made big progress, Paul. Congratulations."

"Yes, but now it stops," I replied in French. "I am like a Jeep in the merde. I am blocked but I can't get out to push myself."

Michel pulled at loose wires, one electrician admiring the capacity of another to leave things unfinished.

"No, I like the floor tiles, very clean. And the counter. Lots of room. It will be a good café."

"Thanks."

He hadn't come just to admire my new flooring, though. He was worried, he said. He switched to English to explain. He'd turned up at the apartment, found lots of my stuff, but no sign of me.

"I knew you weren't in Ré, so I wondered where you were. I have been in the apartment for two days and you never return. I wondered, I mean . . ."

He cocked his head at me like a spaniel waiting for someone to say walkies, and I saw what was going on. He'd asked Florence if she knew where I was, got a surprised "No" as an answer, and they'd assumed I was shacked up with a woman.

"I'm sleeping here, downstairs."

"Here?" He grimaced, looking around at the sheer non-residential bareness of the place.

"Yes. There's a gym on the other side of the Champs-Elysées. I take my shower there every morning. I've bought myself an inflatable mattress. I have some clothes, a sleeping bag, the essentials. It's OK."

"Ah."

I could see that it pissed him off to ask the key questions. Would I be returning to the apartment? Were things on or off with me and Florence?

He started feeling wires again, twisting the three cables sticking out of a hole in the wall into a spindly coral. It struck me that they might be connected to the mains, in which case very soon he was going to be filling the place with an unpleasant burnt-flesh smell that would put off prospective customers. But presumably he knew his business.

"If you want any help . . ." he suggested.

"Help?"

"With the electricity. I am here in Paris to wait for a job. A new film is starting, but I have no money at the moment because I don't have my hours."

"Your hours?"

"Yes, as a film-worker, If you work for enough hours in one

year, you receive unemployment money for the rest of the time. Very good money. But if you don't have your hours you get nothing."

He obviously preferred discussing the nuts and bolts (and wires) of the film industry more than the gory details of my relationship with his sister, because he sat down and explained the incredible French-movie-star-unemployment system. Many big-name actors, he said, are paid the rate they got for their last film as unemployment money from the State when they're not working. So they get the same rate day in, day out, whether they're working or sitting on their yacht in Saint Tropez.

"Same for directors, writers, everyone. That's why we all want to work in the cinema. But only if we can get our hours." The poor guy had the forlorn look of someone who's not quite tall enough to reach the handle on the booze-cupboard door.

"Well, as you can see, I do need an electrician," I said.

"How much will you pay me?"

"How much do you charge?"

He told me his daily rate as a film electrician, and when I'd got up again after my heart attack he said he'd finish the electrics in two days for the price of one, cash.

Which meant that when my first interview candidate arrived that afternoon, there was an electrician in the background busily proving that My Tea Is Rich was a dynamic, waste-no-time business. Staff were being recruited while the tea room was taking shape before their eyes. Michel might have given them the impression that it was OK for some employees to work topless and sing out of tune, but I was too pleased to be back on track to worry about that.

By the end of the day, both Michel and I were feeling a sense of achievement.

I'd interviewed seven job applicants, and scared away only two with my bad French and my non-smoking staff policy. Michel had done all my light fittings and even connected up the air conditioning. We decided to go out for a meal together to celebrate.

It was at this point that Florence chose to call him for a report.

Michel told her where I was living, and added "Yes, on his own," and "Yes, I'm sure."

Then, however, he let slip that he was at the tea room, and, worse still, that he had been working here. He mouthed "Sorry" and handed me his phone.

"Hi, Florence, how are you?" I asked, very chummily, I thought.

"You have Michel working at the salon de thé?"

"Yes. The builders hadn't—"

"So you got rid of my ex-boyfriend and now you use my brother?"

"Use him? I'm paying him."

"I didn't think you were like this, exploiting people."

"Exploiting?" I shot a look of incredulity at Michel, who shook his head as if to say, "Sisters, huh."

"Yes, Nicolas works hard for you and all you do is try to get out of paying him."

"I'll pay him what he's earned, but not what he tried to rip me off for."

"He will sue you if you don't pay him the full ten per cent." It seemed that Nicolas had done some very detailed crying on his ex-girlfriend's shoulder.

"If he sues, he'll only lose even more money. I have the proof that he was trying to defraud me."

"Honestly, Paul, all you think about is money and business."

It hardly seemed worth arguing, but I did anyway.

"It's true that my mind is kind of focussed on trying not to throw all the money I borrowed down the toilet, yes. Down a toilet that your friend Nicolas couldn't even draw straight, by the way."

If our relationship wasn't dead already, it got a fatal kick in the balls as she rang off.

6

D O PEOPLE STILL play Snakes and Ladders? I guess
not—it's much too simple to be made into a computer
game.

But here I was, feeling like I used to as a kid when I slid down
one of those long, grinning pythons. Back at square one. No,
before square one, because at least when I'd arrived in Paris the
previous September, I'd had a job and a decent place to sleep. Now
I had no home, and no job except spending the money I'd
borrowed. The only constant was that, as usual, I was in major
woman merde again.

And the worst person in the world I could have turned to for
advice about women, except perhaps Florence's mum, was Jake the
grunge poet. But in my present masochistic state, I suppose it was
only natural to call him up. We arranged to see a show together
that same night at what he called "this, like, complètement genial
club" in Belleville.

He was waiting for me at a Tunisian café on the corner of an old
shopping arcade that had seen better days—days when there were
actually shops in it, that is. The club, he said, was at the back of the
arcade.

This lower part of Belleville, between the big-brand shopping
zone at République and the prosperity of the Chinese restaurant
area higher up, was lined with budget import shops and hole-in-

the-wall food outlets. The cloying humidity and bare neon light really made me feel that I was in the kasbah in Marrakech rather than a couple of miles north of the Seine. There were veiled women in the streets, and groups of North African men were talking earnestly at regular intervals along the narrow pavements. The streets were much busier in the ethnic areas of the city— probably because if some of these people left the neighbourhood, the immigration officials would never allow them back in again.

Jake was living up here now, he had told me, with the latest in his atlas of women.

"Hey Paul!" he called out as soon as he saw me walking down from the métro station. I felt as if everyone in the whole street stopped to see who was being shouted at.

He was the only European outside the café, although he was dressed in the most Oriental style. He had on a long, loose round-necked shirt with an embroidered collar, whereas the Arab men were all in Western gear. As some kind of concession to the heat, he had cut his straight hair shorter, into a sort of blond shower cap. He certainly looked at ease, slumped back on a white cane chair, an immense Moroccan hokah pipe between his outstretched legs.

"Are those things legal?" I asked as I sat down next to him.

"It is tabac only, man. Try."

He held out the brass mouthpiece on its long tube, but my lungs were burning already from the hot atmosphere. I waved it away.

"Allez, be cool, integrate yourself."

"If you insist." I took the mouthpiece and blew. This caused a satisfying eruption of bubbles in the water bottle and a snarl from Jake.

"You take nothing at serious, man." He took a long puff, as if he needed to prove to the Arabs around us that he for one did not take sucking smoke through a long straw lightly.

"What are you up to these days, Jake?"

He explained in his usual garbled fashion. He was still teaching English, though he didn't have many classes because his business students were all away for the summer. Besides, he had a plan to get out of teaching, he said. This involved "going backwards to go forwards." I could only assume that this actually meant something in the weird non-language he spoke, because he refused "for the instant" to explain.

As far as women were concerned, he was now shacked up with a lady from Algeria.

"Are you nuts? An American living in sin with a Muslim woman?"

He let a philosophical stream of white smoke seep out between his lips.

"Don't inquiet yourself. She's a verve."

"A what?"

"You know. Dammit. Une veuve? Dead husband?"

"Widow."

"Yeah. Widow. Shit. Anyway, the people in her building are totally cool. They're not religious. They're just content that Kalifa is getting some." He started sniggering as if the pipe had been bubbling with a less legal type of smoke. "You ever try a verve?"

"No, I usually stick to my own generation."

"Yeah, well she's only forty, though she looks older 'cause she's had three petits. Anyway, she sure knows how to take her foot."

"Take her foot?" And where does she put it exactly? I wondered.

"Prendre son pied? You understand—enjoy herself. How do we say it?"

I really didn't want to know, I told him. I had enough problems with my own perverse forms of masochism without looking into self-abuse from another continent.

"Anyway, comment ça va for you, Paul? Not très bien, uh?"

"No, not very bien at all."

He nodded wisely and sucked on brass as I talked him through my feelings about Florence's phone call and Alexa's hallucinatory breasts. As I spoke, the city grew darker, the mosquitoes grew bolder, and I had time to sweat out pretty well all of the mint tea I'd ordered.

"OK, if I understand well," he finally pronounced, "you have broken with a girlfriend who is French, and you are attracted by an ex-girlfriend who is also French. It is evident why you are in the merde. You must enlarge your geographic horizons."

I felt like pissing in his hookah to give his tobacco a suitably scornful flavour.

"Yes, well thanks for your advice, Jake. Let me know when you give up poetry and start writing self-help books. What exactly is this concert, anyway?"

"A Lithuanian jazz singer."

"Lithuanian jazz? What's that like?"

"I don't know. Probably like Estonian jazz."

Ask a silly question.

"You know the difference?"

"Oh, yeah. The French, they have no taste for music. They don't know what's good and what's merde. So they listen to anything. That's why France is such a great place for World Music. It's because they can't decide."

"And every type of World Music show attracts different nationalities of women?"

"Exact."

"But you've just said you're living with an Algerian."

"Oh, she's cool with my poésie project as long as I don't bring the women home. Hey, Mokhtar!" He waved towards the café and the young waiter came out to collect his money.

It struck me that Jake was genetically incapable of worrying about anything. If any of the mosquitoes buzzing round us had drunk a drop of his blood, they would have decided that life was too short to bother with all the hassle of biting people and gone to chill out in a drain. The WHO would only need to send Jake on a tour of the Third World, and he would eradicate malaria.

The basement club was as well ventilated as the inside of a jet engine. The low, black-painted ceiling and the lights trained towards the stage had raised the temperature from the ambient jungle at street level to something approaching the surface of the sun. The waistband of my jeans was sopping wet before I'd crossed the entrance hall and dripped myself on to a stool at the bar.

On stage were a lone microphone, a small drum kit and a double bass, all of which I expected to melt at any moment.

Jake's eyes weren't turned towards the stage, though. He was watching the entrance.

"Sure to be some Lithuanian women here, right? Maybe Latvians, also. You got to ask all the women you encounter."

So as the place filled up and we combated dehydration with bottles of beer that seemed to evaporate before we had a chance to drink them, I had a fun time asking every woman who came to the bar what nationality she was. Most of them were French, of course, and only three or four of them took offence at my line of questioning.

The fun ended when the skinny, vodka-slurping singer came on.

I daresay there are some real divas in Lithuania, but this girl was more of a dive-bomber. She squealed and howled, and even the protection of half a dozen beers and everyone else's dope smoke didn't take the pain out of her unprovoked attack on "Sommerr-tam".

"Got one," I told Jake, who was deep in conversation with a Slavic-looking girl.

"Got what?"

"A poem for you. There was a chanteuse from Tbilissi, who sang that the leebing was ee-see . . ."

He stopped me before I could do any more damage to world literature. "That is a merde, man. Tbilissi's not in Lithuania at all. You know nothing in geography."

This, I realized, was true. I could only vaguely remember where I was living, which is always a sign that you should go home.

Besides, the whole Eastern Europe theme was getting me down. I suspected the singer of slipping in a bit of Ukrainian jazz just to spite me.

One taxi ride later, I was back at the tea room, where I flopped full-length on to my inflatable mattress, remembering just too late that I hadn't blown it up before I went out.

Once a masochist always a masochist.

7

THE BIG QUESTION was whether to complicate Alexa's life by telling her my news: like a Picasso painting that's been locked away in the vault of a private collector for fifty years, Paul West was back on the market. She didn't need to worry about giving me a bad conscience if she felt like kissing me again.

Before I could come to a decision, though, she phoned to give me some news of her own. She was in Paris.

"Why don't you come to see me?" she said. "I'm at the film shoot. There are some real French movie stars."

"Where is it?"

"At the Bastille. Will you come?"

"Yeah. Great."

"And bring your business card, maybe you can get a deal to supply food and drink to the technicians. The coffee is horrible here."

I came out of the métro, and turned my back on the new Bastille Opera—well, newish, because it was already looking older and shabbier than the original nineteenth-century one in the Ninth. Several of the entrances had become homeless people's urinals, a large staircase was being used as a tourists' picnic zone, and one whole side of the building was swathed in netting to prevent the blocks of cladding from falling off and killing passers-by. It must have been designed by the guy who trained Nicolas, I thought maliciously.

I walked past a shop selling white-leather sofas, life-size porcelain cheetahs and glitzy chandeliers that would have looked over the top at a transvestites' Abba revival party. This was one of the last vestiges of the days when the neighbourhood had been full of furniture-makers. I'd come along here with Florence once on the way to a Latin club, and she'd lamented the disappearance of the craftsmen, all the time cringing at what she called the "horreurs" in the remaining furniture shops.

Now the street was lined with international shopping chains, plus a smattering of local talent including a gothic Jean-Paul Gaultier building where a wild homeless guy had taken up residence. Perhaps, after his campaigns using smooth sailor-boy models, Jean-Paul was going for more of a shaggy, skin-infection look?

I turned up a side road, where the big chains disappeared and things got more café- and designer-oriented.

The sun was shining straight along the narrow street, filling it with hot, stagnant air. It felt like walking into a tube of chilli sauce. But a hundred metres up the road, on the other side of an unprepossessing door into the "passage" where the shoot was being held, the chilli sauce was suddenly washed away.

I was in a hidden private street, with crumbling apartment buildings lining a cobbled road that led to a shady, tree-filled garden at the other end. The grapevine growing up the white-painted building on my left seemed to be puffing out breaths of pure oxygen. There were traditional craftsmen's workshops here—I could see lengths of brightly coloured leather hanging up in a bookbinder's studio, and hunks of carved wood waiting to be varnished and assembled in a low building full of half-finished chairs.

Where was the film crew, though?

I went to ask a cute, round-faced girl who was loafing on an old cart halfway down the passage. As I got closer, I saw that as well as long bare legs and tight shorts, she possessed a walkie-talkie. A good sign.

"Bonjour," I said. "The film, is it here?" My question sounded a bit weird. Like a guy who's come to collect the "special interest" DVD he's ordered from the sex shop.

"Why?" she whispered huskily.

"I came for Alexa." Which sounded a pretty good name for the dirty DVD.

"Ah, oui, Alexa." Which would have been my best line in the film.

Still whispering, she explained that she'd have to wait until she got the all-clear on the walkie-talkie before she could send Alexa a message. They were getting ready to shoot a scene. I could only assume "they" were underground because there was no sign of life anywhere. There wasn't even an unusually bright light coming out of any of the buildings.

"How long?" I asked.

She shrugged. "I don't know. You can sit here with me if you want."

I wondered what her job description would be on the credits of this movie. Chief cart-sitter?

Or shorts-expander. Those shorts were being stretched to the limit by her smooth yet rounded thighs, which she was scratching thoughtfully with her walkie-talkie aerial.

"Are you her boyfriend?" She looked me up and down, her eyes lingering on what I hoped was an adequate bump in my surfer shorts.

"No." I returned the compliment and enjoyed a few moments admiring the triangle of cleavage poking out above her clingy orange top. She was wearing a small jewelled cross on a chain around her neck, and Jesus was peeking in a decidedly un-Christian way down between her breasts.

"No, you don't look Ukrainian," she said. I wondered how huge my bump would have had to be to qualify for that honour. "You're not French, are you?"

"No, English."

"Ah oui? Can you teach me?" The way she said that was straight out of a dirty DVD, too. The doe-eyed girl asking for instruction in the ways of love.

"Teach me English" is something you frequently get asked as a Brit in France. If it's a woman who wants lessons, it's often a kind of code, and the correct reply is to ask, with an ironic glint in your eye, what she's going to teach you in exchange. I wished it had been Alexa asking me, but these days she was studying Central European vowel sounds by licking the inside of a Ukrainian's throat.

"Do you really have time to teach English, Paul?" Alexa had come up silently behind me and saved me the trouble of answering.

She was dressed in men's khaki shorts and what would have been a green bikini top if it had had a clip at the back instead of a band of material. She exuded that terrifying sexiness that comes from getting shagged well and regularly by someone else.

We kissed each other's cheeks hello, and Alexa introduced me to Virginie, who had obviously grown out of her name a long time ago.

"See you letter," Virginie said in English as Alexa dragged me further down the passage.

"Where are you filming?" I asked.

Alexa hushed me. "The assistant director will get angry if we make a noise, even when they're not shooting. She's a bitch. She told one of us to go and stop the talking in the passage. I guessed it was you."

She pulled me through yet another unprepossessing doorway into yet another shady haven. It was a row of three glass-fronted houses set in a small, silent courtyard. The cobbled yard was crammed full of young half-dressed people sitting about on metal equipment boxes. A torrent of thick cables poured out of one of the houses and into a corner of the courtyard, where a stone staircase went down into some kind of sunken studio. I could make out the tops of metal sculptures poking up out of a pool of white light.

"That's where the stars are. We must be very quiet." Alexa was clutching my arm, holding me back at the doorway, as if there was a real danger of me charging into the centre of the courtyard and performing my off-key karaoke version of "Hi Ho Silver Lining."

"What are you doing in the film?" I asked.

"Assistant."

"Assistant what?"

"Assistant anything. Like the others. It is work experience."

So that was what they were doing. The courtyard was full of unpaid gophers getting work experience in nothing more useful than wearing out their backsides, but dreaming of doing it professionally for the required number of hours a year.

Alexa lowered her voice even further, and pressed her mouth against my ear. "It gets very boring sometimes."

"Taisez-vous, bordel!"

A long-haired woman with an earpiece had poked her head out of the stairway and told us to "shut up, brothel." A common French request. Perhaps their brothels are particularly noisy.

The woman glowered at both of us with equal ferocity. She didn't seem to notice that I wasn't one of the gophers.

"Can't we go and talk somewhere?" I whispered. I didn't fancy sitting on a metal box all afternoon.

Alexa gestured over to a guy who was busy reading the blurb on a can of Coke. She made it clear to him that she was going out for a break. He nodded as if he didn't give a shit.

Virginie waved and winked goodbye, but I didn't get a chance to reply because Alexa was tugging me at a trot towards the street.

"At last, freedom," she said, as we hit the wall of chilli sauce on the other side of the passage doorway. "It's like being a nun."

"Why do you do it, then?"

"Oh, it is good for contacts, and the director is really superb. It is wonderful to see him at work."

"But you can't see anything. He's in the cellar."

"We see him prepare, we hear him explain. Oh, did you bring your card?"

"Yeah." I gave it to her.

"I'll give it to the assistant director."

"But she just yelled at me, she'll hate me."

"No, she yells at everyone. And she saw you. That is the important thing. That is why we are there."

We went and sat at a café that had annexed a huge area of pavement for its terrace, marking off its territory with potted bamboo plants as if to tell the locals that they'd lost access for ever.

Alexa ordered two amazingly thick pink fruit juices for us— "pêche de vigne," or vine peach, whatever that was. The juice came in a bottle, but tasted as if it had been inside the fruit just seconds before.

She sat back and ran a hand down her aching neck. I had to look away. I was thinking that it could have been my hand. And wondering if she wished it was another guy's. But before I could ask whether she'd like some help with the massage, she started going on about bloody Sacha's birthday party.

There had been rivers of caviar, lakes of vodka and champagne, and the street outside had looked like a jam at a Formula One drivers' car park. The armed bodyguards had set up camp on half a dozen rooftops. Sacha's presents had included a Ferrari and a recording studio. And no, not just a large tape recorder for his bedroom, this was a whole building equipped with recording equipment, musical instruments and sound engineers. He was now the boss of Sacha's Studios in Soho.

And if all that wasn't excitement enough, Sacha's dad, Yuri the DVD pirate, had promised to finance Alexa's new documentary.

I didn't dare ask if he'd promised not to bring out a pirate version of it. It might have smacked of sour grapes.

"Thank you," she said.

"For what?"

"For the idea." She held up her juice and we clinked bottles. I made sure I was looking into her eyes. "Na zdorove!" she toasted, and took a swig.

Oh no, I thought, he's turning her into a Red Army tank driver.

"Where we're living in Notting Hill, it is a bit like that passage," Alexa said. "More chic, though." She seemed to have no idea that I might want to talk about us. Or "us."

I listened helplessly as she launched into a description of the film they were shooting. It was the story of an artist who was going through a midlife crisis and couldn't work out if he wanted to run off with his young model or stay with his writer wife, who knew about the affair and was encouraging him to get it out of his system. Very French.

"In the end, the model kills herself."

"Oh yeah, comedy, is it?"

"You English, you think everything must be a comedy."

"Yes, well you French think that everything has to be about love. And that love is so serious that you're not allowed to laugh. Don't laugh, I'm in love. That's a typical French film." Ironically, it was also exactly how I was feeling. Maybe I was turning French.

"So what's an English film? 'Is this good enough to get me a deal to make an action movie in Hollywood?' That's all your directors want to know."

"At least it's more interesting than your director guy working out his hang-ups about his marriage. If they invited him to do a Hollywood action movie, it'd be: when the nation is threatened by nuclear terrorists and a plague of man-eating locusts, the president begins to wonder whether his wife is cheating on him."

Alexa suddenly screamed with laughter.

"I was going to kill you, but you are right," she said. "The assistant director is the director's mistress. And you know who wrote the script? The director's wife." She clapped. "It should be a comedy. The director's mistress helps the director to make a film written by his wife that ends with the mistress killing herself. It is beautiful. This is why I love talking to you, Paul."

"Yeah?"

"Yes, you know nothing about art or cinema but you say more reasonable things than anyone I know."

Leaving aside her barbed remark about my lack of culture, yet again the circumstances were exactly right for a full-on, tongues-and-all celebration of our closeness. But all I had to suck on was the neck of a juice bottle.

"It's great when we talk," she went on. "You give me ideas. And not just ideas for a documentary . . ." She raised an eyebrow suggestively.

"No?" Was this a chance for me to mention my current availability for any new ideas she might want to develop?

"For another one of my projects," she went on. "I can't tell you all the details yet."

"Oh." So this new idea I'd given her hadn't been, for example, to go and spend the rest of the day in bed.

"Don't look disappointed. I will tell you soon. And maybe I can give *you* some ideas."

Oh, she did that all right. I just couldn't find the right moment to tell her about them.

"Now I must go back," she said.

"Go? Already?"

"Yes." She told me that this was her last day at the shoot—she was leaving for London the next day.

"But you always call me the day before you're leaving."

"I know. I'm sorry. Things are in such a hurry for me at the moment. I am organizing my exhibition, trying to start this new film, coming here to make contacts . . . Next time I will call sooner."

"Next time? When's that?"

"Soon."

She stood up, and leaned low to kiss me goodbye. Of course I couldn't resist staring down her tight top at the delightful double portion of beige flesh being held captive in there. When I looked back up into her eyes, she had a half-smile on her face. She knew exactly where I'd been looking, as I guess all girls do when they wear that sort of top.

"I'm sorry, Paul."

"What for?"

"We did not have enough time together today. I have talked too much about my things. But I will see you soon, and we will talk some more. You do not look happy. You must tell me why."

She stroked my hand and turned away.

I wanted to watch her go, but was distracted by a ratty dog that had started to pee on the base of the plant pot approximately three inches from my left foot. I hissed and pretended to kick out at its bony rear end.

The canine rat snapped and growled, as did its owner who suddenly leapt to its defence.

"Hey, don't touch her, she is gentille!" The little bitch was "nice," it seemed. A middle-aged woman in designer jeans snatched the yapping beast out of my reach.

"So is he, Madame," said a voice behind her. Alexa was calling out from a few yards further down the pavement. "He is very nice."

She blew me a kiss and jogged off towards the passage.

What the fuck was that all about? I wondered.

I sat there dripping the last dregs of thick pink peach juice into my mouth and tried to analyse the situation.

Why does she call me the day before leaving Paris and then say we didn't have enough time together? And was her happy babbling about the birthday party and the film shoot a way of avoiding more emotional subjects? Or simply a sign that she was babblingly happy with her life?

I'm not the world's greatest communicator, but she was sending out more contradictory messages than a schizophrenic's video diary.

By the time my bottle had given up its last drops of peach juice, I had come to the conclusion that there were only two things I could be pretty confident of.

One: people are supposed to come to Paris to fall in love. But if I wasn't careful, I was going to let any chance of amour slip away.

And two: it was absolutely no consolation to know that if the worst came to the worst, at least I'd get hired to provide sandwiches for Alexa and Sacha's wedding.

4

Liberté, Egalité, Salon de Thé

1

GOING TO BED with someone for the first time is like eating a clementine. No, I don't mean because you can spit the pips out afterwards.

When you look at a clementine you never know what it's like inside. Sometimes the peel is really tight-fitting, and the fruit is pressing its curves up into the skin. But the clementine itself can turn out to be bone-hard and juiceless.

If the peel is loose, the fruit might be burstingly ripe, or it might be limp and uninspiring. You just never know. Clementines are much bigger teases than apples or bananas.

Of course, one major difference between undressing someone and peeling a clementine is that clementines don't talk to you while you're doing it.

This is one of the many reasons why peeling French women, or undressing them, I should say, is interesting. From the moment you first slide your fingertip into their waistband until you're both lying there breathless, you hear lots of foreign noises.

It must be pretty exotic for a French woman to go to bed with an English guy, too. How many Frenchmen shout out "Tally ho!" "Bizmillah!" or "Foul, ref!" as they hit boiling point? Not that I do any of those, of course.

But I'm getting a bit ahead of myself.

It was ten to eight on the third Wednesday of September.

The tea room had been due to open on the first Monday of the month, though I'd always known it wouldn't. Builders are builders, after all.

It was light, and the streets were just starting to get busy. Women were clipping along in their heels on their way to the office or to open up their chic boutiques. Cars were cruising in search of newly liberated parking spaces. Furtive dog-owners were loitering while Fido chose where to poop. I was standing in the middle of my gleaming new tea room, wondering what essential things I'd forgotten to do.

The days running up to the opening had been a bit of a bungee jump, with me heading straight for the bottom of the ravine wondering whether I was going to get the thrill of a bounce or suffer an embarrassing splat. I still wasn't a hundred per cent sure I'd remembered to attach the elastic to my ankles. Would we open the doors and then find out we had no teabags? Would people buy their food and then ask why there weren't any chairs?

To combat my nerves, I was chomping on an apple. I was peeling it and cutting off slices as I went along, which I'd never done before I came to France. Here they seem to peel everything, including nectarines that cover you in sticky juice right up to your armpits. And as I was hacking off chunks of fruit I was thinking, I'd much rather be peeling a clementine.

But no, I told myself, the previous few weeks had been pretty clementine-free—apart from one very fruity exception—and all the simpler for it.

Clementines can really do your head in if you let them get to you.

Florence had had one last crack at doing my head in.

When she finally returned to Paris in mid August, she called me up from the apartment and asked me to come and take away the rest of my things.

Before I got the chance to do that, though, I had to get frisked by her bodyguard. Or at least that was how it felt. When I rang at the door, I was greeted by a pair of shoulders that had probably had to turn sideways to get into the apartment. Sitting on top of them was a handsome shaven head with a tiny black beard.

"Pull?" he said, as if he wanted to do just that to various sensitive parts of my body.

"Oui, Paul. Bonsoir." I held out a hand, which he duly squashed to the shape and consistency of a roadkill rabbit.

"Jean-Paul," he replied.

Florence was lurking behind him, looking tanned and mouth-wateringly sexy, but acting ultra-cold.

If I'd had time to bother about things like pride, I'd have dressed up a bit to come and say farewell. But when you're doing a late-night removal after a day of shopfitting, you don't have time to slip into anything slinkier than cut-off jeans splattered with varnish and an ancient red T-shirt that had now turned into a pink tent.

Florence introduced the guy as her old Pilates teacher. She'd told me once that she used to go out with her Pilates teacher. The mysteries of my gigantic Corrèze trousers, and why everyone in Brigitte's village thought I was a midget, were instantly explained. This was her superhuman ex, the guy with lashings of upper-body strength but no taste in fabric design. Although this evening he was looking positively swish in jeans and an annoying silver T-shirt designed to let muscular men show off their biceps and nipples. Perhaps, I thought, he had left all his most hideous clothes down in Corrèze to be used for the ritual humiliation of Florence's new boyfriends.

I noticed he was looking defensive, which was satisfying. Here was a guy who could walk past a scaffolding gang and say, "Hey fellas, need a hand?" and they'd rush to find him a hard hat, and he was eyeing me as if I was some kind of Bruce Lee.

So even guys like him can suffer from a someone-else-has-been-shagging-my-girlfriend complex, I realized. It was good to know.

I asked, with fraternal concern, what Florence was going to do about work now. She'd packed in her big-company job to help me open the tea room.

No problem, she said. The unions had forced the company to stop laying people off, and she'd asked to be reinstated.

It figures, I thought. She was going back to her old life, as if I'd never been there to disrupt it.

Our conversation had just breathed its last when Jake, my poet and life counsellor, arrived at the front door. He was helping me with the move. He was going to store, and no doubt use, my excess clothes and my collection of bizarre French cooking implements, and had been parking my hired van while I went up to say hello and goodbye to Florence.

One dilemma, though. Did French etiquette dictate that you kiss your lost love goodbye?

She hadn't come forward to do the cheek-rubbing thing when I walked in, and she'd even crossed her arms as if to keep me away. She seemed to be angry with me, although all I'd done as far as I could see was knuckle down to the work I'd always said I'd do. Oh, and fall out of love or lust or whatever with her. But we were quits there.

I decided to invent my own French etiquette. Announcing a loud "au revoir, Florence," to make it clear to everyone in the room that I was not intending to carry her on to the balcony for one last bout of nude Pilates, I walked towards her. She didn't back off, and even uncrossed her arms. I bent forward from the waist to keep any risk of genital contact to a minimum, and said "mwa" on each side of her face. She did the same, even putting a fleeting hand on my shoulder, which wasn't strictly compulsory.

She smelled, as usual, of sweet coconut, and I suffered a moment of weak-kneed regret that this was my last breath of her, before remembering that my coconut days were best behind me. I had Cheddar and fruit cake and toasted ham sandwiches to think of now.

2

"Is the water boiling, Katy?" I asked. "It has to be boiling to make decent tea."

"Yes, if the urn doesn't let off steam soon, I think it's going to explode."

"I know how it feels."

Katy was an English girl supposedly working as a language assistant at a lycée, but who was free most days because the teachers were too scared to have a real English-speaker in their classes. She reminded me a bit of when I first met Alexa. You could tell that she wasn't a professional in the café business but you didn't care. She was bubbly, smiled a lot and wouldn't assume that customers were there to be ignored or insulted. I hoped.

Katy was standing by the huge stainless-steel urn in the centre of the food counter that ran along the right-hand wall. In front of her was a clutch of small stoneware teapots with "My Tea Is Rich" stencilled on the side. These were arranged to be the first things you set eyes on as you walked into the place. I wanted it to be clear that this was a salon de thé anglais, even if it wasn't all oak, pot pourri and frilly aprons, as the French might expect it to be.

The idea was that after taking in the teapots, your eye would move naturally on to the rest of the gleaming food counter. It was glass-topped, so that you could stare down at all the British gastronomic delights on offer as you queued (assuming there would be enough people to form a queue).

Standing expectantly behind these delights were two decidedly non-British people.

There was a girl from Madagascar whose real name had about fourteen syllables, so she told everyone to call her Jeanne. She spoke perfect French and passable English, and her gestures as she spoke were some of the gentlest movements I'd ever seen performed by a hand. She was a trainee dentist who had come to France hoping to get her qualifications recognized, but had got bogged down in a squabble between the two countries' Ministries of Health. She was doing odd jobs and starting her dentistry degree over again. Unfortunately for her, she was perfect for the tea room.

Next to Jeanne was Yannick, a French version of Bill Gates, with a lank fringe and metal-framed glasses that made you want to say "science student" as soon as you looked at him.

In fact, very few of the gastronomic delights that Jeanne and Yannick were going to dish up were a hundred per cent British. That would have sent the customers screaming out the door. Our curried potato salad was made with the best French mayonnaise. All our other salads came with the least English vinaigrette in Europe. And the ingredients for our toasted sandwiches—cheese, cheese and ham, cheese and tomato, or, if you were feeling especially adventurous, cheese, ham and tomato—had never crossed a national border.

It wasn't until you got halfway along the savoury foods, and were well acclimatized by now, that things started to get a bit more British. I had brought in some genuine Bradford chicken tikka and real Somerset sausages (well browned to stop them looking so limp and inadequate compared to French saucisses).

Only the sweets had no complexes about their nationality. The French love English desserts. Parisian cafés often do crumble (which they eat cold for some unfathomable reason), and carrot cake has plenty of fans on this side of the Channel. These and our selection of tea-time goodies would have tempted a French supermodel to forget her sparrow's-kidney-a-day Atkins diet.

And at the far end of this garden of earthly pleasures, I would be waiting by the till, getting a chance to touch all the lovely money tinkling (or preferably, folding) into the coffers to pay off my staggering builders' bill.

Only when the customers had got all their food and paid their dues, could they go and sit at one of the fifteen industrial-strength Formica tables that I'd had sent over from the UK.

However, all of this was pure theory so far, because it was just before eight and the doors were still closed.

"OK, everyone ready?" I threw my mutilated apple in the bin and looked around one last time. Too late to worry now.

I got a bright "Yup!" from Katy, who was clearly feeling much perkier and happier than me. She had her short hair up in two little pigtails that looked like antennae channelling energy into her smile.

Jeanne looked as calm as I would have done if given the choice between making a pot of tea and poking my fingers around in people's mouths.

Gilles, the taller of my two student chefs, grinned encouragingly from the top of the staircase leading down to the kitchen. He and his friend Julien, both of them in their last year at cooking school, were going to alternate in the kitchen. They had seen Jamie Oliver on Cuisine TV and thought the idea of working in an English café was as cool as riding a scooter through the corridors of Buckingham Palace.

Only Yannick was as nervous as me, and fiddling with his name badge.

We all had name badges. I wanted the customers to feel that the staff were potential friends, and not enemies, as the French service sector often tries to make you think.

All we needed now were customers.

But when I unlatched the door, the first thing I saw was my ex-boss.

Jean-Marie Martin, chairman of VianDiffusion (aka VD) Foods and mayor of the Norman town of Trousur-Mayenne, had been waiting in his double-parked car on the opposite side of the road. He now strode across, ignoring the traffic and defying anyone to knock him over. Nobody dared take up the challenge. Men with his natural authority don't have to wait for cars to stop, even in France.

He entered and looked around the place as if he owned it. Which he did. Well, the walls and floor space, anyway. He'd originally bought these premises and six or seven others in Paris when he'd hired me to open up a chain of tea rooms for his company. After he changed his mind and sacked me, he hung on to the shops and rented them out. When I decided to go it alone, I persuaded him to give me a year's lease with the option of buying the property at market price once the lease was up.

"Hello and congratulations," Jean-Marie declared in his excellent English. "Hello," he repeated on catching sight of Katy. He hadn't lost his habit of trying to hypnotize women.

"Welcome, Jean-Marie." I shook his hand, which was, as usual, poking out of a superbly tailored suit. Today he was in a pewter-grey creation with a lining the colour of recently sliced smoked salmon. His tie was royal-violet silk and had been knotted by a team of precision engineers. The same team had groomed his thin, dyed-brown hair back across his perfectly tanned forehead.

Here was a man obsessed with details, so it was reassuring to see him nod his approval when he looked around the tea room. Almost as reassuring as the hygiene inspector the week before.

"What will you have?" I asked.

"Ah." He smiled for the gallery. "Perhaps the charming young Katy can serve me with a cup of English tea?"

"Of course, Sir, what sort would you prefer?" Like all women, even those a third his age, Katy was gazing into his eyes as if she couldn't wait to be asked for a blowjob. I don't know where he buys his charm, but it's not from the aftershave counter of any shop I've ever managed to find.

Jean-Marie sighed in anticipation of the pleasure to come, and ran his eyes down the list of teas next to the urn.

"Darjeeling? With a *nuage* of milk?"

Katy giggled and did her stuff with the teapot.

"Come, we must talk," Jean-Marie said to me. Which sounded ominous.

As we sat facing each other over white Formica, I was reminded of our last meeting the previous May. I'd gone to his apartment and blackmailed him into letting me use the name My Tea Is Rich, which, strictly speaking, belonged to his company. To get his agreement, I'd threatened, or rather suggested that I was in a position to threaten, to reveal to the press that he'd been importing English beef when it was forbidden in France.

At the time he'd been running for office as mayor in a town where he had no chance of winning without support from two ultra-patriotic parties, so he didn't want any rumours about illegal trade with France's traditional enemy.

Since then, he'd rapidly become a much bigger player in the national political game.

French political parties seem to fracture and re-form with

incredible frequency as one ego outbids another for leadership of various factions. And according to ex-colleagues of mine, Jean-Marie's innate self-belief and circle of influential friends had already projected him to a position where he'd only have to make a few key speeches, and he'd find himself at the head of a breakaway "traditional values" type of party. Anti-crime, pro-family, vague on Europe, distrustful of America and French steak for everyone. What voter with an ounce of Gallic blood in their veins could argue with that?

So I assumed I was in for a politely delivered death threat aimed at quashing any future rumours about English beef.

"I have watched you," he said.

"Oh yes?"

"When I came back to Paris in the summer, I saw how you were working here. In the last two weeks I saw your progress. The décor is excellent." He gestured towards some of the framed pictures on the tea-coloured walls. Instead of going for golf, cricket and croquet scenes, I'd opted for a collection of superbly kitsch photos by a Brit called Martin Parr. There were garish close-ups of fluorescent cakes, a queue at a chip shop, sunburnt holidaymakers with melting ice creams, and a whole bunch of similar shots affectionately taking the pee out of British food.

"And the—how do you say façade?"

"Façade."

"Really? Yes, the façade looks very good. The name—My Tea Is Rich. It looks fine, no?"

"Yes, thanks, Jean-Marie. I know it was your idea, and it was a good one."

"Even if you said it was bad at first?"

"Yes, I know." I nodded shamefully, though I had never actually said that it was a bad name. The word I'd used was "crap." But that was before I realized that the French loved "My Tea Is Rich," because it was a pun on what they'd always learned as a "typical" English sentence—"my tailor is rich." It doesn't mean anything to us Brits, of course, but then we all go round asking "Où est la plume de ma tante?" which only makes the French think that we have relatives who are careless with their writing materials.

"And your, what do you say, slogan? *Le plus British des salons de thé*. I like it."

"Thanks." Here, it comes, I thought. After reminding me how much I have to lose, he's going to tell me exactly how I could lose it.

"We will come to your party."

"You will? Oh, good." This was our official inauguration do a couple of weeks later. I preferred to get things running smoothly before I officially revealed that we were open. It would be good to have Jean-Marie at the party. A minor political star like him would do wonders for PR in the neighbourhood.

"With my wife. And my son."

"Benôit? How's he doing?"

"Huh." A tiny flicker of exasperation cracked his mask for a moment. "After changing from medicine to biology, now he will do—how do you say—*oenologie*."

"Oenologie?" Wasn't that something to do with masturbation?

"Yes, you know, the study of wine. Franchement, il se fout de ma gueule." This sentence about his son taking the piss was delivered in the same growl that he'd used all those months ago when swearing at me for trying to blackmail him. "He is now twenty-five, bordel. He must work."

"Yes. And how is . . ."

I was going to ask after Élodie, his generous daughter, who

had given me so much more than a room of my own when she'd sublet her apartment to me. But Jean-Marie hadn't finished with Benoît. He held out a restraining hand and looked me square in the eyes.

"He must work for you."

"What?"

"Benoît. He must work here."

"Here? But I've got all . . ."

His hand clamped down slowly but firmly on my forearm. His voice became a soft purr.

"We will come on Saturday. With Benoît, and with a journalist who will make a television report about me. You would wish your salon de thé to appear on TV, I think?"

"Sure, yes."

He released my arm.

"Good, you will propose to Benoît to work here. With the charming Katy, perhaps?" He turned to look over his shoulder and smile at her.

What the hell was he up to? I wondered. Benoît gets off with Katy, brings her home to meet the folks, and Dad whisks her away from inept son to some swish château for the weekend? No, surely not. He'd only just seen Katy for the first time. There had to be something else going on here apart from an old guy's taste for young, impressionable flesh. But what?

Jean-Marie clapped his hands to conclude our meeting, and got up to leave.

"Excellent tea," he said, even though he hadn't touched it. Katy blushed. As he passed the till he lay a ten-euro note on the counter. "Excellent service, also." Katy's blush got even redder, which didn't seem humanly possible.

Jean-Marie crossed the road, sweet-talked a traffic warden out of giving him a ticket, and drove off, giving a wave to the gallery of my staff who were gaping at him through the window.

They didn't realize that in all likelihood he'd just cost one of them a job. Still, isn't that the mark of a great politician? They make you unemployed and still you vote for them.

3

A FTER A QUIET first morning, trade quickly began to pick up. The place was never packed out, but from the second day on, we were rarely empty between around nine in the morning and closing time at seven, which was fantastic news.

The problem was that with days settling into a rhythm, I had time to think of other things.

Clementines, for example.

I still had a hell of a lot to learn about them.

Why, for example, when things had been looking promising with Alexa, did she have a beautifully ripe clementine delivered to my door?

At the end of that first week, I got a call from someone who said she'd got my number from Alexa.

It was cute little Virginie, the girl from the film shoot. I mean, here was a clementine who in several key areas showed signs of being all grapefruit. What did Alexa think I was going to do? Take her out and have a polite conversation about working conditions in the French cinema industry?

No, of course not. Alexa must have known what would happen, so I could only assume that she'd given Virginie carte blanche to go where her instincts took her.

And what instincts.

The day after she called—a Saturday—I took her to dinner at a great couscous restaurant near Bastille. It served spicy stews, thick North African wine, and gooey sweets that gave Virginie the chance to show me that she had no complexes about licking her fingers in public. With the first flick of her tongue, she made all the guys at the other tables swoon with envy.

She then took me to a dimly lit bar around the corner where the ceiling was decorated with women's bras. This predictably encouraged a rather suggestive conversation about women's underwear, and what kind Virginie enjoyed wearing.

Across the road there was another bar, with long, low sofas, where two people who were just getting to know each other could relax, lie back in the corner, and see if their limbs and lips liked being rubbed together.

It felt only natural to pop the question, "Your place or yours?" and after a short taxi ride to the Twentieth arrondissement, we were playing chase the hormones up the stairs to her studio apartment.

The best clementines are of course the ones that peel the easiest, and it took all of three seconds for Virginie to peel off and leap on to her bed.

This was where those exotic sounds came in. Every touch of my fingertips produced a new word. Some of them sounded like items on the restaurant we'd been to. Sheesh. Kiiiifff. Muuhaah. Others were real French words, an exercise in slow-motion pronunciation. C'eeest booooon. Doouuucement. And one I had heard before, but was pleased to hear again. Ooouuuiiii.

"Wow," I said when we were both bizmillahed out.

"Do you want to stay?" she asked. "I don't mind if you go home. But you can stay."

"I would like to stay, yes." Sleeping on a real mattress with a real woman would be a novelty for me. And breakfast might be fun, too.

"I must tell you. I'm not really looking for a boyfriend." She was leaning up on one elbow and looking cutely guilty, as a recently shagged woman often does, even when she's got nothing to feel guilty about.

She pulled at the cross that was still clinging on to its snug resting place in her cleavage. I didn't blame it. The cleavage had turned out to be even better than I'd pictured. She had those wonderful breasts that meet in the middle and tempt you to play all sorts of rude games.

"No?"

"No, I just split up with my boyfriend. He was pissing me off, he was so boring." She said he'd been "gonfling" her—inflating her, as the French say. From where I was lying, he'd made a good job of it, too. "I told my friends about you," she went on, "and they said, go on, have some fun with him."

"Well tell them thank you from me." A sudden thought struck me. "Did Alexa tell you that when she gave you my number?"

"No, she's not really a *friend*. I just know her from the shoot."

"What *did* she say about me?"

"Nothing, really."

"Oh."

Virginie misread my confusion, and seemed to think I was offended.

"I could tell she likes you, though," she said.

"I see," I said, although I didn't see at all.

"You don't have to stay. I won't mind. But it could be fun, don't you think?"

"Yes, I think."

"Good. Do you like it when I put my breasts here . . . and here?"

There was no need to confirm verbally that I did.

But I couldn't help wondering. Was this *really* what Alexa wanted me to be doing?

4

A NOTHER THING THAT I now had time to deal with was finding somewhere to live.

It really was not practical stashing my inflatable mattress behind a curtain in the basement every morning. Any of the customers going downstairs to the loo would only have had to carry on along a little passageway to be confronted with the unfortunate truth about their genial host upstairs. He was, to all intents and purposes, homeless.

This was where Yannick, the science student, came in useful. He wasn't yet particularly skilled at getting toasted sandwiches out of the machine, but he had some friends who were looking for a fourth person to share their apartment.

It was down in the Fifteenth, in a part of town that was mostly full of middle-class families and not particularly lively. But Yannick said his friends were fun. They were in their last year at business school, and they were all on work placements in big French companies. Paid work placements, too, which was good news. I didn't want to be the one paying the rent every month.

I made an appointment to go and meet them one evening after closing time.

I should have guessed from the taxi driver's reaction that things were destined to go awry.

"Rue Eugène," I told him.

"Rue Eugène?" He didn't know it.

I looked again at my slip of paper and realized I'd forgotten to tell him the end of the name. After I read it out, he cackled for most of the fifteen-minute journey. I had no idea why.

The building itself wasn't especially amusing. It was one of those typical six-floor French apartment houses that all seem to have been put up in the same two weeks in the 1890s. Or should I say six weeks, to take the builders' delays into account.

A digicode takes you into a hallway with tiny black-and-white tiles on the floor. There's a rack of letterboxes, a couple of which are always bulging with junk mail. Then a glass door with a frame painted to look as if it's made of natural wood. Next to this, on the wall, a bare aluminium entryphone, with a double row of buzzers. Here you choose a name on the list and press the relevant button. The door buzzes, you push and you're in a small stairwell that, if you're unlucky, will have a tiny one-person lift that's been installed to push up the value of the apartments on the top floors. I say unlucky, because if like me you're going up to the fifth floor, you're tempted to use it, and as soon as the concertina door shuts you in there you start wondering whether there's enough oxygen to last the trip.

There are thousands of these buildings in Paris, and I didn't notice the subtle variations until Jake explained them to me.

You have to check whether the mailboxes have been broken into (in this case there were no obvious signs of forced locks), and whether the stairs are unvarnished and dirty (no concierge, or a bad one), covered in red stair carpet (posh residents and snooty concierge) or polished so brightly that you need crampons to stay on them (houseproud concierge who might be up for some extra cleaning work in your apartment).

The lift in this building was new and slid upwards pretty

smoothly, though I had plenty of time to read the notice telling me that it was forbidden to use the lift if the building was on fire. Only thing was, you wouldn't have seen the notice till you got in and the door closed behind you.

And these buildings never have fire escapes. What are you supposed to do if you live on the fifth floor and a fire breaks out in the staircase? I wondered. Douse yourself in Perrier water?

"You are Pool?" A breathless girl with short mousy hair, red cheeks and a slightly insane grin opened the door and waved me in before I had a chance to say yes or no. "I am Marie-Christine," she said.

Two guys were hovering in the entrance hall, staring at me with unnerving anticipation. It felt like a film in which someone gets invited to dinner and they're dinner.

The three of them shook my hand and welcomed me in English of sorts. There was Théodore—small, black-haired, with a dark five o'clock shadow; Matthieu—even taller than me, with blond hair and freckles; and the breathless Marie-Christine, who was conscious of being slightly overweight and seemed to jiggle around permanently so you could never get a good look at her. They told me I could call them "Théo," "Matt" and "Marie Hee," though I was pretty certain that "Hee" was a nervous tic rather than part of her name.

"Come into ear." Fortunately, I was used to French accents and knew that Marie was inviting me into the living room rather than suggesting aural sex.

I sat in one of the four battered leather armchairs facing a tiny TV. The bare floorboards were looking suspiciously clean for a shared house, I thought. No wine stains, and not even a stray magazine, joke plastic vomit stain or charred wig lurking under any of the chairs. (Yes, I have lived in some bizarre shared houses in my time.)

Both the living room and the hallway, which had been lined with neatly arranged shoes and tidily hung coats, smelled suspiciously of housework. Frantic cleaning after a blood-splashed cannibal party, perhaps?

"You on drink?" I guessed that Théo was offering me refreshment and not inquiring about possible alcoholism.

"Yes, please." I accepted a bottle of beer and sat there being stared at by these three people who wanted to eat me.

"So, you're looking for a fourth person to share?" I said to break the silence.

They squinted back at me.

"Footh?" Marie asked.

"You want another person to live here with you?"

"Ah yes, we want an udder."

"You Hinglish or Hamerican?" Matt asked.

"English."

"Good, I like earring Hinglish."

"But you like free ends?"

I didn't know how to answer Marie's question. She seemed to be back in her "come into my ear" territory.

"Free ends?"

"Yes, you know. Hoss, shorn lair."

Maybe this was some new business trend I'd missed out on, I thought. For all I knew, horse-shearing had become an essential part of international trade since I'd graduated from catering school.

"I don't know much about it," I confessed.

They almost fell out of their armchairs in shock.

"You done no free ends?" Théo gasped.

"No, never."

"You wash." Marie jumped up and ran out of the room.

Now I was getting scared. If she came back in with a sponge, soap and a pair of shears, I was out of there, inflatable mattress or no inflatable mattress.

The other two sat smiling at me while we waited. I heard Marie's small feet padding back down the corridor, and braced myself to run.

But she returned with nothing more sinister than a portable DVD player. And when the first pictures flashed up on the screen, I relaxed.

Guitars jangled out, actors with silly bouffant nineties haircuts leapt around in a fountain.

"*Friends*," I said. "Ross, Chandler."

"Yes!" They all cheered. "Fibby, Ha-shell, Showy."

"You no diss, yes?" Théo asked me.

"Of course."

"Oof," he said as if I'd just punched him. But this, I knew, was the French way of saying a phew of relief.

After this early misunderstanding, we all got on fine. I taught them how to say "Chandler," and they plied me with beer. A fair exchange.

They told me the rent, which was acceptable, pointed to various empty parts of the fridge, which were easily big enough to cope with my limited home-cooking ambitions, and showed me my tooth-mug space in a bathroom that was astonishingly free of curly hairs.

What was more, the cleanliness was not down to any horrific communal cleaning rota but the brilliant idea of chipping in to pay the concierge, who would even iron shirts and scrape any pans that had got out of the roommates' control.

It sounded like a great deal, and I was back there with my essential stuff at ten that same evening. Marie even lent me a set of sheets, which almost made me cry with gratitude.

Life, I felt, had just become a little more merde-free.

Silly moi.

5

THE DAY BEFORE the inaugural tea party I got a weird email from Alexa, wishing me luck and advising me not to work too hard.

"Don't forget to take some time for yourself," she told me. "Relax, get pampered."

Did that really mean what I thought it did? Was she telling me to call Virginie for some more fruity R&R?

Not the kind of question you can ask a girl directly.

I replied that I'd got myself well and truly pampered a few days before, and thanked her for passing on my telephone number.

Then Jake called to pass on some very worrying information, in his inimitably uninformative way.

"I don't think your site's branched," he said.

"My what's not what?"

"You know, your site Web. It's not on ligne."

"It's not?"

"No. I was posting my posy . . ."

"You were what?"

"Posting my posy. Putting it on ligne. You know. I'm editing my poems on ligne, right? And, oh man, à propos, I found a super Estonian site. Like, Estonians reunited? All these women. It's genial. You know they're connected to the Basques?"

He rambled on about the linguistic links between Estonians, Basques, Finns and Hungarians and the chances of sleeping with their female populations, while I started to get seriously worried about my Web site. It ought to have been on line already. Last time I'd spoken to the designer, everything was on schedule. Maybe Jake had got the address wrong?

"Jake . . ."

"So Europe should be OK, but terminating with Africa is like really dur, man."

"Jake . . ."

"Like, there's no woman in Paris from Sudan, Somalie, Eritrea. Which is like, too ironic."

"Ironic?"

"Yeah, it's the *horn* of Africa. Horn, horny, right?"

"OK, so how about, I couldn't find girls from the Horn, so I had to make do with porn?"

Very cruel of me, but I knew that taking the piss was the only way of stemming his flow of geo-sexual information.

"Hey, man, I told you, you know, you've got to show un peu de respect for my posy."

"Yes, I'm sorry, Jake. I do respect your posy. But I need to ask you about the Web . . ."

"Oh, damn, gotta go. Boss is arriving."

"You're at work?"

"Yeah, I'm in a course with Madame Brunerie."

"You're in a lesson now?"

"Yeah, I said it would be good for her to listen to a real English phone conversation. But my boss is arriving. At tomorrow. Ciao."

He hung up and I wondered what his student would have learnt. The interesting verb "to post your posy." Oh, and that her teacher was a sex addict.

And still they didn't fire him?

*   *   *

He was right, though. My Web site wasn't on line. And when I called the Web site designer she explained why. It was very simple, really—she didn't know how to put Web sites on line.

"But you are a Web site designer," I reminded her in my calmest French.

"Yes, I design Web sites. But that doesn't mean to say I can put them on line."

"But that is like a train driver saying he can drive a train but he doesn't know how to stop it."

"No, it is not," she said.

"Well, who will put it on line, then?"

"I don't know," she said.

"But I need it to be on line when I have my official opening party."

"Well you'd better find someone really quickly, then."

Her logic was so dazzling, her indifference so perfect, that I had to hit myself repeatedly over the head with my phone as a kind of homage to her genius.

I T WAS SATURDAY afternoon, just before four.

I'd got all my staff in to help out at the party—Katy, Jeanne, Yannick, the two chefs, and a part-timer, Fabrice, a small Corsican guy who hadn't been able to come on the opening day because he'd had to go and sign up for his university Polish course. Not that he intended to study the language—he just wanted cheap students' social-security cover. The Eastern European languages faculties were apparently full of students who never attended lectures and tutors who got paid for doing nothing.

I lined up my troops and congratulated them on a job well done. We had closed the doors after the lunchtime rush, rearranged the tables in a long L-shape, and piled every square inch of table top with quasi-English teatime treats. The counter was given over to teacups and the holy brew itself. The tea urn was decorated with good-luck cards I'd received, including one from my folks apologizing for not coming over for the party, and reminding me that they didn't have enough money to bail me out if things went wrong. Thanks for the confidence, guys.

All of us were kitted out in My Tea Is Rich T-shirts, and as we posed for photos behind our battlements of cakes and sandwiches, we looked a suitably young and keen band of new recruits.

Of course, I'd originally hoped that Alexa would do the photos, but I hadn't even dared to ask her. It would have felt so complicated, given the whole Virginie situation. So in the end I'd just got a guy from the Yellow Pages.

One of the first guests to arrive at the party was Virginie herself. We hadn't seen each other since that hot night, but neither of us seemed to take this as an insult. She kissed me full on the mouth with enough tongue to let all my staff know that we had shagged, and then headed off to the table where we'd set up all the cakes. Though it seemed to me that there wasn't much room in her tight, low-cut trousers for chocolate sponge.

My old colleague Bernard the human walrus turned up, too, and I thought it was kind of him given the tensions between us when we'd worked together. He'd been forced by Jean-Marie to speak English in all our meetings, which had been as cruel as making a real walrus run the four-hundred-metre hurdles. He'd hit every linguistic obstacle and gone sprawling.

"You were in the sun," I said, speaking French to show him that he was on pure leisure time. His forehead and nose were scarlet, offsetting his white cheeks and bristly blond moustache, so that he now looked less like a walrus than a hairy strawberry muffin.

"Yes," he said, "Norway." Visiting walrus relatives, I guessed.

"Well, you can forget the raw fish and eat some nice English food now."

"Nice English food?" He went off chuckling to himself at this absurd concept.

Two more ex-workmates arrived together. Stéphanie, the aggressive blonde who was, as far as I knew, still Jean-Marie's mistress. And Nicole, the quiet financial controller who'd had a quiet crush on me.

As soon as she was inside the door, Stéphanie's critical

purchasing manager's eye was on my teabags, my crockery and the sausage rolls, as if she could see from the shape of them whether I was getting ripped off.

"Pas mal, pas mal," she conceded. "Let me taste your sausage."

"Go ahead." I was flattered. That was probably one of the offers she usually reserved for Jean-Marie.

Nicole brushed her face against mine and said how pleased she was that everything was working out for me. She then went off to the sandwich table where she timidly nibbled through three tons of toasties.

My snooty neighbour, the clothes-shop owner, came in and told me that the tea room didn't look English at all.

"There should be a red carpet, leather sofas, butlers serving the tea." This, I guessed, was why her clothes shop never seemed to have any customers in it. She was stuck somewhere in the 1940s.

"Butlers?" I said. "You just can't find them nowadays."

But lots of French people would have agreed with her. Many of them still think that all Englishmen wear bowler hats and have sex with their wives once a year before the croquet season begins.

Luckily, those French people are fast being out-numbered by their compatriots who think of Britain as a trendy place full of pop stars, sexy young princes and carrot cake.

A few minutes later, with the room now getting full and smoky, came a surprise. Jean-Marie's wife, the surgically enhanced Dior wonderwoman, turned up with her son Benoît in tow. The last time I'd seen her was the night I went to blackmail Jean-Marie, when she'd quite naturally treated me as if I had just peed on her favourite Oriental rug.

Now, though, she was charm itself, which I guessed was equally natural. At Dior wonderwoman finishing school, they doubtless taught future French politicians' wives to be charming to rats and cockroaches, to get them into practice for the type of life forms they would have to schmooze if their husbands were going to succeed. Being nice to an English ex-blackmailer was kids'stuff.

"Bonjour, Paul." The warmth of her greeting was very convincing.

"Bonjour, Madame Martin." I took the outstretched fingers and felt socially inadequate because I didn't have the balls to kiss them.

"Catherine," she said, squeezing my hand. If I hadn't known better I'd have said she was flirting.

She was dressed pretty sexily in her own classic way. Tight knee-length skirt hugging the smoothest of hips, crisp cotton blouse cut to accentuate her boobs, the tops of which were just visible above an undone blouse button. They, like her face, showed zero signs of wrinkles despite their age. And I could have sworn she'd gone up a bust size or two since our last meeting. Surgeon's gift vouchers for her birthday, perhaps.

Still clutching my hand, she congratulated me for having made everything work out so "merveilleusement."

It was unnerving. None of this sounded as if she'd learned it by heart for a Chamber of Commerce garden party. I even found myself doing that thing where, while a woman's talking to you about something totally non-sexual, you start looking for hints as to whether she wants to sleep with you. Are her pupils dilating, is she licking her lips a lot? That kind of thing. Which was just plain ridiculous with Jean-Marie's wife. Apart from the fact that it would have been commercial and maybe physical suicide, I was only two years older than her son.

Ah yes, the son. Benoît was standing behind and above her, smiling benignly into the crowd. He'd cut off his puny dreadlocks and slicked his hair back, so that he now looked like a younger,

IN THE MERDE FOR LOVE

less tanned and million times less self-assertive Jean-Marie. Judging by his expression of vacant curiosity, he had no idea that he was being brought here to meet his new boss.

I escorted Madame to the tea counter, prised my fingers free at last, and poured her a cup of my finest Lapsang before rushing back to the door to confront the horrific vision that had just wandered in off the street.

The guy's hair had apparently been stuck on with glue, his face had been shaved three days before by a blind Parkinson's sufferer, and he had a hopelessly DIY cigarette crumbling on his bottom lip. The only incongruity was the spanking new grey-black suit that suggested he'd just burgled a designer-clothes shop.

"That's my suit!" I wailed as discreetly as I could.

"Uh, yeah, man. I was going to demand you."

"My *Paul Smith* suit, Jake." This was, after all, a man who, if the Earth was conquered by aliens from the planet Slob, would be singled out by the invaders as a god and elected eternal ruler of the Slob empire. Letting him wear that suit was like lending your best teapot to the bull who had just demolished your china shop.

"I'm trying it so I can get myself acclimated."

"To what? The rest of my clothes?"

"No. For a job interview."

"What? Don't tell me they finally fired you?"

He took a long, morose pull on his cigarette.

"No, that's the problem. And it's starting to press. I'm doing this job as teacher of English since four years nearly now. And I feel the toxins rising almost to my brain. So I'm postulating for a new job in relations public."

"Public relations?" I said this less to correct his English than out of pure shock. Surely no company would let Jake have any relations with the public, except maybe in their complaints department. One look at Jake and you'd realize that your problem was never going to be cleared up.

"Yeah. I told you. I have this plan."

"Plan?"

"Yeah. You remember." He leaned close, so as not to reveal it to the tea-drinking, cake-chewing masses. "I want to get ahead by going backwards."

"I hope you're not putting that slogan at the top of your CV, Jake. It sounds as if you're trying to sell rowing machines."

He tutted impatiently and berated me for not being able to understand his "limpid concept."

"I want to walk backwards out of the rat race. Get a better work from which it is easier to get fired, and then I'll get a better chomage."

"Chomage? Dole, you mean?"

"Yeah. It's proportional to your last salary. You get fired from a good job and you get great whoosit? Dole."

"So you're going to get a job in PR just to screw it up?"

"Yeah. Brilliant, huh?"

I had to close my eyes and lean against the doorpost for a moment. This guy's life was so exhausting. It was like an American football match, an endless series of short sprints against brick walls. Except that he never felt the slightest impact.

"Go and eat some cake, Jake. And try not to get any on my suit."

I was about to go and mingle when I caught sight of Jean-Marie crossing the street. He was in deep conversation with a tall, classy woman in a long leather coat, who was letting him grasp her by the elbow. Was he really mad enough to bring one of his mistresses to a tea party where his wife was waiting? I wondered. And where his other mistress, Stéphanie, was making risqué comparisons between English and French sausages? Though this was France, so maybe it was the done thing as long as you didn't actually start shagging the new lover in front of everyone.

I beckoned to the photographer to get ready for action and held out my arms in the pose of the delighted host.

"Ah, Paul!" Jean-Marie gripped my hand and turned instinctively towards the camera. He looked as stylish as ever, as if he'd come straight from a Karl Lagerfeld fitting room. "Let me present Nathalie. She is a reporter. She is preparing a portrait about me for the television."

I turned and got hit by a pair of eyes even more hypnotic than Jean-Marie's. They were curacao blue and apparently back-lit. I felt as though they could see right inside my head. He certainly knows how to pick women, was the thought she would have seen in there.

She was about thirty-five, almost as tall as me in her sexy heeled boots, with a slender face, dark-red lipstick, and blond hair in a loose ponytail that was folded up at the back of her head and held in place with a pencil. She had a gold ring on her wedding finger, but that didn't seem to bother Jean-Marie.

"Enchanté," I told her, using the word almost literally for once.

"I was just telling Nathalie that the tea room was my idea originally." Jean-Marie the shameless self-publicist. "Is that not correct, Paul?"

"Oh yes."

"But Paul has taken it to its . . . fruition." He relished the last word as if it had been a slice of foie gras.

The journalist tilted her head and smiled at me. "It must not be easy for you, an English businessman in France?" She had a slightly posh accent when she spoke English, as many French people do when they've been taught by the generation of teachers who think that all Englishmen wear bowler hats and shag their wives once a year, etc.

"Well, no, but Jean-Marie helped me."

The photographer got another shot of a grateful tearoom proprietor shaking hands with a benevolent politician.

Jean-Marie pulled me to one side. "Have you talked to Benoît?"

"No, not yet."

"Well, I cannot stay long here. I will speak to him quickly." With a last smile for the lens, he went inside, and the crowd naturally parted for him.

This left me alone with the lady journalist. Most of my past meetings with Jean-Marie had had far less pleasant outcomes, I thought.

"So you're making a report about him?" I asked, and groaned inwardly. This had been explained to me approximately thirty seconds earlier. "I mean, just him and not, uh, all politicians?" From bad to worse.

She smiled warmly, as if to forgive me for stepping in my own conversational merde.

"There is enough of him for a television portrait, do you not agree? Or a series, if you let him write it." She laughed loudly. If she was his mistress, she wasn't just a starry-eyed fan.

"He mentioned that we could film in your café," she said. "You know, you talking with him and saying how you created the concept together?"

I got the picture. Jean-Marie, man of the community, friend of the small businessman. But why not? As he said, I wasn't going to shoo the TV cameras out of the tea room.

"Yes, that would be great."

"Do you have a card?"

"Of course. Even better, take one of our office-delivery menus. Maybe we can bring you some lunch one day?"

She nodded, and those eyes burned right into me again. It struck me that what I'd said could have been interpreted as a chat-up line. Not a bad one, for once.

Oh merde, I thought. What was my brain up to? Surely I wasn't coming on to Jean-Marie's wife *and* his new mistress? With one of my own recent bedmates standing just a few feet behind me in the tea room.

There was only one explanation, only one excuse—Alexa's confusing messages had turned me into a clementine addict.

7

B EFORE I COULD pour myself a nerve-steadying cup of tea, I got ambushed by Jean-Marie and his wife, who combined to shove a panicked-looking Benoît in my path.

"Benoît will come to see you on Monday," Jean-Marie growled in French.

"Mais Papa . . ." Benoît objected.

"He will come to see you for a job. Twenty hours per week, minimum."

"What?" Benoît seemed to think this was a breach of his human rights.

"It can include working all of the day on Saturdays if necessary." Jean-Marie held a threatening finger up in Benoît's face. There was more than just a part-time job at stake here, I could tell. There was accommodation, use of the car and the country house, even an inheritance maybe. Heavy parental stuff.

I could see exactly where it was heading—Dad forces son to work. Son decides to piss off boss to get back at Dad. Paul "nanny" West has to watch as protected Papa's boy gets his belated teenage rebellion out of his system in the middle of an English tea room. Merci bloody beaucoup.

Jean-Marie put his politician's smile back on and marched towards the exit. Madame made as if to follow him, then stopped and put a hand on my arm.

"Please treat Benoît well," she implored me, a tiny care line appearing between her electrolysed eyebrows. "I will be *very* grateful."

I wouldn't have been surprised if she'd reached down and given my balls a thank-you tweak.

I was still reeling from the effects of Jean-Marie's family circus when Stéphanie came up behind me and spat crumbs in my ear.

"Ce cheese n'est pas anglais." She brandished a half-eaten toasted sandwich at me.

"Well don't bloody eat it, then," I replied, giving her an authentically anglais reply to chew on.

Over at the tea urn I found Jake trying it on with Katy.

"Tu n'es pas Lithuanienne?" he drawled in his instantly recognizable New York accent.

"Non," Katy giggled.

"Hmm." Jake stroked his chin and stared at her in search of clues as to her origins. "Belarusse?"

"You bastard Jake!" I interrupted.

"Oh hi, Paul."

I turned to Katy. "I bet he asked you if you were Latvian too, didn't he?"

"Yes, but . . ." Katy was looking slightly confused.

"How dare you ask my staff if they're Latvian," I barked at Jake.

"Oh come, Paul, I didn't . . ."

"Did he ask you about any other of the ex-Soviet Republics?" I demanded. Katy took a step back, and seemed to wonder about the wisdom of working in such a politically sensitive tea room.

"No," she said.

"Well, he would have. It would have been, "Are you Georgian?" "Are you sure you're not bloody Ukrainian?" First he steals my suit, then he wants my staff. She's English, Jake, for Christ's sake."

Katy fled to the basement mumbling something about needing more teabags.

I took a long gulp from the nearest cuppa and it did its customary calming trick. I'm sure we Brits wouldn't need all our Prozac, Valium or cannabis if we'd just carried on drinking tea instead of switching over en masse to double iced lattes. There's something genetic in the bond between British blood and Indian tea.

A warm cup cradled in my palm, I surveyed the roomful of contentedly munching, chattering people. I knew about half of them, but the rest were strangers, either brought along for the ride or just Saturday-afternoon shoppers who'd gatecrashed on the off chance of sampling my scones.

The photographer was flitting about, snapping at their happy, cake-filled smiles. All in all, things had got off to a fantastic start. Even Benoît would be hard pressed to screw this up, especially if I banished him to apple-peeling duties downstairs.

"Sorry, Jake. I'm feeling a bit pent up."

"No problem, man. But hey, you really don't mind about the suit, uh?"

It was looking surprisingly stain-free after a good half-hour in his presence, I noted.

"No, Jake, I don't think I need it right now."

It struck me that the world is divided into two sorts of people: those who have to tuck their shirt in, and those who don't. People who have to dress up in a suit and tie every day, and those who can express their own identity. That, I decided, was what I was going to do for a while.

"It's good to be on the side of the untucked," I said.

"Uh?"

For once, I was the one coming out with the meaningless profundities. I explained my theory about the tucked-in shirt, and Jake agreed, even though he probably wasn't really aware of the concept of tucking one garment into another. He just kind of let them overlap.

"Yeah, you've found what you're researching for." Jake sounded almost envious.

"Except where women are concerned," I corrected him.

Jake bellowed a laugh that rattled the teacups. "Yeah, you're in your usual merde there, man. But not as bad as me. I mean, I was actually trying to pick up an Anglaise back there."

"Draguer une Anglaise? Pourquoi pas une Française?" Virginie had come over and was giving us her cutest pout.

"A Française?" Jake was aghast. "No way. They bring nothing but merde. Ask Paul."

He certainly was going to be a real find for the French public-relations industry.

8

I'D OFTEN FANTASIZED about having another conversation with Alexa while both of us were naked in bed.

Although, for obvious reasons, in my fantasy there was no English Channel between us. And there certainly wasn't a sleeping Ukrainian lying there with his nose in Alexa's armpit. Still, I reasoned, life isn't always like our fantasies, so I had to make the best of things.

"Hello, Paul." She was whispering. So I naturally assumed she wasn't alone.

She yawned. The duvet swished and I could picture exactly what was going on over there in her London bedroom. Her non-phone arm was stretching up as if to stroke the ceiling. The guy beside her would sense movement and home in on the warm, waking flesh.

"I just wanted to let you know how the tea party went," I said. Of course I had to have a reason to phone. We were now way out of the zone where you can call just for a chat.

"Yes?" She sounded only half-interested, but then she was still half-asleep.

I gave her a quick run-through, and was pleased to hear that Jean-Marie's name didn't make her suddenly perk up. Last time she'd met him, his charm had had her practically levitating.

"The photos aren't that good, though. It'd have been much better if you'd done them."

"Yes?"

"Would you have liked to do them?"

She groaned. It was too early on a Sunday morning for abstract thought.

And it was too frustrating having a naked woman groaning in my ear when there was nothing I could do about it.

I say naked, but of course for all I knew she could have been wrapped from head to toe in coarse woollen chastity pyjamas. Yes, I thought, perhaps it would be better to change the image in my mental videophone to something more like a nun or an Egyptian mummy, in place of the long, smooth, perfumed body that I was now imagining.

"Would you have . . . ?" Her voice trailed off. I guessed it was probably too early for complex English grammar, too.

"Liked you to do them? Yes, of course. I should have asked you, I know. But I didn't."

"Oh."

Dead end. What should I talk about now to stop her falling back to sleep? I hadn't read the paper or listened to the radio so it was no use trying to exchange banter about the issues of the day. I didn't even know whether her new stepdad's football team had won.

"Hey, my God, Alexa." I'd just had a horrifying thought.

"What?"

"The French word beau-père. It can mean two things, right? Stepfather and father-in-law."

"Yes." I could almost hear her muscles stiffen defensively. "So what?"

"Nothing. It's just that, you know, if you introduce Yuri to your French friends, you won't need to explain which one you mean. Because he's both."

This was, I realized, quite probably the most ridiculous remark ever made by a naked man to a naked woman, even this early on a Sunday morning.

"Thank you, Paul, now I am really glad you woke me."

Dead end again.

And when you get to a dead end you have two choices. Turn round and go home, or try to kick a hole in the wall. I decided to go for the kick.

"Alexa, I want to ask you a question."

"I hope it's not about French vocabulary."

"No. Listen, Alexa." This was such a serious question that I even stopped scratching my balls to ask it. "Why did you set me up with Virginie?"

"Virginie?"

"Yes. The girl from the film shoot." Surely she wasn't trying to remember who that was?

"What do you mean, 'set me up'?"

"You know, you told her to call me and invite me out."

"Invite you out?"

"Yes, you gave her my number."

"I didn't give her your number."

"You didn't?"

"No. Oh, yes. I did."

"Ah, well then."

"But just for her to give it to the assistant director, to recommend you. When I returned to the shoot, they were filming and they didn't want anyone to go into the courtyard. So I gave your card to Virginie and then I went home."

Oh merde, I thought, so she didn't mean to set me up with Virginie after all.

"Why didn't you come back to the café terrace?" I asked, hoping to drag the conversation away from other women.

"I did, but you were gone. So I went home."

Silence. She hadn't picked up on why I'd been asking about Virginie, thank God. And she wasn't whispering any more, either. Maybe she was alone after all. Yes. Those chastity pyjamas dematerialized, and in my mind's eye she was naked again.

"Why?" Alexa asked.

"Why what?"

"Why do you ask me why I have given your number to Virginie?"

Double merde.

"No reason. By the way, did Newcastle play yester—"

"You slept with her."

"No I didn't." Always deny everything, I say, at least until the Polaroids are waved under your nose. Even then you can claim that they've been digitally doctored.

"Huh, you went out with her and you didn't sleep with her? I don't believe you. She's very sexy girl. And she liked you."

"Would you mind if I had slept with her?"

"Do you want me to mind?" Hey, now she was even more awake than me. This wasn't fair. 'Anyway, you *did* sleep with her. This is why you said in your mail that you were pampered. You slept with her. You shagged her."

Shit. There was the Polaroid. And I'd sent it to Alexa myself. Quel twat.

"Forget about Virginie," I said, wishing that my voice had the power to make her do just that. "When are you coming back to Paris? It's your photo exhibition soon, isn't it?"

"I don't want you to see my exhibition."

She mispronounced the word. Ex-HIB-ition, she said. It wasn't that she'd decided she didn't want me looking at her photos. She just didn't want me to see her ex-hibition, her former hibition, whatever that was.

It took me a second to work out what she was saying. And even then I didn't understand why she'd said it. Of *course* I was going to see her photos. It's not every day that a friend, an ex-lover, has an exhibition. And I was even going to be in it, wasn't I? In that photo she'd taken of me in front of the Courrèges shop. No way was I going to let her have an exhibition without my support. I'd take some friends along, buy a print, try to make the show a success for her.

But by the time I thought of all that she was gone. She'd rung off, and when I called back she was on voicemail.

Well done, Paul, I told myself. A great morning's work and it's only half past ten.

"Pol? You are OK?" My flatmate Marie-Christine's reedy voice came floating through my bedroom door.

She sounded worried, no doubt because she'd heard someone in my room yelling as if he'd just poured paint-stripper all over the Mona Lisa.

"Meeeerde!"

9

THE FRENCH WILL tell you that "le client est roi." The customer is king. But we all know what they did to their kings. Louis XVI's guillotined head ended up bouncing across the Place de la Concorde, with several thousand French people laughing at it.

And Louis's wife, Marie-Antoinette, is still a hate figure in France today because when the starving mob protested that they didn't have enough bread to eat, she said that they should eat brioche, a sort of sweet milk bread. Yes, she was executed for recommending an upgrade.

Basically, "le client est roi" is as empty a phrase as My Tea Is Rich. And my main worry about the tea room's long-term prospects was that the staff had started living by the real mantra of French service industries—that is, "the customer is a waste of time."

This attitude has given rise to some classic techniques in bad French customer service. Benoît was a natural at the most common of them—ignoring the customer totally. If he was polishing the tea urn or refilling salad bowls when a client came in, he would steadfastly deny their existence unless they leaned across the counter and grabbed him by the ears.

If they were less violent than this, and just said "excuse me," he would inform them politely that he was very busy and would see to them as soon as he'd finished the vital task he was doing.

I had to explain to him that there was no point refilling salad bowls if he scared away all the prospective salad buyers, and it was only after I'd given several demonstrations of how to stop doing a routine task and say hello to a client that he actually admitted I might have a point.

Even after my lesson, Benoît and all the other counter staff could not help lapsing into another French habit that they seemed to have got from the Three Musketeers—"All for one and one for all."

Let's say that a customer returned to the counter after paying and told Yannick or Jeanne that they hadn't got exactly what they ordered—they'd been given a cheese-and-tomato toastie when what they'd actually asked for was a cheese-and-*armadillo* toastie.

Suddenly everyone else behind the counter would stop what they were doing and join in a general debate about how this could have happened, and whether "tomato" and "armadillo" were differentiated clearly enough on the menu, before going on to reminisce about the lunchtime when someone had ordered a jacket potato with baked beans and got a jacket potato with baked *spleens*.

Meanwhile, the other people in the queue could damn well wait.

All my eager workers—even the friendly Katy—looked forward with particular relish to a daily routine of customer abuse just before lunchtime. At eleven fifty-five on the dot, they took it in turns to savour the pleasure of booting any remaining drink- and snack-only clients off their tables. Buy lunch or get out, they'd tell them, whisking away half-full teapots and practically stuffing uneaten biscuits down the customers' throats.

I had to talk them through it again. No, I said, the message is, are you thinking of staying for lunch? If so, our special today is an armadillo—that's armadillo, not tomato—tikka kebab. And then see if they take the hint. We only eject them—apologetically—when we physically need the table because someone is standing there looking lost with their lunch tray and nowhere to sit.

If the customer whinges about how in a real French café you can stay as long as you want over a cup of coffee, they should smile, I said, and ask the client if they'd ever dared to order a drink in a French café while sitting at a table laid for lunch. I'd tried insisting on my customer's rights like this once and been told to fuck off to McDonald's.

We want our clients to return, you see, I told my staff. It sounds obvious, but it's a message that hasn't got through to the whole French service sector.

However, sometimes it wasn't the staff's fault. Occasionally I had to admit that le client was a bit of a dickhead.

The tourist was about thirty, and was kitted out with everything the English-speaking visitor in Paris needs for a long weekend in hostile foreign territory. A hurricane-proof anorak, a guidebook with a finger inserted at the chapter dealing with this neighbour-hood, and a permanently suspicious expression. He also wore a gigantic moneybelt-cum-parachute with a pouch for a little water bottle that had a long plastic tube protruding out of it, so that he could stuff it in his mouth and suck rather than having to stop behind enemy lines and actually pull out the water bottle, which might leave him open to ambush. The tube was flapping about in front of his chest like the aerial on a satellite location system. Which may well have been its second function.

It was about eleven-thirty on a Friday morning. He walked into the tea room, looked warily about, and edged towards Benoît, who was standing there day-dreaming with his cheek pressed to the warm tea urn.

Benoît had fallen in love with the tea urn and loved fiddling with its tap, or just polishing its rotund stainless-steel body. I had nothing against this unnatural infatuation. On the contrary—I was pleased that he was showing enthusiasm for *something*. He'd always seemed such a total drip.

"Quelles sont les options végétariennes?" the tourist asked. He had a strong English accent but his pronunciation was very clear. This was obviously one of the life-saving phrases that he'd practised before crossing the Channel, along with "appelez l'ambassadeur' and "où est mon anorak?"

Benoît stopped foreplaying the tea urn and gave his attention to this new intellectual challenge. He'd never been asked about vegetarian options before. Being French, he'd never even imagined that things like that might exist. But he coped well. He pointed up to the menu on the wall and told the guy in slow, clear French that there was lots of veggie stuff there—cheese toasties, salads, baked potatoes—he just had to take his pick.

The tourist gave this a moment's consideration.

"Mais pourquoi vous ne marquez pas les options végétariennes avec un signe végétarien?" he asked.

"Signe végétarien?"

"Oui." The guy mimed writing a green V.

"Ah." Benoît leaned forward and confided to the guy that we wouldn't dare mark anything veggie because that would scare off the French customers. He caught my eye and winked. He was learning fast.

The tourist wasn't convinced.

"Est-ce que vos pommes de terre sont végétariennes?" he asked.

No, I thought, they're carnivorous potatoes. You try sticking your fork in one of them and it'll have your arm off.

Of course I knew what he meant. Were the *fillings* veggie? But then a dish of baked beans is a dish of baked beans in any language. He must have known that they weren't frog's kidneys in a horse-blood sauce.

Initially, Benoît was stumped. His logical French brain had crashed when confronted by someone asking whether a vegetable was vegetarian. Fortunately, though, French kids study philosophy at school up until the age of eighteen, so he was able to perform a spectacular leap of lateral thinking.

"Why don't you just have a cheese-and-tomato toastie?" he suggested.

"Est-ce que le fromage est végétarien?" the veggie asked.

This time, Benoît almost fainted with mental exhaustion.

I knew why. Vegetarian cheese? The French would not get their heads round this concept if you offered them a swimming pool full of champagne every day for the rest of their lives.

I came over to catch Benoît in case he actually passed out.

"No, it's French cheese," I said, in English. "You never know whether the rennet is animal or vegetable. But if you've eaten one mouthful of cheese over here, then this is exactly the same."

"Hmm." The tourist stood there mulling this over. The only sign of life he gave was a slight twitching of his water-bottle tube.

It was lucky, I thought, that it was early and we didn't have a queue of people to serve. Half an hour later and every member of my staff would be gathered around him doing their "all for one" problem-solving thing.

It was at that moment that I understood French waiters.

They're in a rush to serve twenty tables at once and they get confronted with a guy like this asking about vegetarian options. A French waiter in a hurry would quite naturally think, vegetarian option number one: ram his head down the toilet.

Because apart from the time-wasting element, there's also a kind of impoliteness going on here. A chef spends years at catering school, months planning a menu, hours buying ingredients and cooking them, and then a family of tourists orders three plain omelettes and a plate of spaghetti. With ketchup. It's as if Michelangelo had sketched out the Sistine Chapel and then the Pope wanders in and says, "You know, I think I'd prefer a plain coat of eggshell all over."

"Look, you speak really good French," I told the guy, "but there's no point speaking the language if you use it to say things they'll never understand. They honestly don't care about vegetarianism. They think that anyone who doesn't orgasm over undercooked beef is a total philistine. To them a vegetarian coming to France is like someone who takes a vow of chastity and then goes to live in a harem. They think vegetarians are nuts. No pun intended, of course."

I knew that I'd fallen into the trap of treating a customer like a dickhead, but I really thought the guy needed to understand the country he was visiting, otherwise he was in danger of starving to death as soon as the emergency rations in his utility belt ran out.

"But you should mark the vegetarian options on your menu," he replied.

"I can't. It's against French law," I told him, falling back on stereotype.

"Are you *sure*?"

"No, you're right, I'm *not* sure. I'll call the police and ask them if you want."

To my surprise, the guy didn't stomp out in a huff, he simply grunted, turned to Benoît and ordered.

"Un toastie avec fromage, s'il vous plaît."

"Comment?" Benoît hadn't quite emerged from his coma yet.

"Un toastie avec fromage, s'il vous plaît."

Oh come on, I thought, be French. Moan about my rudeness, yell at me until you win the argument, don't just give in.

Who was it called the French "cheese-eating surrender

monkeys"? We Brits are the mild-mannered, mild-flavoured, vegetarian-cheese-eating surrender Corgis.

"Oui, Monsieur." Benoît flipped open the toaster and slotted in a sandwich.

"Est-ce vos jus de fruits sont *organic?*" the tourist asked, and I felt a sudden craving to go and squeeze some oranges.

But I was the one who'd learned a lesson.

French waiters are professionals, I realized, and too many of their customers are so damn amateurish.

For a professional waiter, dealing with amateur customers is like a tennis pro who never gets the ball knocked back to him. Of course he could content himself with serving ace after ace, but where's the fun in that? Good waiters enjoy the game, they like an opponent with style.

They send over a brisk request to order, the customer returns with a crisply hit choice from the menu, the waiter meets it at the net and crashes in a volley about wine, which the client can only lob back in the form of a plea for advice. The waiter smashes home the vin du mois and the point is won. There are similarly tight exchanges about dessert and coffee and everyone gets a good workout.

But what if the customer doesn't even understand the whole concept of the serve? What is this round, bouncy thing that is being hit towards me, the tennis virgin wonders, and what should I do with it? It's no wonder that waiters occasionally get frustrated and overcharge amateurs for wasting their time.

Hang on a minute, I thought, what's going on here? Someone get me a mirror. I think I'm mutating into a French waiter.

5

That Was No Lady, That Was Your Wife

1

WHEN A MARRIED lady invites you to join her at a museum, you assume it's a perfectly innocent invitation, don't you?

Even if she gives you the museum's address instead of its name, which did strike me as a bit weird.

Weirder still, when I walked out of the metro station I came face to face with a row of topless ladies, all of whom were wearing large black crosses or red hearts over their crotches. Some of the women had their hands thrust down behind these crosses or hearts, and the expressions on their faces suggested that they were astonished to find that they had no knickers on. Others, their mouths locked in a gaping "O," were pointing their unnaturally large boobs at me as if I was the target in a milk-squirting contest.

They were photos, of course, although some of them were nearly life-size. And they were the first in what looked like a whole, long boulevard of similar photos.

What kind of museum could there be up here? I wondered. The national vibrator gallery? The breast implant collection (otherwise known as the unnatural history museum)?

When I stopped in surprise at the first of these photo displays, a man in a tight leather jacket stepped out of the doorway and told me that these ladies were lapdancers and that they were all waiting for me downstairs.

I found this hard to believe for two reasons. First, only one person knew that I was coming up to this neighbourhood today—the married lady. And secondly, through the little golden-framed door I could see a dingy staircase that really didn't look as if it led down to a big enough basement to contain all of the ladies in the photos. But when I expressed my doubts that they could *all* be waiting down there, the man got angry and called me a rude French name that implied, inaccurately, that I was a small vagina.

I didn't know why he was so upset at the loss of one potential lapdancee. Over on the other side of the Boulevard Clichy, two big tourist coaches were spilling out their human loads along the row of sex shops and lapdancing clubs. And they obviously weren't the first coaches of the day. Giggling, ogling groups of foreigners were wandering slowly along the street trying to picture what went on behind all those ladies' crosses and hearts. Most of them kept at two or three yards' distance, but some were bound to go into the clubs.

At this point, I really should have asked myself why I'd been invited to a rendezvous up here, but I didn't. I only wondered why it was that the sex clubs were interspersed with kebab bars. Perhaps the ladies in the basements needed regular high-protein snacks to maintain their gyration speeds.

I kept walking past the alternating displays of sex and Mediterranean food until I found the right street number, and only then did I seriously begin to question the motives of the married lady who was waiting inside.

The museum looked just like one of the sex shops, except that the objects in the window had little multilingual signs explaining what they were. Not that an enormous wood carving of an erect penis needs much explanation.

This was, a neon sign proudly announced, Le Musée de l'Érotisme.

If the pictures of naked women in the window had been more modern, I probably wouldn't have dared to stop and look at them at such close range. But hey, this was a museum, it was culture. So, like the tourists, instead of giggling or looking furtive, I furrowed my brow and pondered upon the sociological importance of these particular nudie pics.

Although everyone, including me, had problems keeping a straight face when they caught sight of a seat on show in the central section of the wide glass façade. A normal dining-room chair had been covered with fake leopard-skin, and a section of the seat had been cut out. Into this hole, a kind of mill wheel had been fitted. As it revolved, it sent a series of plastic tongues flapping up through the hole, the idea presumably being that a naked woman would be sitting there getting a good tongue-lashing. But judging by the dirt sticking to the tongues, I thought that the chair would be more likely to give her thrush than thrills.

And this was where I was to meet a married woman. What did it all mean?

Well, if it had been Jean-Marie's wife, I'd have presumed it was a kind of ironic foreplay and run a mile.

But the invitation had come from Nathalie, the TV reporter, who'd told me she was preparing a travel item about quirky places in Paris, including my new English café and this museum. I didn't see much of a link between the two, but maybe that's why I'm not a reporter.

I'd been expecting a more conventionally quirky museum. There are some very quirky ones in Paris. The Tobacco Museum (Oh, Daddy, look at that lovely tumour!), the Perfume Museum (Hey, a bottle of perfume. Wow, another bottle of perfume, etc.), the Doll Museum (mummy, why is that man taking photos of the Barbies?).

But Eroticism, I thought, why not? What could be more Parisian? Apart, perhaps, from a dog-merde archive.

Things got even more explicit inside the museum's sliding doors. Before I'd even paid the hefty entrance fee, I'd seen a "phallic owl" (a realistic, six-inch-tall porcelain bird with, quite inexplicably, a human penis growing out the top of its skull) and a fountain consisting of a crouching naked woman with water spurting out of her mouth and nipples and one strong jet giving her a colonic irrigation. I could understand why I'd never seen one of those in the French branches of Habitat.

The general feeling, though, was that all this was a million miles from the sordid world of massage parlours and sex clubs. There was a young Italian couple bending down to get a close-up rear view of the fountain, a small group of Japanese girls (or maybe Koreans—I'd have had to ask Jake to be sure) taking phone photos of some raunchy etchings.

I didn't even feel self-conscious about being a single male until I caught sight of a prime saddo on the stairs leading up to the first floor. Thirty years old, baseball cap, denim jacket, no tourist accessories like a day pack or camera, his eyes not on the photos in the stair well but constantly checking out the visitors, an expectant look on his face as if a woman was suddenly going to accost him and say, hey, want to try *this* with me?

Yes, apart from the baseball cap, a few extra years and the expectant look, he looked a lot like me. Now I understood why people came here in couples or groups.

Time to find Nathalie, and fast.

I caught up with her on the second floor. She was gazing intently at a set of Nepalese wooden dildos, which looked as if they hadn't been properly sanded down. I hoped they were fertility symbols rather than sex toys. One quick session with those and you'd need twenty-four hours of microsurgery to remove the splinters.

We said hello with a professional handshake, and started to walk around the museum together. Which wasn't much less embarrassing than going round on my own. In a normal museum you can comment on the incredible age of something, or how you used to have one of those when you were a kid. Here, though, the only appropriate comments would have been things like "Look where she's putting *that*" or "I can see why *he's* smiling." And when you don't know a woman very well, it is pretty difficult to make intelligent conversation in front of exhibits like a ten-times-lifesize resin model of a vagina.

None of this seemed to embarrass Nathalie, though. She strode purposely from room to room, chuckling at the commentaries and making notes into her dictaphone.

"Très bizarre," she dictated. "The Indian paintings show men with long, thin penises. The drawings of Japanese men all have monstrous members out of all proportion to their bodies. Inferiority complex?"

"Have you ever done any modelling?" she asked me in English, her eyes flicking towards a Samurai who was hung like a kimono'd elephant.

"Only plasticine."

"No, I mean . . . Oh, sorry, I forgot, English humour. Self-mocking, I am sure."

Whatever that meant.

We moved on to a cabinet full of earthenware water jugs with obscene decorations. One of them had a handle in the form of two people having oral sex, and a spout in the shape of an erect schlong.

"Oh, pre-Colombian," an American tourist said to his wife. "Probably Aztec." He seemed to think he was at the Louvre.

"No wonder their civilization ended," the wife replied. "I'd have died of thirst before I drank out of that thing."

"That's not what they say about American women," Nathalie whispered.

Meanwhile, she asked me to tell her how I'd come to live in Paris and open up a tea room.

I talked her through my initial problems settling in in France while we stood in front of a collection of distinctly limp jade phalluses.

As we tried to make sense of a surreal modern drawing of a woman apparently sticking her head up her own anus, I told her how the French team assigned to the tea room by Jean-Marie had spent most of their time being a pain in the butt.

And I was only slightly distracted from my description of Nicolas the architect's cock-ups by a Thai statue of a robed man with penises instead of hands.

"And you personally, do you feel welcome in Paris?" Nathalie pushed her glasses up on top of her head to give her hypnotic eyes a direct X-ray view into my brain.

I reassured her that, apart from a few false starts with receptionists, waiters, the ID card people, certain shopkeepers, estate agents, several of my ex-colleagues, and the city's entire dog population, I'd settled in pretty well as an Anglais in Paris.

"Ah, talking of Englishmen in Paris, look at this."

We leaned in close to examine a photo marked "The Prince of Wales Room." This, it turned out, was the future King Edward VII's permanent pied-à-terre in a Parisian brothel. The enormous bed and the proudly grinning Madame were proof enough that Queen

Victoria's eldest son was a bit of a lad, but I was more interested in the extraordinary "love seat" that, according to the label next to the photo, the prince had personally designed for his den.

The base was a chintz-covered divan, on which a man was apparently supposed to kneel. Above this, on sturdy wooden legs, halfway along the base, there was a raised cutaway seat with two high arm rests. This, presumably, was where a woman would sit with splayed legs while the kneeling prince pleasured her, hanging on to the arm rests to get extra leverage.

Or maybe he would be sitting back while she did the kneeling. I didn't particularly want to know. All I knew was that he probably didn't ask his mum's throne-makers to knock that particular piece of furniture together.

"I had no idea that you English had such imagination." Nathalie, her head tilted to one side, was trying to work out the mechanics of getting the best out of the love seat.

"His dad was German," I admitted modestly.

"And do you live in an apartment like that?"

"Afraid not. There was no room at the whorehouse for me."

"Oh, how sad. Where do you live, really?"

When I told her, she laughed.

"Why does everyone do that?" I was starting to get serious hang-ups about living in the Fifteenth. OK, it wasn't the trendiest part of town, but was it really such a source of merriment?

Nathalie explained. When you tell someone you live in the rue Eugène Gibez, she told me, it sounds to French ears as if you're saying "rue Eugène, I fuck there" ("j'y baise"). Which explained why every taxi driver I gave my address to unfailingly replied, "lucky you."

Bloody typical, I thought, that I should end up living in that street among central Paris's 4,800-odd thoroughfares.

"And is this true?" Nathalie ran her finger over a bike saddle with a suggestive pink slit cut into the leather.

"Is what true?"

"That you . . . fuck there?" That nanosecond pause before she pronounced the key word should have been in one of the displays here as an example of genuinely erotic erotica.

"Well . . ." I wondered whether to lie about the distinct lack of flesh-on-flesh action that my flatshare had seen.

"Have you heard of the . . . Hôtel Gibez?" Again, she left an oh-so-meaningful pause. Her eyes locked on to mine and I knew that this was no real hotel. It was a declaration of intent.

2

I GATHERED THAT Nathalie had done this kind of thing before. She guided me briskly across the main boulevard and down the hill to a hotel set on a busy street corner.

It looked like a typical mid-range Parisian hotel. A converted nineteenth-century apartment block with a blood-red awning over each window and its name spelled out along the whole width of the ground floor. Hôtel Réage, it said, and the dark-blue plaque by the main door boasted three stars.

I wondered whether she'd reserved a room, and whether that would have been incredibly sexy or just a bit spooky.

But as we crossed the threshold, the confidence went out of her stride and she gripped my arm.

"You ask, please. I hate this part," she whispered.

The lobby was tiny but plush. Half of it was taken up with a wooden staircase leading to the rooms upstairs. It was clear that people didn't come here to hang around in reception.

The décor was classic bordello, or what I imagined classic bordello to be. The Prince of Wales's photo had been in black and white, of course, but the colour scheme would probably have been exactly the same as this hotel. Dark-crimson walls and carpet, with light fittings, mirror frames and all other accessories thickly painted in old gold.

The receptionist behind the cramped counter didn't look at all like a Madame, though. He was young and Spanish, dressed plainly in a white shirt and black tie.

His manner was just as discreet as his uniform. He must have known what Nathalie and I were up to, but he didn't show it.

He greeted us with a quiet "Bonjour, Madame, Monsieur."

"Vous avez une chambre," I began, "pour . . ."

Should I say "one night," I wondered, or would that be taking the pretence too far? He must have seen that we didn't have our pyjamas with us.

"Pour deux?" the receptionist tactfully filled in the blank.

"Oui." I turned round to share my relief with Nathalie, but she was engrossed in some tourist brochures on a revolving stand by the exit.

As the receptionist debited my credit card, he started to explain about breakfast times and how to get to the dining room, at which point Nathalie finally lost interest in the brochures and told him firmly that we wouldn't be requiring breakfast, merci beaucoup.

He took the hint, handed over the key, and ten seconds later we were heading up to the first floor.

Walking up the stairs behind a woman can be a very pleasurable experience in Paris, where the girls generally take great care of their rear contours.

The Paris metro is not as far underground as the London Tube, so there are a lot fewer escalators, and a lot more stairs. The staircases are wider, too. In the time it takes to get from the platform up to street level, you'll often have a selection of derrières to choose from, and in the course of a week of commuting you'll see a vast and wonderful array of differently shaped backsides that make you glad to be human. I'm sure Parisian women get as much fun out of it as the guys.

But all this is idle fantasy, a way of making your commute less routine. Things are far more pleasurable when you are walking up the stairs of a Paris hotel in mid afternoon behind a rear end that you know for a fact you're about to see—and grab hold of—in all its undressed splendour.

And I couldn't get it out of my head that this was an older, and by definition more experienced, rear end. My first married one, too.

After the museum, this was becoming quite an afternoon of cultural discovery.

As Nathalie was obviously no novice at this hotel-sex game, I felt that it was important to play the seasoned veteran when we got into the room, so I resisted the temptation to turn on the TV to see what cable or satellite channels were on offer.

I did, however, sneak a peek in the minibar while Nathalie was in the loo. But she was out of there more quickly than I'd expected and caught me at it.

Oh no, uncool, I thought, until she gave a girlish squeal of delight and declared that I was a genius.

"Champagne," she purred, "yes, très classe."

She then invited me to come and undress her, switching over to French and calling me "vous," as if we hadn't been introduced, when in fact we were indulging in Mother Nature's most intimate way of saying hello.

I wondered why I didn't merit a "tu." But given the choice between unbuttoning her blouse and discussing French grammar, I decided to save the linguistic questions for later.

Great lingerie, I thought to myself as she squirmed out of it. If she wore this kind of stuff every day, her husband was a very lucky guy. Except when his wife was shagging other men, of course.

Very inventive use of champagne, too. Not much of the chilled liquid ended up in the glasses. Most of it got poured over various sensitive parts of our bodies that fizzed and bubbled until we kissed them dry.

She had a surprisingly excellent body. I'd often wondered what happens to a woman's body between, say, twenty-five and thirty-five. And the answer in Nathalie's case was, nothing serious. She'd had two kids but the only clues that gave this away were a few wrinkles beneath the breasts and around the belly button. And she had a really flat stomach—another gold star for the French medical system, I concluded, helping women to keep in trim for all this post-natal, extra-marital sex.

Being such an experienced lady, Nathalie certainly knew what she wanted and knew how to get it, as the song goes. But, as the song carries on, she also wanted to destroy passers-by. Well, their eardrums anyway.

Several times I was sure that her screaming was either going to smash the windows or reach a crescendo, but each time it died back down again and I was left wondering whether the show was over.

I almost suggested adjourning to a hotel near the airport. With an Airbus landing every minute, we wouldn't be disturbing anyone.

"Don't worry," she reassured me later, "it is not your fault. I can't orgasm if I can't scream."

From where I'd been lying, it had certainly sounded like screaming, but I didn't want to quibble about exact decibel levels.

In any case, the Frenchman in me was at work, and I was concentrating on more intellectual matters. Nathalie was calling me "vous" again. And as we really had become very familiar with each other over the past half-hour or so, I felt at liberty to ask her why the formality.

She blushed scarlet. They really are obsessed with their

language, I thought. She hadn't shown the slightest pinkening of the cheek while we were making love and now she was as red as a nun at a nudists' trampoline display just because I'd asked her to explain her use of pronouns.

"C'est très sexy," she confessed.

"Just saying "vous" is sexy?" So this was why "French lessons" was a euphemism for shagging a prostitute. Perhaps the hookers just read you a chapter from a grammar book.

In fact, it was more complicated than that. Nathalie told me how upper-class husbands, wives and lovers often call each other "vous" in daily life, which in her opinion added a kind of thrilling contrast between the politeness of the way they usually spoke to each other and the vulgarity of what they did to each other in bed. The best thing, she said, was going from "vous" to "tu" just at the moment of climax. The switch was almost enough to give her an orgasm in itself. Pity she hadn't told me before.

"It is like being brutally seduced by a workman in a chic ballroom," she added. This was not an idea that had ever turned me on, but each to her own.

As it happened, our room looked very much like a ballroom. Decorated in a similar baroque way to the lobby, but with a huge crystal chandelier above the bed and thick purple drapes that almost obscured the windows even when they were held open by their gold braids. Like a ballroom, it was a place where you were meant to be in twilight.

The only bum note, in my opinion, was a gilt-framed photo staring down at us from above the bedhead—a black-and-white portrait of a leering, smoking man whom I recognized as the French singer Serge Gainsbourg.

Nathalie saw me frowning up into his nostrils.

"He was a great lover," she said. "Once on live TV he told

Whitney Houston that he wanted to fuck her. I am sure he called her 'vous.'"

"So as not to be too impolite, you mean?"

I've never figured out how this small, ugly drunk was a sex symbol in France. But then I'm not a French woman.

"All the rooms here are named after famous French lovers," Nathalie said.

"You've been here before, then? With your husband, of course?" Her laugh told me the answer to that one. "Why do you do it?" I asked. "Cheat on him, I mean?" I knew as I spoke that I sounded somewhere between a naive schoolkid and a priest. A total hypocrite as well—the guy who's just had sex with her coming over all moralistic.

She considered the question for a while, stroking my thigh as she did so.

"With you, I suppose I am simply cheating on my husband to prove to myself that I am still alive."

"Oh, there's absolutely no doubt you're alive," I assured her.

"And you, who are you cheating?" she asked, giving me a teasing smile. I could tell that it was meant as a joke but I suddenly felt myself being dunked in a puddle of melancholy. "Oh, no," Nathalie said, seeing my expression. "Someone has been cheating *you*."

This wasn't really how I saw things with Alexa, but I found myself lying back and letting it all out. How we'd met when she was waitressing during a waiters' strike, how she'd taken me on a tasting of France's most disgusting cheeses and sausages, how I'd screwed things up by accidentally screwing someone else. The whole story.

It felt bizarre, opening my heart about Alexa to this woman I was lying in bed with. But it also felt totally natural. After all, there is no better place to receive an encouraging hug while you're telling your sob story.

"What makes her so special for you?" Nathalie asked.

At first I didn't know how to answer. I'd never asked myself in those terms.

Alexa was beautiful, sure, but in a less classy way than Florence, for example. She was sexy, too, though certainly much less upfront about it than Virginie or Nathalie.

I had vivid memories of the curve of her nose, the colour of her nipples, the smell of her hair, the taste of her sweat. But I hadn't experienced any of those recently. I'd hardly even talked to her, and whenever we did speak we usually ended up arguing.

So what was so special about her?

"She's just her," I answered feebly.

Nathalie, though, nodded as if this was a profound piece of wisdom. "She has something?" She was speaking English now.

"Yes. She just fascinates me. She's got all these things she wants to do. And she's totally determined to do them, but she's still really supportive about what I want to do. And I'd love to be able to help her, too. We just kind of . . ." I couldn't think of the right word.

"Work?" Nathalie suggested.

"Yes. We could work."

"Then you must decide what you really want. It is like me. I do not want to leave my husband. I would only leave him if I fell so deeply in love with somebody that I could not stand to stay at home a moment longer. Perhaps that is why I content myself with these little *aventures*." She laughed. "Oh dear, Serge thinks we are stupid."

I turned to look at him, and it was true that Monsieur Gainsbourg's leer didn't seem to be expressing the greatest respect for our discussion about the intricate workings of the human heart.

"Just shut up and shag," he seemed to be saying.

Though from what I've heard of his songs, his lyrics are usually more subtle than that. Except for the bit in "Je T'Aime, Moi Non Plus" when he describes anal intercourse as "I come and I go in between your kidneys." Full marks for anatomy, but romanticism—nul points.

Nathalie took Serge's leer at face value. "What I really want now," she said, switching back to French and rolling on top of me, "is for you to pour some more champagne over me and make me shout."

"Comme vous voulez, Madame."

She shuddered as the old vous-do magic did its trick.

3

HAVING A STABLE relationship was doing wonders for Benoît. (His partner being the tea urn, of course. I was assuming here that it reciprocated his feelings.) He went from strength to strength, and started doing a full thirty-five-hour week, acting as a kind of gentle-giant team captain.

Once you got to know him, everything about the way he moved suggested quiet confidence, rather than laziness, as I'd first interpreted it. When he poured a cup of tea, you got the impression that he'd really thought through the importance of this particular cup of tea, and his relaxed smile as he handed it to you told you that you'd made the right decision in ordering it.

He had come to understand the correlation between a happy customer and the ringing of the till. And pretty soon he was even able to get on with serving one customer while all around him were flocking towards someone else in the queue who'd raised an armadillo/tomato problem.

So when Jean-Marie called me up for a progress report, I was perfectly happy to tell him the truth. I let him know that I'd had to fire one of my other staff—Fabrice the "Polish" student. In fact, he was a terrible timekeeper, but I thought it best to put the moral onus for his dismissal on Jean-Marie. If he was capable of recognizing such things as moral onuses, it'd be a point in my favour.

And I told Jean-Marie that Benoît had surprised me by

slotting in really well. He'd put up with his boring kitchen duties, cured his bad habits, and now seemed to be in his element. What's more, he was the one who finally worked out how to put my Web site on line via my email provider, so I owed him a debt of eternal gratitude.

Jean-Marie was delighted to hear all this, though there was still an impatient edge to his voice as he said so. Something else was bothering him.

"Nathalie, the TV reporter, have you seen her?" he asked.

"Yes, I have." All of her, I wanted to add. We'd met up once more since our après-midi at the hotel. One Sunday afternoon she'd come round to my place in I Fuck There Street, pretended to be English to my delighted flatmates, and then come into my bedroom to shout things in her very own language.

She'd spent the best part of an hour chewing on a pillow but this still didn't muffle the sound enough for my roommates, who reminded me later that that kind of thing didn't go on in *Free Ends*. Shame, I said, that they didn't offer Jennifer Aniston's part to Nathalie. She'd have upped the ratings without even being in the same room as the main action.

"Is she going to do a report about My Tea Is Rich?" Jean-Marie sliced into my daydream.

"I don't know." This was true. We hadn't spoken about it since the museum. Maybe all she wanted was my body. Not that I begrudged her its occasional use. "Why do you ask?"

"Well . . ." I guessed Jean-Marie was deciding which version of the truth, and how much of it, to tell me. "We were going to film for my portrait but she, how do you say, pulled me off?"

"Called it off?"

"Yes. She pulled it off. She said that she was working to do something different."

"Well I haven't heard from her recently. Do you want me to ask her what she's working on?"

The idea of calling Nathalie and maybe meeting up for another screaming session was quite a pleasant one. There didn't seem to be any other women in Paris—or the other European capitals for that matter—as keen as her to sleep with me.

"Yes, why not? Good idea." Meaning that it was what he'd planned all along. "You know," Jean-Marie added, his voice more spritely now, "if Benoît enjoys himself, maybe I will buy the salon de thé for him."

I assumed this was a joke.

I duly left a message for Nathalie, and she dropped by at the tea room early the next morning.

Unlike Virginie, she was very good at what the French call "mondanité," that is, making normal conversation in public with someone you've shagged as if you'd never shagged them. An essential social skill in chic circles, apparently.

We talked at the till while Benoît and Katy's ears twitched with the effort of pretending they weren't eavesdropping. I don't think it would have occurred to them that I had had erotic encounters with Nathalie, though, because she spent most of her time talking about Alexa.

She showed me an entry in the small weekly Paris events guide, *Pariscope*.

"This is your Alexa, isn't it?"

I read the four-line announcement in the exhibitions section. An "exposition photo," at a place called the Espace Photo Beaubourg, described with a long, suitably arty sentence that I didn't quite understand. Something about a voyage through men seen by a woman's hidden eye.

A woman's hidden eye? Sounded very dubious to me. It could have been the name of one of the gross sculptures at the erotic museum. Especially when combined with the title of Alexa's exhibition, which I understood all too well: *Des hommes, rien que des hommes*. Men, nothing but men.

Brilliant. So Alexa had created a new version of that tent installation where Tracy Emin embroidered the names of all the blokes she'd ever slept with. Except here I'd be able to admire their photos, too.

How lucky I was that Alexa had said she didn't want me to see it.

"Is it her?"

"Yes," I said.

"Do you want to see the exhibition?"

"Not particularly."

"Oh, don't you think it will be good? You said there will be a photo of you. I thought maybe it could connect with the story of your tea room. Give me another location. But if you think it will not be very good . . ."

A cruel trick for fate to play on me. A TV reporter is interested in my opinion of the one exhibition in the whole of Paris I didn't want to go to. And if there was the slightest chance that Nathalie might be interested enough to give Alexa TV exposure, then of course I had to make damn sure that Nathalie went along.

"No, I think it'll be very good," I said. "I just think I'll be sick with jealousy."

"Oh . . ." Nathalie very nearly gave my hand a consoling stroke. But she stopped herself at the last moment and turned slightly away from our eavesdroppers. "Well, we can go together tomorrow, then you will at least be there with a lover. Even if *her* photo is there with twenty of her lovers."

She seemed to find this irony highly amusing, unlike me.

If only Alexa knew how much suffering I was going through just for her.

4

M EANWHILE, I HAD to put myself through some pain of a different kind.

It had been all too easy to set up a small business in Paris. I'd imagined that I'd have to spend days crawling on my knees from one government office to the next, begging a series of sadistic pen-pushers to add their stamp to my dog-eared application form until I finally got to the last hurdle, only to be told that the ink had faded too much on the first stamp and that I had to go back to the beginning and start again.

But no, all I did was go along to a massive domed building called the Bourse du Commerce and pick up a form. I returned at the same time next day with the filled-out form and a cheque for less than the price of a small bottle of Chanel No. 5, and I was the président of my very own company.

The only bit of the form that I was slightly concerned about was the section where you had to choose exactly what kind of business you were setting up. There were various types of limited-liability companies with different tax régimes and different ways of screwing money out of you if you went bust, but I didn't intend to go bust anyway, so I opted for a "micro-entreprise," which sounded small enough not to attract too much attention from the bureaucrats.

How wrong I was.

*　　*　　*

Signing that form was a bit like pricking your finger with a needle then dipping your hand into the Amazon.

The first piranha to reach me was a guy in a sleeveless fleece and a check shirt.

It was late, just before closing time, and I was resting my feet, reading the newspaper over a cup of Orange Pekoe. I didn't really pay any attention to the guy at first, except to do a double-take at his impeccable colour coordination. Sand-brown fleece, beige-and-green shirt, khaki chinos, light-brown suede shoes. Even his hair matched, a kind of chestnut-and-grey flecked combination. Here, I felt, was a guy whose sock drawer was graded in a strict spectrum pattern.

I returned to reading the football pages. I couldn't work out why there was never any mention of Alexa's new stepfather. He buys one of the biggest clubs in England, and no one talks about him? He had to be even shadier than I suspected.

But my attention wandered back to the sock-drawer man again when I realized that he was arguing loudly in French with Benoît, who wasn't an arguing-loudly kind of guy.

"You must translate everything," the sock-drawer guy was saying. "*Cup of tea*, for example."

"But every French person knows what a *cup of tea* is."

"How do you know this? Perhaps I do not know this?"

"Don't you know what a *cup of tea* is?"

"No."

"Yes you do, you ordered one when you came in."

"Perhaps I was just curious to know what this unknown thing was on the menu."

I realized I had to intervene. Benoît was clearly up against a mind more fiendish than he could possibly imagine. A French bureaucratic mind.

I introduced myself and asked what the problem was.

The guy didn't introduce himself. He simply snapped back a question. "What is a moog?"

"Moog?"

"Oui, *moog* of tea."

"Ah, mug," I corrected him.

"Oui, mag."

"Mug."

"Mog."

"Mug."

"Maaahg."

"Oui, c'est ça," I congratulated him. "Un *maaahhg* est un grand *coop*."

"Coop?"

"Cup."

He snorted triumphantly. "You see, even you do not know what a *cup* is. This is why you must translate it as tasse de thé. You must translate everything on your menu."

He introduced himself as an inspector from the Ministère de la Francophonie, the government department that tries to protect the French language from attack by such foreign invaders as "le marketing," "le Walkman" and, it seemed, "le cup of tea".

He flashed his card at a wide-eyed Benoît and me and informed us that it was illegal to have a menu that did not give French translations for every foreign ingredient or dish.

"What, even sandwich?" I asked. I pronounced it à la française, "son-dweetch," though the French spell the word as it is in English.

"No, of course not."

"OK, so if it is an English word that is used in French, or known by the French, I don't have to translate it."

"English? But sandwich is *French*." His cheeks flushed for a moment, but realized they were disrupting his colour scheme and quickly returned to their normal shade of grey-green.

"What? Sandwich is English."

"Ho!" This was by no means a laugh. It was a cry of indignation. He appealed for support to Benoît, but by this time the poor lad was gaping at us mutely, stroking the tea urn for moral support. "It is like les frites"—French fries—the inspector went on. "The whole world knows they are French, except the English who say *they* invented them. As do the Belgians, but who cares about them. We French have been eating sandwiches for much longer than you. The traditional baguette is the perfect bread for a sandwich."

Apart from his wild rewriting of culinary history, he'd left himself open to attack here, and I darted in.

"No it's not. It's the worst bread in the world for a sandwich. You can't get it in your mouth." I mimed the impossible task of closing your teeth on a baguette sandwich without first crushing it flat. "And when you squeeze it, all the ingredients fall out the other end of the sandwich on to your trousers."

His eyes narrowed at me. "I thought we were having a linguistic conversation, Monsieur, not criticizing French table manners." When a Frenchman uses "Monsieur" at you in the middle of an argument, you know you've offended him badly.

"I wasn't criticizing French table manners," I assured him. "But sandwich really is an English word."

"Nonsense. What is its meaning? Something to do with sand, no doubt?"

"It's the name of the man who invented it."

"Ah oui, Monsieur *Sandwich*, a cousin of Monsieur *Fish and Chips*?" He bowed as if acknowledging polite applause at his rapier wit. Even Benoît accorded him a nod of appreciation.

I could see that I was rapidly sinking into the quicksand of an intellectual discussion that was only going to drag me under. This guy was a professional quibbler, after all. His clothes and his ID badge proved it.

And as everyone knows, once you're in quicksand, the last thing you should do is flail about and hope you can fight your way out.

Trouble is, some of us are just born flailers.

"Well, it's an English word so I'm going to translate it on my menu," I told him.

"You will not translate it. It is French."

"It is an English word and I demand the right to translate it."

"I forbid you to translate it." By this time we were practically nose to nose.

"I will translate it, as 'traditional English food with two slices of bread and, er, something between.'" My French let me down at the end but the blow struck home.

"That would be a gross misrepresentation. The law forbids incorrect translations."

"Oh yes? Well, we will see what *Bruxelles* says about that. Or *Brussel* as the Flemish residents call it. *Bruxelles* is just a bad translation, n'est-ce pas?"

The inspector took up the gauntlet and threw it back in my face. "I will return, and if there is one mistake in the French translations on your menu, you will be obliged to reprint all of them, or face a heavy fine."

No one throws gauntlets in my face and gets away with it, even if my face is the only part of me still sticking up out of quicksand. "Oh yes?" I replied. "We will take the train together to *Brussel* to discuss the case."

As the glass door clanged shut behind him, I'm sure both of us were feeling that peculiarly French sense of satisfaction at having created mutual outrage. Nothing at all had been resolved, but we'd had a damn good row and each of us had emerged feeling sure we were in the right. I was as exhilarated as a poodle strutting away after a damn good yapping match.

"Do you think we will have a problem?" Benoît asked.

"No, we'll never hear from him again," I said, and almost believed it.

The injustice of it, though. During my time in Paris I'd seen dozens of well-meaning but hopelessly inaccurate translations on menus, and no one went around giving out fines for those.

I'd eaten at places offering "omelette with fungus," "jumped potatoes," and "mangled steak."

OK, they were translations into English, but ignoring them was just double standards. And the French were getting away with linguistic murder every day.

For example, it always made me cringe when I heard a French person call a sweatshirt "un sweat." Despite the fact that they wrote it "sweat." It was like re-writing Shakespeare: a rose by another name would smell of sweat.

And they couldn't get sports right, either. They called football "le foot," basketball "le basket" and skate-boarding "le skate." They obviously didn't know that English words actually mean something, and if we'd put "skate" and "board" or "basket" and "ball" together, it was because they combined to create a new concept.

My favourite of these bad English abbreviations was one I heard from an old estate agent, who described a toilet as "les water," which he pronounced "wat-air." Short for water closet, of course. Would I like to see "les wat-air?" he asked. I thought he wanted to introduce me to the neighbours, until I realized that they couldn't be living down that little hole in the floor.

No, I decided, the language inspector wouldn't bother me again. What with all these howlers and the horrifically English words coming in with the Internet and phone technology, he had far too many anti-French invaders on his plate.

Unless, of course, bothering English-speakers was his tasse de thé.

5

I HAD UNDERESTIMATED the importance of Alexa's exhibition.

But then there was no way I could have guessed how important it was unless I'd known, for example, that Parisians call their new national library "the chocolate biscuit."

Which they do.

Officially, the library is named after ex-president François Mitterrand, but Parisians call it the "BN," which is the brand name of a popular chocolate biscuit. And an abbreviation of "bibliothèque nationale."

Parisians seem to have a similar aversion to saying other ex-presidents' names, too, even Charles de Gaulle, who has all sorts of places named after him. And not saying his name causes a lot more confusion than just mistaking a library for a biscuit.

This is because Paris has two main landmarks named after the General. The city's biggest airport is known the world over as Paris Charles de Gaulle. Your baggage stickers have a big CDG on them to prove it. But Parisians call the airport Roissy, which is the name of the little town that was lucky enough to get an airport as a neighbour.

Meanwhile, at the top of the Champs-Elysées, beside the Arc de Triomphe, there's a massive metro and regional train station called Charles de Gaulle Étoile, which Parisians call Étoile, after the roundabout that runs around the Arc.

It is, of course, by no means uncommon for foreign visitors to want to go to one of these two places. So it is just as common to hear a conversation between a linguistically challenged tourist and a metro ticket-seller that goes something like this:

Tourist: "Uh, hello, I mean bon-jaw, I, uh, want to go to, uh, *Charles de Goal?*"

Ticket-seller (speaking quickly through perspex window above noise of busy metro station): "Roissy ou Étoile?"

Tourist: "Uh? Er, bon-jaw, I, uh, want to go to *Charles de Goal?*"

Ticket-seller (at exactly the same speed and volume): "Roissy ou Étoile?"

And so on.

My problem with Alexa's exhibition was that there is exactly the same confusion over the Pompidou Centre.

Georges Pompidou was the president who took over from de Gaulle at the end of the 1960s. But he died in office, just as a new art museum in the shape of an inside-out toaster was being built in the centre of Paris. So the city named the museum after him, and all us foreigners know it by its official name, the Pompidou Centre. Parisians, though, call it Beaubourg, the name of the neighbourhood of medieval buildings destroyed to make way for the museum and the hideous apartment blocks around it.

All of which goes some way to explaining why I didn't immediately latch on to the fact that Alexa's show was in one of the small temporary exhibition spaces inside the Centre Pompidou. Which is a totally huge honour.

Nathalie was understandably impressed when she saw Alexa's name alongside the stars in the permanent collection.

"Is she the daughter of a famous artist? Or of the director? Or maybe she is sleeping with him?"

She saw me flinch and apologized. The worst thing was, she hadn't been joking. She really didn't understand how someone so young could possibly have an exhibition in such a temple of the art establishment.

"Perhaps she's just very good?" I suggested, disappointing Nathalie with the simplicity of the idea.

We were directly underneath the museum's towering, multi-coloured metal structure. From a distance, and especially if you come at it through the medieval Marais district, it looks like a modernistic scar on the ancient city, but close up it is spectacular.

It must have taken quite some cojones to put all the building's innards on the outside like that. And quite some spanners, too. You can actually see where the beams are joined in gigantic robot elbows, with immense bolts that look all too easy to undo.

Even though it was late afternoon, there was a queue of twenty or thirty people waiting to get into the building to see the main exhibition, a Pop Art show that would probably cause the deforestation of half of Sweden to provide enough Andy Warhol posters for the museum shop.

Nathalie flashed her press card and we pushed straight to the front. My second time in as many months, I thought. You really know you've arrived socially in Paris when you never have to queue for exhibitions.

"We're looking for des hommes, rien que des hommes," Nathalie told the young, black security guy, enjoying the double entendre.

We had to go down to a basement, and the staircase bore all the scars of a 1970s building that has millions of visitors clomping around inside it. But even so, the idea that Alexa had a show on here was pretty awesome.

I still couldn't work out why she hadn't wanted me to come along. Half of the Paris art establishment must have been at the opening. One English café owner wouldn't have been noticed. Unless he'd got drunk on free wine and tried to kiss the artist's naval before collapsing beneath a white-on-white photo and entertaining the dignitaries with a tearful refrain of, "That's me, that is."

OK, so maybe I could see why she hadn't invited me.

The show was in a large, square room, with white walls, rough grey carpet, and about thirty atlas-sized colour portraits confronting you as you walked in. At least half of these were of Alexa's dad, alone or with one of two or three different guys who were identified only by their first names. They seemed, to judge by the affectionate poses, to be her dad's lovers.

These pictures were brutal close-ups. They were grungy, often blurred, with sweeps of colour where a hand had been raised or a bright shirt had soaked up the light of the flash. In most of them, her dad was grinning at the camera or his lover, but occasionally she'd caught him in a microsecond of melancholy which jarred against the general mood of gaiety, in all the senses of the word.

The rest of the photos were of a guy who hadn't known he was being photographed. He was usually walking along a Paris street gazing at nothing in particular, or sitting in a café waiting for someone, or, once, squinting towards the camera as if he couldn't quite make out what he was seeing.

These photos were grainy and grungy, too, but seemed to have been taken from a distance, occasionally through a window or between moving cars. And they weren't "gay" so much as breezy. A young guy in Paris, staring out at the city, eager to see what it had to offer.

It was Nathalie who gasped "That's you."

To say that I was stunned would be an understatement. I was like a wrestler who's just collapsed after a headbutt to the abdomen, and then feels the weight of his twenty-stone opponent crashing down to hammer the last remaining molecules of air out of his lungs.

I walked round and round the room, gaping at myself and trying to make sense of the bubbling goulash of emotions raging inside my stomach.

When had she taken all these pictures?

Why hadn't she told me?

Why hadn't I noticed?

The photo of me outside the Courrèges shop was there, but ironically it was the one where you saw me least clearly. All you could make out was a cloud of whiteness with a face smiling out of it. In the others, you were spying on me through binoculars, getting a good look at every detail of my face against the blurred background.

The only thing I could think of was that, when we were going out together, she'd got to all our meets ahead of time and snapped me as I arrived. I remembered that she often used to be fifteen minutes late. Now I saw that she'd spent that quarter of an hour taking pictures of me waiting.

It was all incredible.

Nathalie spent a couple of minutes burbling about focus and light and intensity, and then settled down to join me in trying to solve the central problem of the whole thing, the real Pompidou Centre of a question, with its innards on the outside and its inner workings hidden away.

Where the hell was sexy Sacha, the Ukrainian lover boy?

"Two possibilities," Nathalie said, pulling me into the centre of the room to stop me circling aimlessly like an eagle with too many rabbits to choose from. "One, these are the men in her life, and you are one of them. Two, these *were* the men in her life, and you are not one of them any more."

She put her hands up in a gesture of surrender, a French way of signalling ignorance in the face of life's mysteries.

"Merde." I don't know why it came out in French, but it summed up pretty accurately how I was feeling.

"Ask her," Nathalie said, pointing towards the door.

I looked around, expecting to see Alexa striding in, having just taken yet another sneak photo of me.

But no, Nathalie was pointing at the visitors' book lying open on a small square table.

"I can't just write 'Where's Sacha, then?' can I?" I was standing over the table, pen in hand, in even more anguish than usual when faced with the prospect of having to write something pithy and intelligent.

"No. That would be cruel," Nathlie agreed.

A middle-aged attendant in her white, Centre Pompidou-logo'd T-shirt was sitting behind the visitors' book watching us as we shared our bout of writer's block. Her eyebrows rose millimetre by millimetre with each of our groans of frustration, then started to descend at the same speed as she fixed her gaze on my face and recognition dawned.

Finally I wrote, "Thank you so much, Alexa' and signed with a kiss.

The attendant was smiling up at me.

"C'est vous, non?" she asked.

"Yes," I confessed, feeling like the actor getting recognized the day after his debut episode in the soap.

"You are one of her father's lovers," the woman added, spoiling it all.

"No, Madame, he is my lover." Nathalie gave the woman a lascivious grin and we made a theatrical exit.

"Wait here," Nathalie ordered. Dumping her large leather handbag in my arms, she strode across the hallway to a door decorated with the plastic silhouette of a lady with a wide skirt, no breasts and no feet.

I stood in the middle of the wide corridor, feeling stupid about feeling stupid about having to hold on to a woman's handbag.

Of *course* people wouldn't think it was mine, I told myself. And even if they did, so what? A man has every right to carry the handbag of his choice.

I finally worked out a way to hold on to it that implied it wasn't mine, without revealing that I felt totally ridiculous having to hold it—arms folded, one palm held upwards with the handle of the bag resting on my unclenched hand. A pose that said, See, I'm just waiting for the owner to return from the toilet and reclaim it.

Having solved this tricky problem, I let my mind stray back to my more serious worries. Alexa, the photos, Sacha, me. It was a jigsaw with too many pieces.

"Paul?"

She'd changed and not changed at all. She was paler—after all, it was early November, and summer was a long way behind us. She was wearing her battered old leather jacket, which clung to her like the armour of a Roman gladiator. But the jacket now seemed to be part of a look. Not a formulaic, catalogue style—this was a me-rocker attitude. An extra ear piercing here, a splash of red-gold eye makeup there. The London, I-am-who-I-am-and-fuck-you-if-you-don't-like-it look. Anarchically sexy.

"Alexa. What are you doing here?" Yes, there were a million intelligent questions I could have asked her, and I chose the one at the bottom of the list.

"Guess." She nodded towards the exhibition. Same old Paul, she seemed to be thinking.

"No, I mean . . . Oh, dammit, Alexa, you know what I mean."

"Yes, but what are *you* doing here, Paul? And where did you get that handbag? It's very chic. It suits you."

There were also a million other questions I'd have preferred her to ask.

"It's, uh, for my mum," I improvised, wishing that someone was there to write me a script. "A Christmas present from Paris."

"A very *early* Christmas present."

"Yes, I always do my Christmas shopping early. Saves panic buying on Christmas Eve, I find." I really ought to have held the bag up to the camera, TV-shopping style, and waited for the price and phone number to show up on screen.

"And are you also buying her a half-empty bottle of Evian?" Alexa asked. Nathalie always lugged around her own water supply in case she accidentally wandered across the Mediterranean into the Sahara.

"No, no. She's here, now. In the ladies'." I glanced over at the toilet door and sent out a silent prayer to all the gods of public-toilet facilities that Nathalie should not emerge at that moment, to reveal that either I was a hopeless liar or my mother was not only Parisian but had been a miraculously precocious parent.

"Oh, I see."

My prayer had been heeded and Alexa actually started to

believe me. Though of course in a couple of minutes, when Nathalie did come back, she was going to disbelieve me very seriously indeed.

Shit, I thought, why hadn't I just told her that I'd brought a TV reporter along to see her show? Here I was digging myself into a pit of lies when I could have been the hero standing atop a sandcastle of efficient networking. Or something like that.

There was only one thing for it.

"Wait here," I told Alexa and sprinted towards the toilets, my handbag almost taking the ear off a passing art-lover.

I burst into the ladies' toilet and found that the gods had not only answered my first prayers, they'd also set things up to keep my humiliation to a minimum.

Several women gave me shocked looks as I let the door slam behind me, so I quickly wished them "Bonjour, mesdames," a greeting that disarms most potential conflicts in French life.

One of the women was Nathalie, frustrated by that great injustice which proves that the gods of public-toilet facilities are all male, namely that there are never enough loos for the ladies. She was third in line for one of the two cubicles.

"Nathalie, sorry, got to go." I thrust her handbag at her.

"Go?"

"Yes. Business. Jean-Marie. He just called me. Very urgent. Sorry."

I got the hell out of there before she could think of a reply.

Another miracle—Alexa was still waiting for me. I held my hands out as if they were magnets that could pull her up the stairs, and told her that we really, really, needed to go and talk somewhere more peaceful. Now.

"But I was going to my—"

"Please, Alexa." This time my prayer was accompanied by the appropriate joined-hand gesture.

"But your mother? Don't you want to wait?"

"Mum? Oh, no. No, she suffers from terrible constipation. She'll be hours."

6

THE CAFÉ BEAUBOURG is a trendy place with a full-face view of the Centre Pompidou. It has some of the snootiest waiters I've ever been snooted by in my life, but upstairs on the mezzanine the lighting is dim and the Philippe Starck chairs are so hard and metallic that you're almost propelled forwards across the table into the arms of the person sitting opposite you. So if you're going to have a conversation with your ex about why it is absolutely essential that you both stop farting about and admit that you are meant for each other, this is as good a place as any to do it.

And my priority numéro un, I kept telling myself, was simple—just try and stick to the truth for once.

"My mum'll call me when she's finished," I told Alexa.

Yes, bad start. Not only was I bullshitting again, I also felt that it really would be wise to steer the conversation away from the subject of my mother's alleged bowel problems.

"But if she can't get a signal?"

"It's OK, we can see the exit from here."

"What does she look like?" I wondered whether Alexa was taking the pee, but there was a look of real concern on her face that made me want to leap across the table and kiss her to death.

"She's like me but with tits. But listen, Alexa, about the exhibition . . ." It worked. At the mention of her photos, Alexa stopped staring out the window. "It was fantastic. And I don't just mean because I was in it," I added quickly. "The photos are all great. And in Beaubourg, too. You must be so proud. Though I think I can understand why you didn't want me to see it."

"You can?"

This one short sentence sparked something off. Silence fell over us like a blanket of snow. We were speechless but speaking volumes. It felt as if words and pictures were flying across the table between us like bytes down a phone line. Memories, misunderstandings, anger, affection, and in my case at least, several megabytes of hope.

I don't think I've ever looked into someone's eyes for so long without blinking. At least, not since I used to stare at my Kylie Minogue poster and ask her if she liked young English boys.

"Paul?"

A huge fist of nerves grabbed me by the throat. What if she was about to say, sorry, mate, I married whatisname yesterday and I'm three months' pregnant?

No. No wedding ring. What a beautiful thing a bare ring finger is.

And pregnant? No. Well, not three months, anyway. Way too slim.

"What did you want to say to me that was so urgent?" She seemed almost breathless.

"Just one thing, really." Except that now I couldn't work out how to phrase it. I was the new recruit who pulls the pin out of the grenade and then forgets how to throw it. Not that I wanted to throw hand grenades at Alexa. Far from it.

"Yes?"

I stretched my fingers out a millimetre closer to hers on the table. If they so much as twitched I wasn't going to say it. Only trouble was, I was still looking into her eyes so I couldn't see whether she pulled away or not.

"It's. Oh, shit." Where should I start?

"It's so shit?"

"No, no. It's not shit at all. Well, yes it is. That's the thing, you see, Alexa. Without you, it is so shit."

She laughed, but I thought—I hoped—I saw the tiniest prickle of a tear in the corner of one eye. Of course it might have been an allergic reaction to the cigarette smoke in the room. But a hint of a tear was all I needed to give me the courage to go on.

"Yes, Alexa. That's it. That's what I've realized. I've been dashing about setting up the tea room and stuff, and it's soaked up most of my energy for the last three months at least, and I broke up with my new girlfriend because of it, and through it all, what I've realized is, without you, if you're not there somewhere, it's all . . ." I waved my hands above the table, trying to express the whole gassy emptiness of things that take up space in your life but don't necessarily have much substance. "It's all just . . ."

"Shit?" The tear hadn't grown or receded, but now she was smiling.

So was I. God, it's so much easier when you just tell someone what you feel, I thought. Why the hell do we waste so much time not telling them? What self-defence mechanism is it that makes us inflict so much pain on ourselves?

"Well, not totally shit, of course, because the tea room is working out, it's fun."

"And shagging Virginie was nice, too, I expect?"

"Yes, maybe almost as nice as shagging big blond Ukrainians. I don't know. I haven't tried it. But that doesn't matter. It's all meaningless. It's you I want. Need. You know. Love."

Wow, that word hurt a lot, but it was better out than in.

We Brits have it much harder than the French. They've got their word "aimer," which means to love, sure, but it also means to like. So you can get away with telling someone you love them without nearly so much risk and commitment.

I'd had it done to me. A woman says "je t'aime" and then quickly adds "bien" on the end, and suddenly it's just, "je t'aime bien"—"I like you a lot."

I guess we could achieve the same deflating effect in English by saying "I love you" and then tacking on "in that wig." But generally, when we use The Word, even as ham-fistedly as I'd just done, it actually means something.

"You are sure you're not just feeling flattered because of the photos?" Alexa asked.

"No. Well, yes. Incredibly flattered. Why didn't you tell me you'd taken so many?"

She shrugged. Not an annoying Parisian shrug of indifference. This was a gesture of helplessness.

"When I was taking the photos, I couldn't tell you that I was taking photos of you because that was the charm of it. You didn't know what I was doing. And then, when I thought I could tell you, because we were really finished, then . . ."

"Then I pissed you off with my stupid phone calls so you didn't want me to see them. I know, I'm sorry."

"No, it wasn't that. It's so complicated. I'm with someone now."

I know, I wanted to say, and he's a rich blond hunk, but so what? Rich blond hunks tend to get over breakups quicker than other people. It's in the very nature of rich blond hunkdom that they're never alone for long.

"And, oh." She pressed her fingers against her eyebrows as if she was trying to clear her sinuses. "It will sound terrible, but Yuri, Sacha's dad, you know he will finance my film."

This was what you might call a bucket-of-icy-water-down-the-boxer-shorts moment. Not only was Sacha a rich blond hunk, he was a rich blond career move, too.

Though it seemed to me that there was one essential point she was missing.

Surely, no matter how important the film was to her, she wasn't going to stay with Sacha just because his dad had promised to finance her? What would she do after the film was made—say she was going to leave him if daddy didn't back the sequel?

"Alexa, let's have dinner together. We've got to keep talking. This is important."

"I can't, Sacha's waiting at my father's apartment."

"Call him and say you'll be home late. You've got to go out with the director of Beaubourg, anything. Please."

She took a deep breath. She was going to have to give one of us a punch in the mouth. Which one was it going to be?

"OK." She reached into her jacket pocket for her phone. "And you call your mother and say sorry for leaving her."

A fair compromise, I thought. A punch for him, a slap for me.

T HE FIRST TIME I ever kissed Alexa, she tasted of French
farmer. She'd just eaten Reblochon, a runny cheese that
gives off an aroma somewhere between old sock and cow dung.
But I didn't mind—I'd just eaten andouille de Vire, a sausage that
smells even more pungent.

This time, a year later, both our mouths were like empty jars of
caviar, so we had definitely come on in the world.

We were standing on the Pont des Arts, a spindly, wind-blown
pedestrian bridge from where you can look along the Seine
towards Nôtre Dame, which, from a distance, seemed to be a
horned animal waiting in the undergrowth to pounce on one of the
many bateaux mouches heading up the river towards it.

Closer to us, almost immediately below the bridge, was an
arrow-shaped garden on the prow of the île de la Cité. This, Alexa
told me, was where King Henri IV used to seduce his lovers.

"I expect there weren't as many tourists and homeless people
back then," I suggested.

"You're really not romantic, are you, Paul?"

"No, not at all," I said, kissing her.

"You know," she went on, "I like Sacha a lot, I really do."

"I'm glad." And I meant it, too. There it was. Proof. Poor old
Sacha had been relegated to the "like" division. He wasn't in the
"love" league. "But I *love* you, Alexa, and I want to be with you.
And I'm old enough to know what I want."

First time I'd ever used my age as an argument with a woman. Bloody hell, I thought, was this maturity finally arriving? Or old age?

Back in the Russian restaurant Alexa had taken me to, I'd tiptoed into the potential minefield of why she shouldn't stay with someone because his dad's rich, and I'd come out of it pretty well unscathed. It was a dilemma that had been bothering her, too.

However, she'd hit back at me with a real heat-seeking missile of a question.

OK, she asked, what if she did drop everything, move out of Yuri's house in London and find alternative funding for her film. Would I still be there for her?

She'd taken a slug of ice-cold vodka and breathed her worries at me in all their chilling detail.

"The first time we were together, you slept with another woman," she said.

"I was unconscious at the time."

"OK, we have discussed this. Then you slept with Virginie."

"I thought she was your way of telling me to forget you and find someone else."

"Another girl as a goodbye present? I am not so generous. But OK, we have discussed this, too. But do you see what I mean? I am not ready to leave London yet. I am trying to organize this same exhibition there. Will I call you in Paris and get a woman who has picked up the phone from the side of your bed?"

"No, of course not." I was going to add that I never let anyone else answer my phone, but it wasn't the right time for a joke like that. The air was too full of vodka and heat-seeking missiles. "I know what I want now, Alexa, and it's you. And only you. I'd never have slept with Virginie or any of the others if I'd been with you."

"Others?"

Whoops.

"Yes, you know, Florence, my ex-girlfriend, the one I just broke up with." No need to confuse things by mentioning Nathalie. Besides, I was serious. If someone had suddenly burst into the restaurant and told me I'd won the Shag Anyone In the World lottery, I'd have chosen Alexa, thank you very much. Unless, of course, there'd been a massive cash prize attached if I agreed to shag a reality-TV star, in which case I'd have put on a dozen condoms and donated the money to the Alexa film fund. But only if Alexa agreed.

"Forget the others," I told her. "Yours and mine. The reason why I ride out into the salt marshes at midnight to talk to you, the reason I phone you up with stupid questions at dawn on a Sunday, the reason I somersault over scooters, the reason I went along to your exhibition even though you asked me not to, is because I've decided what I really want. You."

This was what had earned me my first caviar kiss of the evening. And this was why we were clutched together on the Pont des Arts, watching Paris's golden street lights flicker over the dark waters of the Seine.

I whispered in her ear. "Come with me to my apartment, now, please."

She tensed in my arms. Then I felt a breath of warm air on my neck as she relaxed. "Yes."

I squeezed her then like someone who's just been reunited with a kidnap victim. She'd been taken away from me and now she was back.

"WHERE DO YOU LIVE?" she asked as we scanned the road for the white roof light of an unoccupied taxi.

"Do you promise not to laugh?"

"Yes."

I told her. She laughed.

And she was the one wanting promises from *me*.

Luckily my front door was brand new. The landlady had had a new, indestructible metal frame fitted around the old varnished door, and if you treated it gently, it opened and shut with no more than a whoosh of air and a barely audible clunk.

There was the problem of getting across the creaky floorboards of the entrance hall to my room, but when I poked my head round the open front door, I could hear faint DVD laughter from the living room. Whoever was in tonight was engrossed in *Friends*.

I really did not want to go through introductions to my roommates.

Hi, this is Alexa and I'd like to go to bed with her as soon as possible, so goodnight.

We arrived at my bedroom door with the giggles but without interruption. I stifled any potential rattling from my keys and swung my room door open for Alexa to go in.

But she didn't. And it wasn't because she wanted to be carried over the threshold.

As soon as I'd squeezed past her, I saw why.

There, squinting at us from my bed, was a half-asleep, half-naked Nathalie.

Oh, merde, merde and encore merde.

Alexa was staring at me with the bitter shock of a fiancée who finds out that you postponed your engagement party so you could go to a swingers' night with her mum.

"Alexa, this is Nathalie. She's someone else's wife. Nathalie, this is Alexa." At least, I thought, something could be salvaged if we all respected a few social conventions.

"Vous êtes Alexa?" Nathalie, a sophisticated woman, grasped the full horror of the situation instantly. She pulled the duvet up over her shoulders, as if covering a few inches of flesh might make things more decent.

"And someone else's wife sleeps in your bed?" Alexa had a tear in her eye again, but this one wasn't accompanied by a smile.

"No. No, not at all. It's not my room. I don't have a room yet. I'm sleeping in the lounge. But I thought I'd use Matthieu's bed. He's my roommate. He's away, you see. Nathalie is his wife."

Sounded pretty damn convincing, I thought.

Alexa wasn't quite convinced, though. Well, not convinced at all.

"Paul. Stop talking complete crap!" she snapped.

"She is right, Paul, stop talking crap." This was Nathalie, nodding maternally from the bed.

The women were ganging up on me, but I saw that they were right. Now more than ever it was time for truth.

"OK, yes, I'm sorry, Alexa. This is Nathalie. I have slept with her a couple of times, but that was when I thought you weren't interested in me any more. She's married, I didn't invite her here tonight, I don't know why she's here and I don't think we're going to sleep together again. Right, Nathalie?" Nathalie nodded agreement. "That is the truth, Alexa, I swear it."

I might even have pulled it off if Alexa hadn't looked down for a moment as she tried to work out where she stood in this bedroom à trois.

She pointed to the dark object standing at the foot of the bedside table.

She didn't even need to say anything. She just shook her head resignedly, glowered at me for a second or two as if putting a curse on me, and marched out of the room.

The heavy front door slammed and shook the whole neighbourhood.

It was the bag, of course. She'd seen the handbag standing there, with the bottle of water beside it. Rather like a side view of Nôtre Dame, in fact, a monument to this whole new generation of lies that had reared up in front of Alexa and convinced her that everything I'd said that evening had been bullshit.

I could have explained. I could at least have said "I can explain." But no one who says "I can explain" ever gets the chance to explain, do they?

"Well, you idiot?" Nathalie folded her arms sternly at me.

"Yes, I know," I said. "I've really screwed up this time."

"No, you imbecile. Go and stop her. Run!"

Of course. Why didn't I think of that?

6

Ex and the City

1

T HE GREEKS GOT it right. There are times when the gods are with you and there are times when they sit on top of their mountain pissing with laughter at all the shit they've caused.

The toilet gods had led me into a trap. They'd allowed me to think I was getting away with my hopeless lies just long enough to aim a steaming bucket of merde at my head.

When I came out the front door of my apartment, an old lady in a blue raincoat was getting out of the lift. This was Madame Gibert, our next-door neighbour on the landing. She was even holding the door open for me.

I did a swift mental calculation. I usually preferred to take the stairs, but this was a new lift, and seemed to go up and down pretty fast. I could hear Alexa's heavy footsteps on the stairs. Would the lift be faster? The fact that the door was being held open for me seemed like a sign from the gods.

It was. Get in, they were telling me, and you're ours, all ours.

I got in, hit the zero button, lurched down a foot and stopped.

I could only think it was revenge from the lift gods because I visited them so rarely.

My neighbour seemed to have a different interpretation of the disaster that had just struck me.

"Non, non, non!" She began to harangue me through the glass wall of the lift about people not waiting for the door to shut properly before they start punching the buttons. "It got stuck like that last week, and this summer, Madame Lagrange from the third floor spent one whole Sunday trapped in there because the repair men were on holiday, and before that, the little crétin on the second floor banged the buttons so hard that . . ."

All I could think of was that Alexa's footsteps were now getting desperately faint.

I hit a few more buttons. Zero again, one, four, five, anything to get the bloody thing to move, but this only raised the neighbour to a new level of hysteria.

"Non, non, non, non!" she howled. "You are going to destroy it once and for all. Call the emergency number, call the emergency number written on the door."

My phone. Of course. It was switched off, and it took me two goes to get the pin number right, then at last it was ringing.

"Come on Alexa, please, give me one last chance." I begged the phone to get through to her, but it stopped trying as soon as it reached her voicemail.

I left a message explaining everything—the bag, the fact that Nathalie was a TV reporter, why I wasn't running after her—but I'm not sure how audible it was. The neighbour thought I was speaking to the lift people, and my pleas and apologies were set to a backing track of her whining on about this making three emergencies this month, and she for one was determined to "get rid of this menace to the tenants."

Alexa probably thought I was calling to say I'd been evicted for sexually harassing a mad old French woman—for the third time.

My roommates thought it was all great fun. It reminded them of a *Friends* episode where "Hoss" wanted to get it on with "Ha-Shell" and an ex-girlfriend of his was in the apartment. Or was it the other way round? They had a little argument about this on the landing while I squatted in the tiny lift and tried not to scream at them that this was not some fucking episode of some fucking soap, this was my real fucking life that was being fucked up.

Nathalie kindly came and sat on the stairs for a while. Fully dressed, I'm glad to say. She told the others to bugger off and leave us alone. She even offered to go round to Alexa's place and explain. But I said no, it probably wasn't a good idea. Alexa had had enough of other women for one night.

Although I did suggest that a sworn, signed statement testifying to the fact that I hadn't planned for her to be in my bed might come in handy at some point.

Yes, why had she been there, anyway?

Her husband, it seemed, had unwisely left her alone in Paris while he took the kids to visit his mum. So Nathalie was free to sleep where she wanted. She'd got my roommates to let her in, she said. She'd assumed I was still with Jean-Marie and would be in need of serious relaxation after meeting him, because he was being a general pain in the butt at the moment. He was pushing ahead with his plan to get to the top in party politics by turning his guns on the député—the MP—of the Eighth arrondissement, and whipping up all kinds of attention-seeking trouble in the neighbourhood to discredit the incumbent.

This, Nathalie said, was why she had put off doing a film about Jean-Marie. She was checking up on him, trying to get a bigger story—the real story instead of some TV showcase that would just serve as part of his campaign.

Two hurried and sympathetic guys in silver overalls arrived and thanked me profusely for not peeing in the lift.

"Never get in a lift if you're hungry, thirsty or need the toilettes," they advised me.

"What if you're chasing after your girlfriend?" I asked.

"Depends if you want to catch her," one of the guys replied.

They laughed and I didn't, because it reminded me how much I'd wanted to catch her.

Half an hour later, Nathalie and I were staring up at the glass-fronted loft where Alexa was probably sleeping. There was no light, no sign of life. The whole courtyard of converted warehouses was dark and silent.

No one answered my five long, hard prods at the bell. We could hear it buzzing up there like a giant fly trapped in an aquarium. If anyone was at home, they were either ignoring the buzzer or full of sleeping tablets.

"Maybe I could shimmy up that drainpipe," I said.

"I don't not know what shimmy is, but climbing up would be stupid. You must let her have a rest, and return here in the morning." Nathalie was already walking towards the exit. "Come," she said, "we should go to bed now."

We did, too, but only to sleep. We both agreed that it would be a friendly, T-shirts-on night rather than something raunchier.

And even though it was difficult waking up next to a beautiful woman and persuading myself that one little morning shag was out of the question, I thought how great it would be if people could just bed down together now and again for a bit of company. Even if you only sleep with someone in the eyes-closed, snoring sense of the word, it's good to feel that they're there with you.

*   *   *

Just after dawn, we were buzzing at Alexa's door again.

And still there was no reaction.

I called Alexa's mobile number—voicemail. I called her Paris number, and I could hear the phone trilling two floors above us until Alexa's voice cut in.

"Bonjour," she said. She informed me in French and English that she would be away for at least the next two weeks, and suggested I call her in London.

"She's gone," Nathalie said. "Perhaps she even went immediately last night. She is very, very angry with you, I think."

"Yes. Do you reckon I'll ever be able to calm her down and explain?"

"I don't know. She must be very—what is the word? Blessée?"

"Hurt, wounded."

"Yes. You have hurt her. You must win her confidence again. Are you good at diplomacy?"

No, I thought. If I was a diplomat, I'd get caught trying to help the foreign ambassador's wife dig a lost earring out of her bra.

3

I T WAS NATHALIE who convinced me to wait a few hours before rushing to the Gare du Nord on my diplomatic mission.

"First you must tell your employees where you are going, and reassure them," she said. "Then you must take some clean clothes. Alexa will think you are very romantic if you go immediately, but she will also think you are a smelly imbecile."

So I didn't get to London till late afternoon, when the damp, grey dusk was descending on the double-decker rush of Notting Hill Gate.

I hadn't been back in town for months, and I almost fainted from shock when the traffic lights turned red, the little green man lit up, and no one tried to knock me over as I crossed the road.

I picked my way along the pavement, instinctively scanning for dog merde, and felt confused when my lasers hit a blank. No dog merde in the streets? No drivers running red lights? Was this a real city or some sanitized Urban Experience theme park?

Nathalie had blagged Alexa's address out of the Pompidou Centre people. It led me to a little mews that didn't look like part of a capital city, either.

It was a wide, cobbled cul de sac, about fifty yards long, lined on either side with squat, old-looking townhouses. Some were bare brick, others had been whitewashed. One house had a teak coffee table outside, another had a pram. There were large potted plants guarding practically every door, and even the little individual dustbins looked quaint and rural compared to the massive wheelie bins that most Londoners have.

I couldn't figure out why an ultra-rich East European would be living in yucca-plant Bohemia and not in a stucco palace in Kensington or a flashy loft overlooking the Thames. Nevertheless, before I'd even looked at the house numbers, I guessed which was Yuri's—it had to be the one with the silver Mercedes sports car parked outside.

You could almost hear the other residents bristling with indignation at this scar on the face of their deurbanized community. Apart from the lights in the windows, the "no parking at any time" signs were the most visible things in the whole street.

I walked past the house, trying to look as if I belonged in the mews, and gave the front windows a casual but attentive going-over.

An open-plan kitchen was apparently empty. The entrance hall behind the half-glass front door was brightly lit and as unpopulated as the kitchen. The two upstairs floors were in darkness, except for the blinking red light of a burglar alarm.

I turned round at the end of the mews and beat a tactical retreat. Time for a think.

And time for a drink.

There was a pub on the corner of the street leading down from the Tube station. Sitting in the window I would be able to see anyone coming out of or going into the mews.

Offering a prayer of thanks to the gods of all-day pub opening hours, and hoping that they weren't in league with the gods of disappearing girlfriends or violent fathers-in-law, I bought myself a frothy-headed amber pint and a packet of salt and vinegar crisps and sat down to ponder on how my life had gone so far off track in just twenty-four hours.

Here I was, with my Paris tea room starting to cruise, abandoning everything to sit in a London pub and spy on the house of a DVD pirate in case the girl I was stalking turned up.

How many days was I going to keep it up for? What was I actually planning to do?

I had no idea.

Even if I did eventually come up with some masterplan, there was no guarantee it would work. Alexa might not give me a chance to try out my amateur diplomacy. I'd seen for myself how well she'd mastered that key phrase in English life—"bugger off."

It was all totally insane.

But at the same time it felt like the most sensible thing I'd ever done.

4

I'M SURPRISED THEY don't call it the Hanging Gardens of Covent or something similarly exotic.

Honestly, Covent Garden felt like the Third World, with all those cycle rickshaws tinging their bells at me, touting for custom. No, not even the Third World, because these days most Asian cities have done away with this type of sweated labour.

It was the same with the poor guys standing on street corners holding their advertising placards. In Paris, you often see student hostesses handing out leaflets for restaurants, phone deals or department stores. I'd forgotten that here in Central London, you see real sandwich men, or guys holding placards on street corners—not students but bearded, backpacked homeless guys who clearly need the money to pay for more than their phone bill and their next pair of Timberlands. What a job, freezing your butt off all day as the caretaker of a sign saying "2 pizza's 4 the price of 1, 50 yards on left."

How soon till we saw shoeshine men and street dentists in London, I wondered. Or lepers.

My mate Chris had suggested we meet up in an Indian restaurant near Covent Garden market. It was still early evening, so I had time to get a table, order a beer, and regret that I'd agreed to eat here.

I knew it was going to be bad as soon as I saw the décor. It seems to me that the quality of Indian restaurants is often in inverse proportion to the price of the furnishings.

This place was Delhi meets Copenhagen—long, communal benches, minimalist cutlery, Bollywood posters, and light fittings like great robotic scorpions hanging over people's heads but not actually lighting very much. The music was Oriental lounge, and the prices were truly international in that they were so big they made me wonder whether they weren't in rupees. A starter was the price of a two-course meal with a carafe of wine in my local café in Paris.

The menu itself was sheer poetry—everything was marinated in this, delicately steamed in that, its spiciness tempered with the other, but I had a hunch that it would all taste like re-heated bull's testicles in masala-flavoured sperm.

I'd forgotten how much of Central London was all style and no substance.

"Paul! Welcome back to civilization!"

Chris snapped me out of my gloom. He was my best mate when I was working in London, but we'd lost touch over the past few months. It was the price of being a nomad.

I stood up to shake his hand but he grabbed me in a bear hug and slapped my back as if I needed consoling after losing my teddy bear. And we Brits make fun of French guys for kissing each other, I thought.

"You're looking good, Chris." He was, too—expensively neat brown hair, three-facial-a-week complexion, a sort of inverse Jake, a young cufflinks-and-formal-overcoat City slicker with a flat leather shoulder bag to show that here was a businessman who was too active to monopolize one of his hands carrying a briefcase.

"Yeah? Well you look like shit, Paul mate. What are you doing in London?"

It took me two beers and an age-long wait for our refried starters to explain.

Once he was up to speed, the first thing Chris did was insult me again.

"Christ, Paul, you are what is known in the City as a prime wanker. Why don't you just call her and say you'd like a chance to explain?"

"Tell her I'm in London?"

"No, don't do that. From the sound of it she'd just bugger off with this guy to Reykjavik."

"Reykjavik?"

"Or Minsk."

"The capital of Ukraine is Kiev, you dork, don't you know anything about geography?" Jake would have been proud of me.

"Whatever. Just call her, say you're still in Paris—you don't want to scare the shit out of her—and give her a bit of the old Paul West bullshit."

"No, I've finished with bullshit. I want to tell her the truth."

"Then you're even more of a wanker than I thought, mate. You don't tell women the *truth*."

The trendy young Indian waiter, who was dressed and coiffed as if he couldn't wait to go out clubbing, came and slotted a group of six women on the bench beside us. Instinctively, Chris and I had a sly look to see which of the six we'd sleep with if given the chance.

The girls, though, had other ideas.

"Hi guys," the one nearest to me trumpeted. "You're cute. I might shag you later."

All six of them hooted with laughter.

"We promise not to have anything with garlic in it, then," Chris said, determined not to lose the fight for sexual supremacy.

"Who said you were going to be kissing my *mouth*?"

Which sounded like a knockout punch to me.

The girls, like Chris, seemed to be fresh out of the office. They were in formal work gear, and had just undone a blouse button or three to give their boobs and navels room to enjoy some fresh air.

Two of them were very attractive, in a slightly over-weight, over-made-up, fussy-hairstyle way. And all of them, after a year of svelte French women, who rarely go out in gangs of more than two, seemed somehow larger than life to me. Louder than life, too.

They killed off any chance of Chris and me discussing my problems, because they were listening out for the slightest word that could be turned into sexual innuendo and throwing it back in our faces.

"Exhibition? You an exhibitionist or what? Gonna show us your dick?"

My God, I thought, we are being sexually harassed. We couldn't say a word without being reminded of what went on below the belt. I was just glad that I was taller than them. If we'd been two demure girls getting that much hassle from a gang of six male Viagra addicts, we'd have started to get scared.

We battled on with more general subjects, and Chris filled me in (luckily I didn't actually ask him to "fill me in") on what he'd been doing for the last few months.

His employers, an Internet travel agency, had gone bust, so he'd moved to a phone company. This had been bought out by venture capitalists who'd laid everyone off and then taken back on a skeleton staff, including Chris. They'd then sold on key parts of the business, making everyone redundant again. Chris had seen the way things were heading, leapt on the bandwagon with the venture capitalists, and was now merrily asset-stripping his way across the country.

"Lot of job satisfaction, is there?" I asked.

"Hey, don't knock it," he said. "You know all these pro-
grammes we have on TV at the moment—they find some poor
bastard counting traffic cones in Wolverhampton, relocate him and
his family to a village in the Dordogne and then have a giggle
when he tries to learn French so he can . . . I don't know . . ."

"Open an English tea room?"

"Right, yeah. Well, everyone wants to be on those shows. Half
of the UK wants to bugger off and live in the sun. So I reckon,
why not help them on their way? We downsize them, free them
from the rat race, they move abroad and live happily ever after. I'll
be heading out there myself one day. Meanwhile, the lemmings
leave room over here for the rest of us to make shitloads of
money."

"Or work in call centres and take shitloads of anti-depressants."

Normally I might have proposed a toast to earning shitloads of
money, or buggering off to live in the sun, but Chris's economic
analysis was getting me down. Even further down, that is.

Apart from the fact that somewhere in what he was saying there
was an insult directed at me and my tea room, he was having to
yell his sociology lesson over the Indo-Danish background music
and the squawking hen party next to us.

Chris started to chat up the woman next to him, who was, I had
to admit, a very nicely rounded girl with hair a cheesecake shade
of blond that I hardly ever saw in Paris. Amazingly, she turned out
not to be a mud wrestler or a bricklayer, as her skill with
obscenities suggested, but a business analyst like Chris. Soon
they were sharing the kind of business analysts' secrets that had to
be giggled in each other's ears.

The woman next to me, who would also have been pretty
attractive if she didn't insist on yelling like a soldier and flaunting

her excess kilos (or pounds) by wearing overtight clothes, took the cue and began chatting to me, but I am proud to say that, even though we were all now several pints of lager further down the river to drunkenness, I resisted any temptation to ask for more details of this garlic-free non-mouth-kissing they had been talking about.

Instead, I gave my neighbour, and those of her friends who weren't busy canoodling with Chris, a quick run-through of the events of the previous evening that had brought me across the Channel. I was, I made it clear, in London on a mission of lurv.

"Oh. My. God. That. Is. So. Sweet." My neighbour was practically sobbing into her aloo saag.

"So you've given everything up for her?" This came from the most attractive of the girls—another blonde—for whom on another night I might have offered to give up everything.

"No one's ever given up everything for me," my neighbour wailed. "My Keith never even gave up wanking."

This seemed to wipe my predicament from the girls' collective memory, and they joined forces to pour vicious female scorn on poor old Keith, who, it seemed, had been caught watching a lesbian-action DVD one weekend when he thought his girlfriend was away, which could happen to anyone.

The one thing the waiter was good at was keeping us supplied with liquid refreshment, presumably to cover up the food's taste and consistency, or lack of both. So it came as no surprise to discover, at some point later in the evening, after saying a heartbreaking goodbye to several large-denomination banknotes, that I was parading towards Piccadilly, arm-in-arm with two women who, although this was now—what? November? December? Greenland?—bloody cold, anyway, were dressed for an August night out in Cyprus. One had an off-the-shoulder top, the other a blouse thin enough to show off the stitching in her white bra. They each had an Indian beer in their free hand, and now and again one of them would bottle-feed me with it, which seemed to be the only way to stop me laughing and shouting.

I don't know what I was laughing and shouting about, but everyone else in the world seemed to be doing the same thing. The street was packed with us. There was probably more alcohol than blood in the bodies charging up and down that pavement.

Gangs of us were milling about with that same determined randomness you see when you look at an ant colony. And on one street corner, two soldier ants from rival colonies were trying to punch each other's heads while their queens spat at the males to "give the cant a slap" and "fakkin twat im one."

We cheered them on for a few minutes, only losing interest when a howling siren came to spoil the fun.

I noticed that my own two queen ants and I were following a set of small bare footprints on the pavement. So women were not only coatless but shoeless out here? Or maybe after midnight, everyone just stripped off and had a sex-and-boxing orgy. I pulled my two companions along in pursuit of the feet, but the trail dried up. Girl Friday had apparently gone into a club.

Chris was trying to drag his new ladyfriend towards one of the several million taxis that had gathered to evacuate casualties. She either didn't want to go or couldn't work out how to get her body to follow him, because she sprawled headlong in the gutter, pulling Chris down with her, and they decided to stay there, cackling up at the street lights.

"Give us a snog before you go," someone bawled in my ear, which suggested that maybe I was meant to be leaving with Chris and his new lady love.

Yes, I had something very important to do. A mission. I

couldn't remember what it was, but it was there in my mind and it did not involve being here in Piccadilly.

"Chris! Why am I here?"

"Why is any of us here, mate? To get pissed and have a bit of fun before we die." From his relaxed location in a London gutter, he gave me an answer that would have done a French existentialist proud. He was then violently sick into a drain, before washing his mouth out from the bottle of beer that he had somehow managed to keep from spilling or smashing when he fell.

No wonder, I thought, that coming into the West End in the daytime feels like visiting a hangover.

M Y BLURRED EYES squinted at the writing on the little screen. My brain made a courageous attempt to enhance the image, and failed. After a superhuman struggle, it finally concluded that in my phone's opinion it was seven o'clock. Which meant that it was either six or eight, because there was an hour's time difference between Paris and London. Which way did the time difference work? No, it was too early and too painful to figure that out.

Anyway, I had to concentrate on more important things.

Like, how exactly should I kill myself?

Just stopping breathing seemed to be the easiest option. Every time my ribs moved to let air in or out, I was reminded that my liver had been soaked in pure alcohol then set alight. The charred remains were sending SOS messages echoing through my empty skull, where my dehydrated brain was lolling like a dead bat.

I was lying on a carpet in the "won't choke if he vomits" position that I trained myself to adopt at the end of drunken nights out. The carpet was still white, and remarkably dry, which was encouraging.

The only trouble was that the architect who had designed this building—and from what I could see of it, a lot of designing had gone on—had forgotten to include foundations, and it was wobbling about like a sumo wrestler's backside.

Luckily, as a kid I did quite a lot of skateboarding, so I was not afraid to stand up on a surface that was trying to pull itself out from under me, and I skated, with only two or three topples, towards what looked like a door. It was hard to tell, because everything in the apartment was made to fold away so as not to clutter up the three cubic millimetres of living space. The whole place was made of doors.

I was, I realized, in the two-room Docklands apartment that Chris had so wisely bought when the rest of us were saying, Who wants to live in a designer shoebox in the East End? And now he would have been able to sell it and buy a whole French village, because lots of people wanted to live in a designer shoebox this close to the River Thames.

I eventually found myself in a bathroom that was so damn ergonomic that I had to open the laundry basket, shower cubicle and toilet before discovering a medicine cabinet. This did not, unfortunately, contain a booklet giving hints on how to give myself a head, liver and kidney transplant, but it did offer up tubes of fizzy stuff that gave me back the will to live.

What a great thing his shower was. On, off, fast flow, slow flow, hot, warm, cold. I almost wished that Florence's mum could be there to witness its beautiful simplicity. Though thinking about Florence's mum was bad enough sober, so I hit the cold button and shocked her out of my system before she could do any permanent damage.

Before leaving the apartment I stopped off to peer into the bedroom. There was Chris, on his back, twisted up in his duvet, his mouth wide open as if he was hoping to swallow any falling light bulbs. Next to him lay the large, cream-coloured body of a woman wearing nothing but a Chinese tattoo at the base of her spine.

For a split second I felt envious. Then hugely pleased with myself. The complications of waking up with yet another woman were just not worth it.

As far as I could recall (which wasn't very far at all), we'd gone to a club with the girls from the restaurant, and had a good laugh, and I could probably have wangled my way into someone's bed. But then there's no great merit in scoring when everyone is so drunk they would shag a dustbin.

Dustbins, yes. Now I remembered what my real mission was— to get to those dinky dustbins in Notting Hill.

I wasn't feeling at my best when I staggered out into the street at Notting Hill Gate. That London Tube jiggles about a lot. And it's very considerate warning people to mind the gap, but did it have to warn me so loudly? The canned voice gave me such a shock that I nearly fell down the gap I was supposed to be minding.

It was still before eight London time. Why is it, I wondered, that during a hangover, when my body most needs healing sleep, it always wakes me up so bloody early?

But at least this meant there was less chance that Alexa had already gone out for the day. I'd only have to hang about for a few hours before being able to confront her and beg forgiveness.

In fact, though, I didn't have to wait for hours at all. My first breath mint had only just had time to turn my tongue into an ice floe when a large man came out of Yuri's front door.

As students of perspective will know, when objects come towards you, they get bigger, so by the time he was right in front of me, this large man would only have needed a dab or two of green make-up to audition for the Incredible Hulk. He'd have needed a black wig too, though, and stick-on eyebrows, because his head was totally hairless. He was Humpty Hulk.

I was standing quite innocently at the entrance to the mews, and could easily have been an undercover yucca-plant inspector, but the man didn't even ask. He reached out a massive green arm (or was the colour just my imagination?) and with what felt like one single movement, propelled me past the silver Mercedes and into the house.

Before I knew what was happening, I was sitting at a scrubbed-pine kitchen table with a mug of coffee in front of me.

Everything in here except my mug seemed to be made of stripped pine—table, chairs, wall units, an enormous dresser. I wondered whether the Ukrainians weren't somehow related to the Welsh. I'd have to ask Jake, if I ever got out of here alive.

"You not shout, OK?" Humpty Hulk warned me. Much more quietly than the Tube people, I had to admit. "Every buddy aslip." He spoke as if he'd trained at the Arnold Schwarzenegger school of English diction.

"Shout?" I felt my testicles trying to hide up inside my pelvic bone. It sounded as if there might be some violence on the cards after I'd finished my coffee.

"No. You shaddap."

"OK." Although I couldn't really promise. I'm not generally good at receiving violence.

"You want spik wid Alyexa, you wet mebbe one hour."

"Alexa?"

"Yeah. You want spik wid air, no?"

"Yes. How did you know that?"

He grunted a laugh through clenched teeth and beckoned me to follow him with a jerk of his tree-trunk-sized neck.

In one corner of the kitchen there was a little computer desk. Hulk woke the computer up, clicked with a surprisingly light touch on some icons, and soon we were watching a black-and-white film of a woman urinating. It was a rear view, and the girl had hoisted up her skirt, pulled her thong to one side, and squatted down right outside someone's townhouse. The camera focussed in on the white glare of her backside. Just above the cleft of her buttocks she had a Chinese tattoo.

The film was silent, but when the camera pulled back it was obvious that one of the two men with her was laughing loudly. He was bent double and his whole upper body was shaking so hard that his bag slipped off his shoulder and got tangled round his neck.

Next to him, facing the camera, was another guy whom I recognized from Alexa's photo show. Moi. I was shouting something that we couldn't hear, and the Hulk provided the soundtrack.

"Alyexa, Alyexa," he crooned plaintively, his smooth face registering something close to amusement.

He hit the space bar and the film stopped.

"We know you want spik wid Alyexa. You want spik wid air at tree o'clock dis morning."

"Oh God. What a dickhead." So this was what my drunken inner self considered to be good diplomacy? "Oh, no." An even more horrific thought than having serenaded a whole mews in the middle of the night had dawned on me. "I didn't actually talk to Alexa last night, did I?"

"No. You all run away when we tell you to stop wid da shoutink."

"Thank Christ for that."

"So you spik wid air today, den you don't wek us up at tree o'clock no more, OK?" Now his face was registering his real emotions about having drunken Brits serenade him with shouts, laughs, and the splash of urine. "It was only Alyexa stop us, or we go and break your face."

Leaving aside for the moment how close I'd come to having my face broken, here was positive news.

"So she knows I was here last night, and she still wants to talk to me today?"

"Mebbe."

"Does she know I'm here now?"

"No. She knows you was here at tree o'clock. Is all. I see you arribe just now, I decide to stop you from shouting no more. Alyexa, Alyexa . . ." He grunted his laugh again. "You sit, you wait, mebbe she spik wid you, mebbe not."

"She's still asleep?"

"Yeah. She's tired. She was awake at—"

"Tree in the morning, yes, I'm really sorry."

My head was hurting enough now, and I didn't like to imagine how much more it would have hurt if a tin dustbin lid, however dinky, had been rammed repeatedly against it last night.

So I sat at the table, watched breakfast-TV presenters gabbling merrily about nothing, saw some football highlights flash across the screen, wondered vaguely again why Yuri didn't get the same media coverage as other foreign club chairmen, and waited.

It felt like days. But it might have been decades.

Because when Alexa finally walked into the kitchen, not only was her hair now henna'd and shoulder-blade length, her whole face had aged thirty years.

What's more, time had transformed her into a purple-robed hippy, with a faint whiff of incense about her, and the piercing look of someone who's been wearing black make-up at the corner of her eyes every day since she was fifteen.

"Bonjour, Paul," she said, not unkindly.

This, even I realized, was not Alexa. It was her mum.

If it's true that studying your girlfriend's mum is the best way of seeing what your girlfriend is going to look like in twenty or thirty years' time, then Alexa's long-term prospects weren't bad at all. She was still slim, graceful, and showed no signs of a Madame Jean-Marie-style craving for eternal youth.

I was doubly impressed, because again, Yuri had surprised me. Not only did he live in a discreet mews cottage, he also had a real middle-aged woman for a partner instead of a surgically enhanced porn star.

"Bonjour," I replied, and apologized in my best French for the previous night's disturbance.

She nodded, acknowledging the apology without completely forgiving the crime.

"Belle maison," I added.

"Oui, it is a very tranquil street," she said, a barbed flash of irony in her eyes. She took a fine china cup and saucer from a cupboard and poured herself some coffee.

"Why do you want to see Alexa?" she asked.

She called me "tu." Was this because I was, even subconsciously, part of the family? Or because I was just a young idiot who was unworthy of a "vous"?

"Je l'aime." I made sure I didn't add on "bien" or anything superfluous.

"Ah." This stopped her as she was about to put the coffee cup to her lips. She mulled over the idea for a moment, then drank. "Tu l'aimes?"

"Qui."

"Really?" She locked on to my eyes. I looked back unflinchingly.

"Oui."

"Ah. Then you must tell me who you are."

Who was I? Good question. I didn't know how to give a short answer—this wasn't "What's the capital of Ukraine?" after all. So I gave her full—or only slightly edited—highlights of the previous year, starting with the day I first met Alexa, going through all the unconscious-sex episodes and the political disagreements, and ending with the handbag, the caviar kiss, the married-woman-in-the-bed accident and the avenging lift gods. With a little epilogue about bad Indian restaurants and too much beer on an empty stomach that is more used to good French food. No harm throwing in a little flattery of her home country, I thought.

Before she could give her verdict, we were interrupted by the entrance of a short fifty-something man with cropped silver hair, a Newcastle T-shirt, an Adidas tracksuit and a gold wristchain as thick as a French croissant. He nodded—icily—to me, kissed Alexa's mum on the neck, and darted out of the house. The Mercedes engine started up as soon as the front door closed, and the sports car rolled away.

That, Alexa's mum explained, was Yuri, off to the gym.

I was puzzled. "His T-shirt. It said 'Newcastle Allstars.' Who are they?"

His football team, she said.

"Not Newcastle United?"

No, she told me. Newcastle Allstars, an American football team in a town that she pronounced "Noocastell onder Lim." As in Newcastle under Lyme, a small town near Stoke on Trent. Which kind of explained the lack of media interest in Yuri.

She didn't think I ought to laugh, she said. Yuri hadn't shown it, but he was not happy with me for waking him up. He had only refrained from sending out Viktor (the Hulk) to silence me because Alexa had said that it was partly her fault that I was shouting out there.

Her fault? This was interesting. Did it mean she was ready to forgive me?

Alexa's mum seemed to decide that the preliminary hearing was over. She finished her coffee, got up and said she was going to fetch Alexa.

And only Alexa, I hoped. I didn't want to have my trial with Sacha as the jury.

6

THE WHOLE TIME-WARP thing started up again when Alexa walked into the kitchen ten minutes later.

She was now looking five years younger than normal, like an A-level student about to go for university interview. Her hair was fresh from the shower, and combed flat, and she was wearing a black trouser suit. She looked great, as usual, but it was as if she had dressed to mute her sexuality, to deflect any erotic signals that she might give off. And she usually gave off a lot.

Again, I had an etiquette problem. This time it was a purely English one. The morning after binge drinking, did you kiss the people you'd woken up in the night?

"Je peux te faire la bise?" I asked, meaning that I wanted to give her a kiss on the cheek.

She leant forward and we did our "mwa's," except that I took the daring step of actually kissing her cheek. She didn't slap my face.

"I'm so sorry for last night. We were drunk."

"I hope so," she said.

"And I'm sorry for the night before that, too. I got stuck in a lift."

"Yes, I think I have understood some of your message. What happened?"

I told her about my two hours getting harangued by the neighbour and typecast as a sitcom plotline by my roommates.

I was relieved when she laughed.

I handed over the letter from Nathalie, which was still in my pocket and only slightly crumpled. She didn't make any attempt to open it, which might have been a good or bad thing.

"You look different," I said. "Great. Not that you don't usually . . . you know. But have you got an interview or something?"

Yes, she said, a gallery was interested in putting on her photo exhibition, and she wasn't sure how to dress. In France, even in meetings with people like the director of Beaubourg, an artist was expected to be scruffy—"artistic," unconcerned with such bourgeois problems as looking good. But in England, she said, people seemed more formal. Did I think this was the right outfit? It was like a job interview, wasn't it?

"Which gallery?"

"The Saatchi."

"The Saatchi Gallery? Holy shit, Alexa, that's incredible. That's, like, brilliantly incredibly brilliant." My alcohol poisoning seemed to have reached whichever lobe it is that deals with choice of vocabulary.

"It's brilliant? Is that all you have to say?" she asked.

"All? I mean, what else is there to say? You're a star. You'll be famous. It's incredibly brilliantly incredibly . . ."

She cut off this new attack of alcohol poisoning by starting to cry.

"Alexa. What did I do? Didn't I whoop loud enough? What more can I . . . ?"

Shit, now I could feel my own tears sprouting up from somewhere. And it wasn't like when you get to the end of *Terminator 2* and Arnie says he's got to have a bath in the molten metal, or in *Love Actually* when the guy walks into the restaurant and proposes in Portuguese, because I had no idea why we were both getting all weepy.

"What exactly is in this letter?" Alexa asked.

I told her about Nathalie's sworn statement. I could remember almost every word.

"There is always an explanation," Alexa said. "Why can you never do things the simple way, Paul? Like Yuri. He said to my mother, come to London, you choose where we will live, and basta. No other women, no handbags, nothing."

"So she chose the house?" The pot plants and the stripped pine were a little clearer now.

Alexa laughed.

"Oh yes, my mother chose the house. Yuri says it is much too small. He wants a bigger house, like the ones on the other side of the big road."

"What, in the royal estate there? But they're palaces. Half of them are embassies." I guessed that she was talking about the gigantic mansions in the park round the back of Kensington Palace, where Princess Diana used to live. There were more security cameras on that estate than there were sparrows.

"Yes, exactly. Yuri wants to buy the ex-Russian embassy—it has space for six or seven cars to park outside. When we had Sacha's birthday party here, the neighbours called the police."

"Too much Ukrainian jazz?" I knew all too well what that could do to the soul.

"No, because of the cars. The police said they can't do anything because it's a private street, so now Yuri parks his car here all the time to annoy the neighbours. He thinks they're being racist, but they're not, they just hate cars. It's like the city. They live in it but wish it didn't exist."

"Yes, but is that where *you* want to live, Alexa? In the ex-Russian embassy, with space for your six or seven cars?"

"For the moment, Paul, I want to live in London. And I want to do my work. Which is not simple with you coming in and out of my life all the time, and then shouting my name so the whole street will hate me."

"But if you weren't out of my life I wouldn't have to shout."

"I'm not out of your life."

"You're not?" What a great little sentence, I thought. It wasn't exactly "je t'aime," but it was hell of a long way from "bugger off."

I heard a noise on the stairs. Oh no, I thought, here comes the guy who is well and truly in her life, and frequently in other parts of her I didn't want to think about right now.

"Is that Sacha?" I whispered.

"No. It must be Maman." She looked as if she was about to cry again. "Sacha spends most of his time at the studio."

"Ah," I said, clamping my fingers to the edge of the table to prevent the merest shudder of glee from showing.

I tried to look sympathetic, but it was bloody hard when all I wanted to do was dance around the kitchen. What a jerk, I thought. He could be spending every night snuggling up to Alexa, and he prefers fiddling around with tape machines. Or groupies. Or both. As long as he was missing out on the chance to fiddle with Alexa, I wasn't complaining.

"You see, my life is not simple. And it is less simple with you coming to London in the middle of the night to confuse me before my interview."

I don't know where ideas come from. Chemical impulses, aren't they? Well, there were plenty of chemicals in my brain that morning, and I felt a sudden jolt in my head as the toxic blend distilled an idea.

"Simple?" I said, suddenly seeing things with breath-mint clarity. "You want things simple? Here's simple." I grabbed her hand as I said it. "You have your interview this morning, for which you look wonderful, by the way. Anyway, it's not an interview, it's an invitation. They want to meet you. They love your photos. They know you have a show on at Beaubourg. All that's very simple."

I grabbed the other hand, forgot what I was about to say, and then remembered just in time to stop myself looking like a dickhead. "I'm going back to Paris now, to sort some stuff out. Then I'm coming to live in London, to be with you. There, that's pretty damn simple, too, isn't it?"

"No," she moaned, flushing my idea away and making things a lot less simple.

7

I NEVER SUSPECTED that I might get pregnant. It's not something you usually have to worry about when you're a guy.

But apparently it worried the French government a lot, because they had sent me a letter informing me that I had to pay for maternity insurance for everyone working in the tea room. In the case of myself and more than half of my employees, this was like insuring a whale against injuries incurred while playing table tennis.

But there it was, a demand for a small fortune in "cotisations." The word sounded like a form of medical treatment, but it meant contributions or subscriptions.

And the maternity-leave demand wasn't the only official letter I'd received. I also had several organizations demanding "cotisations" for various other types of social-security schemes, pension funds and complementary medical insurance. All the people I'd paid off in the summer were back again, wanting more.

For some reason, I seemed to be paying into three different medical schemes. All I'd need was a week off with flu and I could retire on the proceeds.

Then there was the nice letter—a personally signed one for once—reminding me that I had to get my menus translated, and adding that the name of the tea room was also illegal. "Mon thé est riche" had to be written somewhere on the shopfront.

Yes, like there's a translation of "Pizza Napoli" on the front of Italian restaurants, I wanted to reply. This was just anti-English discrimination. I put the letter on my "call Brussels" pile.

Worse than this, there was a letter that I'd left unopened for almost a month which informed me that the council was thinking of widening the pavement in our street (good) and creating a motorbike and scooter park outside the tea room (bad). Very bad. These bike and scooter parks worked on the dog-merde principle. Once one scooter came and parked there, every other two-wheeled vehicle in the neighbourhood thought it was OK to flock round and smother the pavement. There might be official space for ten two-wheelers, but we'd soon have fifty of them blocking our doorway and stopping people queuing up.

The letter said I had a month to object. Which left me about twenty minutes to do so.

Oh God.

I was trying—and failing—to "sort my stuff out" before going back to London.

Alexa had told me not to bother.

"I cannot have this responsibility," she'd said. "You cannot make me responsible for stopping your business. It is too much."

"I always take full responsibility for all my actions," I assured her, "however stupid they are." Which didn't reassure her very much.

In any case, I said, I wasn't going to "stop the business." I was just going to delegate for a while. Simple.

Simple as peeing into a test tube from the top of a ladder.

But then, as anyone who has ever tried it will testify, the secret is to stay up the ladder and keep on peeing until you hit the test tube. I'd just have to sit there tearing my hair out over the admin for as long as it took to sort the really threatening stuff out from the merely infuriating.

But if I really was going to leave Paris for a while, the most important thing to sort out was Benoît, the babysitter who would be looking after my little offspring of a tea room. I knew he could heat up the baby food, and I just needed to be sure that he wasn't the type who would freak out and hide under the settee if he had to change a nappy. Like, for example, if people started leaving their motorbikes in the middle of the tea room.

It turned out he'd heard about the scooter-park plan.

"How come?" I asked him.

"It was Papa who told me. You know he is very implicated in the politics of the arrondissement."

Of course. Nathalie had told me about Jean-Marie moving in on the local MP. But remembering this only added a new level of complication to my admin headaches. Was Jean-Marie capable of having a scooter park parked outside my tea room? And if so, why? To force me to sell the business to him? No, surely not.

After all, I was employing his son. More than employing him, I was educating him in the facts of life. OK, so he mistook hot-water heaters for sexual partners, but lots of mammals did similar things. Dogs and chair legs, for example. I'd even seen one of those home-video shows where a hippo tried to get it on with a tractor.

All in all, Jean-Marie had no cause to piss me off with petty municipal manoeuvrings.

I hoped.

This was one thing I'd have to make completely sure of before I could get back to Alexa.

8

"NEVER TRUST A PHILOSOPHER. Especially an existentialist. If you fall in a hole, he will not help you. He will only laugh and say that life is like that."

Jean-Marie was in a garrulous mood and leading me suspiciously far away from the supposed subject of our meeting.

"It is true," he said. "You know Simone de Beauvoir? The wife of Sartre? During her, how do you say, obsèques?" I shrugged ignorance. "The ceremony when you are dead?"

"Funeral."

"Yes. During her funeral at the cimetière Montparnasse, someone fell in the, how do you say, the hole where they put the dead person?"

"Grave."

"Yes, someone fell in the grave, and broke his arm. And I can imagine all the other existentialists looking down, leaving him there, and saying, Oui, oui, c'est la vie."

He jabbed me in the ribs, inviting me to laugh along at his philosophical joke.

I had to admit it was the right place for stories like that. We were sitting over a couple of teatime beers in the Café de Flore at Saint-Germain des Prés, the famous Left Bank bistro where Sartre and his heavy-smoking friends used to come and philosophize.

For such a historic monument, it was a surprisingly unpretentious place. Small, brightly lit, with discreetly art-déco decor and scarlet-covered leatherette seats. It was full, too, mainly with well-heeled Parisians. There was, I noticed, a higher than usual proportion of old guys with long grey hair in this café, all of them sitting alone. The last of the philosophers, perhaps.

The chit-chat around us was personal stuff, though. There seemed to be less philosophical debate going on in the café these days. Mainly, I guessed, because to come here and discuss the fact that life has no real value, you'd have to be worth a fortune—a beer was almost triple the price of most other places I went to. I'd seen it as soon as I walked in. There were at least four or five waiters, plus a maitre d'. You had to charge top whack to pay all their salaries.

Jean-Marie suggested we meet here because he was due to have a discreet rendezvous with a senator as soon as a debate ended. The senators never knew exactly when they would stop talking, so he had some time to kill.

"It is a game," he said philosophically. "He makes me wait, but that is politics. We have so much respect for the old politicians. It is not like soixante-huit, aah . . ."

This mention of the student revolution of 1968 sent him off into another philosophical dreamland. He even lit up a cigarette, which I'd never see him do before. Somehow I couldn't imagine him wanting to get smoke particles on his immaculate suits.

"I saw him, you know."

"Who?"

"Sartre. En soixante-huit."

"You were on the barricades?" I failed to keep a note of intense disbelief out of my voice. Jean-Marie had risked scuffing his handmade shoes in the cause of revolution?

"Oh, everyone was on the barricades. Sartre, too. He was a little man, very ugly, but always surrounded by women. I was on the barricades because all the most beautiful girls were there. Naturally, this was before I was working for my father."

"He wouldn't have approved?" I'd heard about Jean-Marie's dad, the butcher who had set up his meat company and cleavered his way to the top of the industry.

"Ho!" Jean-Marie choked on a lungful of smoke. "No, my father detested the intellectuals," he said when he'd recovered. "Ask them what they were doing during the war, he said. Talking. In their café talking, when other men were fighting in the Résistance."

"Was your father in the resistance?"

"Oh, every Frenchman of his generation was in the Résistance," Jean-Marie ironized. "I am surprised that the Allemands occupied France for so many years, with all those millions of Frenchmen fighting against them."

"But your father was *really* in the resistance?"

"I don't know. You did not ask men of his generation what they were *really* doing during the war. He was selling beef and horse. But to whom? Pff!" He stubbed his cigarette out. "You English are lucky. You were not occupied. You did not get the opportunity to . . . how do you say? Trahir son pays?"

"Betray your country."

"Yes, you are lucky. It is not a happy test."

His mood had changed from existentialist to half-pissed.

While he ordered some more beers, I watched a group of middle-aged Americans who'd just walked in and were looking round as if to say, is this really the place? What's all the fuss about?

"So, Jean-Marie, about this scooter park?"

"Ah, yes. Huh!" From the tone of his voice he was as opposed to the idea as I was, which was a surprise.

"What do you know about it?"

"I think it is perhaps a salopard with influence in the arrondissement who knows that I am the propriétaire of the salon. Oh, Paul, my English is so bad since you leave the company. Are leaving the company?"

"Left." Since you fired me, I could have said. "So you're against the idea?"

"Oh yes, of course!" He swatted the idea away as if he was clearing the air of motorbikes. "A shop with this in front loses much value. It is terrible."

"Do you think you will be able to stop it?"

"Ah . . ." He raised his arms non-committally, but the grin on his face suggested that his rival wasn't the only person around here with influence.

I breathed a literal sigh of relief. "I thought you were trying to force me to sell the business," I said.

"You want to sell?" This came out as an offer rather than a question.

"No. Well, not yet." I explained about going to England for a while, and wanting Benoît to take charge while I was away.

Jean-Marie stared at me open-mouthed, giving me serious doubts about the wisdom of my idea. It was as if I was the pilot of a plane and had just announced that I was off for a pee and was leaving my pet rabbit at the controls.

"Paul," he finally said. "This is . . ." But he couldn't think of the word to finish his sentence. Ridiculous? Crazy? Suicidal? "Benoît is . . ." Immature? Incompetent? Incontinent? "You have . . ." Lost my business? Lost my mind? Lost any hope that Jean-Marie would ever finish a sentence again?

He grabbed my shoulders and kissed me on both cheeks.

"I knew it," he said.

"Knew what?" I was still looking around the café to see whether anyone else had witnessed this sudden embrace.

"You are a . . . what do you say? Model? Yes. A model for him. He is completely changed since he works . . . is working?"

"Has been working."

"Ah? Has been working for you. He has found his way. Trouvé son chemin. I am very happy. No, I am in debt." He nodded gravely, the joyful look on his face trying to make way for the earnestness of his declaration. "You cannot trust a philosopher, but you can trust me. When you are in London, I will take care of him. He will not, how do you say . . . ?"

"Fuck up?"

"Yes. He will not fuck up."

He held out his hand and we shook on it.

And even though he was a politician, a smooth-talker who had shafted me (metaphorically) on several occasions and tried to shaft Alexa (literally) on another occasion, I felt that I could trust him. Probably.

"You know, Benoît even tells me he is in love," he said.

"Really? That's great."

I didn't have the heart to tell him it was with a tea urn.

9

"I 've got my ticket. I'm arriving next Sunday night."

"I have a dinner with my mother."

I hadn't been phoning to invite Alexa out for a night on the town, but her reply sounded like some kind of self-defence.

"Look, it's OK, Alexa, I'm planning to stay in London for a while, so we'll be able to see each other some other time. There's no hassle." The one thing I didn't want was her thinking that I was going to set up camp in her mews and make her life a misery. If necessary I'd go to a hypnotist and have a reminder implanted in my subconscious about the inadvisability of yodelling up at her window at three in the morning.

"This is a big thing," Alexa said.

"I know, but it's the only way for me to prove that you're important to me."

"More important than your tea room? You've worked so hard for it."

"I know. And the best bit of work I've done is deciding to give Benoît more responsibility. He'll keep things going while I'm away. So don't think you're making me throw everything down the waste disposal, because you're not. Do you believe me?"

"Yes." We both gave this idea some space. "You know . . ." she said.

"Know what?"

"I'm not seeing Sacha any more."

"Oh."

My mood whooped with joy and went soaring up into the blue autumn sky. It swung like Tarzan through the trees, and kissed every monkey it bumped into. It landed firmly on two feet and scored the winning goal in the last minute of the World Cup final. It was carried aloft by adoring fans through the streets of London.

My mouth, though, just went "Oh."

"You sound sad," Alexa said.

"Well, only because I guess you must be . . . because your relationship didn't work out." Diplomatic answer or what?

"You think I should get back with him?"

"What?" Bugger diplomacy. "No, Alexa. Let's get one thing straight. I am sorry if he's caused you any pain, but I am deliriously happy that you've split up with him. It's brilliant news. Brilliantly incredibly brilliant. I'm just too polite to go whoopee." Out loud, that is.

She laughed.

"Have you moved out of the house?" I asked, crossing my fingers, toes, eyes and kidneys.

"No."

"Oh." This time my mood was in tune with my mouth.

"But he has," she went on. "He's living in the apartment above his studio."

"Can I say 'Whoopee'?"

"If you want."

I did. "It gives us a chance, doesn't it?" I said. "All of this?"

"Yes, it does," she said. "Ça nous donne une chance." She spoke to me in French for once.

And in French, "chance" has two meanings—chance and good luck.

*   *   *

After this, there was only one threat to Benoît's captaincy of the tea room, and that was from someone who really ought to have been more supportive.

It was the day before I was due to head back to London.

Katy was dealing with a common problem in the Eighth arrondissement—Da Vinci refugees.

The fans of *The Da Vinci Code* who went on organized tours were OK, because they were shepherded from place to place by a guide. But the ones who tried to follow the book on their own inevitably got lost, because the topography in the book is, let's say, not exactly of satellite-photo standard.

And also because some tourists were just a little bit stupid.

"The Loover was crap," a seven-foot-tall American declared teenager while waiting for Katy to pour him a large Coke. He was several tons overweight, an impression that was heightened by an inflatable ski jacket which was puffed up only marginally more than his cheeks.

"We don't use words like crap," his mother said by reflex. She was more interested in the cakes, and judging by the size of her rear end, which was all I could see of her—well, it was practically all I could see, period—cakes were one of her major interests in life.

"What do you mean?" asked the father, who was miraculously thin. An Atkins dieter, perhaps, or stomach staplee? He was draped in an olive mackintosh as if a private-eye disguise would help him follow the Da Vinci trail.

"I mean, like, you'd think they'd have, like, a reconSTRUC-tion? A dead guy on the FLOOR? Like, why else do we GO there? I mean, doh!"

"It's an art museum, son," his father said.

"How many calories in those fruitcakes?" the mother asked.

She apparently thought you ordered a whole cake rather than just a slice.

"Poo," Katy answered, having picked up the French way of expressing ignorance, which is to blow a raspberry.

"And, like, the Mona Lisa wasn't even THERE. I mean, WHAT?"

Even I was confused at this. If there's one thing that definitely is in the Louvre, it's the Mona Lisa. It's as there as Tom Cruise is there in a Tom Cruise movie.

"Yes it is," the father said, quite calmly, as if his son talked crap all the time and just needed to be contradicted to get out of the habit. "It was the painting that everyone was taking photos of with their cell-phones."

"What, that Jackondee thing?" The kid grimaced as if Katy had plopped a worm in his drink.

It was here that Benoît stepped across from the till. Strictly speaking, this was one of the "all for one" Musketeer moves that I disapproved of, but Katy was showing the signs of stress that you often see in sane people who have to serve idiots, most notably a trembling of the eyebrows as the brain tries to escape from the situation by gnawing its way through the front of the skull.

A few weeks earlier, Benoît might have been suffering the same way in this situation, but now he knew how to take control.

"La Joconde is the French name for the Mona Lisa," he said.

"What? That little bald chick is HER? I mean, eew!" The kid mimed fainting with horror.

"Well, she is very old, you know," Benoît replied, totally deadpan.

"We don't use words like chick. What's a scone?" said the mother.

"And it's so SMALL, too. Like, it's not even BIG."

"Do you mean the scone or the Mona Lisa?" Benoît asked.

The father opted out of the debate about art and concentrated on filling the family's trays and getting his son's mouth filled with something other than gibberish.

The mother and son sat down, taking up two seats each, and as the father paid, he asked Benoît what was probably meant to be a discreet question.

"Isn't the American Embassy up here somewhere?"

"It's not far," Benoît told him.

"No, no, no!"

This exclamation of pain and despair came from Jake who, as he often did on weekend afternoons, was sitting over a free cup of coffee, scribbling on printouts from his poetry Web site.

He leapt out of his seat and went to rant in the tourist's face. He was still wearing my suit, which was holding up really well seeing that it had probably been dragged around Paris every day for two months.

"You have gone to Saint Lazare and have not found the quai for Lille, didn't you?" he ranted.

"The what?" the tourist asked.

"The quai? Dammit. The platform? You have gone to Saint Lazare railroad station and have not found the platform for Lille, n'est-ce pas?"

"No," the tourist said, bemused.

"Well, you will."

"What do you mean?"

Fortunately, Jake was being confusing enough to take the other guy's mind off the fact that he was being spat at with literary fury.

"You goddam Da Vinci tourists. That book is all false! You don't take a train to Lille from Saint Lazare. It's from the Gare du Nord! And don't you know that the American ambassade is only a few metres from the Louvre? The car escape in the book would be half a minute if it was geographically exact. Have you not seen the big building with the American flag at la Concorde? That is the ambassade, man. It is not here on the Champs-Elysées!"

"Oh, thank you for the information." The tourist tried to get away from the drooling madman and go to his table, but Jake wasn't finished.

"Oh yes, he is very good at codes, this Robert Langdon, but he does not know his own flag!"

Now, Jake was a regular (very regular) customer (or charity receiver, anyway) and a friend of mine, so Benoît wasn't sure how to deal with him. I had to show him that even friends have to be kept under control.

I went over and placed myself directly between Jake and his victim.

"You must excuse him," I told the tourist guy. "He's a writer who's just a little bit jealous because he doesn't sell as much as Dan Brown."

"No—" Jake tried to correct me, but I shut him up with a pleading look.

"And he's also a bit of a geography specialist, so he takes these things to heart," I added, trying to usher the guy towards his table where the rest of his family were drooling with impatience.

"Oh, yeah, you write geography textbooks?" the tourist unwisely asked Jake.

"No, I—"

Again I cut Jake off. The last thing I wanted was to cause this poor American family to suffer abdominal spasms after experiencing one of Jake's explicit poems about intimate female geography.

"His work's not ready for publication yet," I said, and dragged

Jake back to his table to lecture him about not scaring customers if he wanted to keep his free-drinks deal while I was away.

I even offered him a free-room deal.

"If whichever nationality of woman you're living with now throws you out, you can crash at my place. I'll be leaving a key here."

I was surprised to see Jake blush.

"Yeah, well . . . merci, but . . ."

I was even more surprised to see him lost for words. His words always came out in a bizarre mixture of languages, but they usually came out fluently enough.

"What is it, Jake? Don't tell me you're sleeping in the street in my suit?"

"No, no, au contraire, on the whoosit. On the opposite." He blushed again.

"You've arranged to swap my suit for an apartment?"

"No, no. I'm going to, you know, loo one."

"Loo?"

"Louer, you know, rent. I'm going to rent an apartment."

"You are?" This was a guy who'd freeloaded ever since I'd known him, and for years before that, from what he'd told me.

"Yeah. With . . ." and he clammed up again.

"With? With what? Drug money?"

"With, oh merde. With Virginie."

I almost died.

"What, little Virginie?"

"Yeah."

"*French* Virginie?"

He blushed even redder than ever, and gave a huge, existentialist shrug. Yes, it seemed to say, the absurd has happened, life is like that.

"Well, you kept this a secret, didn't you, Jake? A French girl?"

"Yeah, but you know, she's . . ."

"Oh, I know she is. Very."

"And, like, I . . ."

"You what?"

"I . . . merde. Je l'aime." He said it as if it was an admission of defeat. "After I rencountered her at your party, I saw her again. Then I found I was writing poems about her tout le temps. I couldn't arret to think about her. And she wants to go out of her studio. And I can loo an apartment now that I will become directeur of studies."

"What?" This was a secret, too. "You're going to be director of studies at your language school?"

"Yeah, well, it's like la guerre des tranchées, you know?"

"Trench warfare?"

"Whatever. Yeah. You know, the survivants get the promotion."

"But that's great, Jake. Congratulations. This calls for fruit cake all round."

The tourist woman looked up expectantly. I was tempted to say that the three pieces she already had on her plate were enough, but as she and her family were the only customers, I extended the offer to her.

Besides, Jake with a real job, and an apartment, and in love—with a French woman? This was as big a revolution as the one back in 1789.

And the revolution didn't end there.

As I was putting the slices of fruit cake on plates and telling Benoît and Katy what the celebrations were about, out of the corner of my eye I saw Benoît edge away from his tea urn and place a hand on Katy's shoulder.

She didn't brush it away or ask him what he was doing. She bent down and kissed it.

So Benoît had finally learned the difference between a woman and a water heater? I was almost paternally happy for the guy.

And then, to cap it all, came one of those visions that stay with you all your life.

You're walking along a beach when you look down and find the ring that you lost there ten years before. You're sitting in a bar in Casablanca and the love of your life walks in.

This one was even better.

I looked out of the tea-room window to give Katy and Benoît the chance to enjoy another secret kiss without their boss ogling at them, and I saw a small brown poodle crapping on the pavement outside. Normally I would have rushed out to kick the little beast into the next street, but for some reason all my reactions were frozen. I watched the woman who was holding the dog's lead—a late-middle-aged, dyed-blonde lady in a fur coat and black high heels—pull a Galeries Lafayette plastic bag out of her coat pocket, stoop down and, using the plastic bag as a kind of glove, gather up the little pile of merde. She walked in pop-video slo-mo to the nearest litter bin and dropped the bag in.

A posh Parisienne scooping her poop?

It had to be a sign.

The city didn't need me any more.

7

Maybe It's Because I'm Not a Londoner

1

THERE ARE SOME concepts that the French don't understand.

Lined writing paper, for example. In France, paper that isn't blank is squared. As if there's always the off chance that you'll want to break off from writing notes and design a mosaic.

And they have no idea about office coffee mugs. If you want a coffee in a French company, you usually go to the coffee machine, which will probably have real coffee-bean coffee but will of course serve it in a plastic beaker. If you get offered non-machine coffee in a posher office, it'll usually be in a plain white espresso cup.

So a French worker arriving in a British company will have no idea that their whole working life from now on will be dominated by a thick, fist-sized mug with "Sex? I'd prefer a caramel latte!" written on it.

This was what occurred to me when I walked back into the offices of my old company, Waterloo Foods—or Waterloo TM as it was now known. It was here that I'd launched the Voulez-Vous Café Avec Moi chain of "French" cafés, just before Jean-Marie had headhunted me.

And the first thing I saw, after getting through the airport-style security in their new reception area, was a guy crossing a corridor with a clutch of mugs in his hand. Off to the kitchen to make tea and coffee. It's a sight that you never see in France. I smiled as if I'd just spotted an old friend.

Not that the guy with the mugs was an old friend at all. I didn't recognize him.

I didn't recognize the corridor, either. The drab old colours had been replaced by Mediterranean blue for the walls and coral pink for the carpet. I was walking through a blackcurrant-and-raspberry yogurt.

Everything about the place was brightness and dynamism. There was even a poster by the kitchen door reminding staff that just clenching your buttocks fifty times while waiting for the kettle to boil could burn up fifty calories.

I was burning calories twirling my rock-star backstage pass in my hand. Everyone had to wear one nowadays, it seemed, though I couldn't quite bring myself to hang it round my neck. I was still in French "I'm too cool to make myself look like a dork" mode.

"You've got to put that on, Paul mate." This was Charlie, my boss, erupting out of a doorway as I passed.

I'd called him up the previous week on the off chance that he might be able to take me back on and, much to my surprise, he had said that I could start whenever I wanted.

And finish whenever I wanted, too.

Because no one actually worked for the company any more. At least, not as employees. There were only consultants, managed by other consultants, reporting to the group of consultants who'd bought the company a few months earlier and made all two hundred employees re-apply for their old jobs. Only a small percentage had made the grade, and the total staff was now just eighty or so, most of them newcomers.

In France a company trying to do this would have made national headlines, but here it was just another takeover.

I wasn't complaining, though, because the new system worked in my favour. I owned my own company, My Tea Is Rich, so I could instantly become a consultant for Charlie, with no admin hassle at all. He had, he told me, a very Anglo-French "problème" that I'd be the perfect man to solve.

So here I was, back in a suit, back in London—Paul West, international troubleshooter.

We shook hands—no hug, thank God—and Charlie escorted me along to my new office.

He was looking very butch. He was forty-five, grey and balding, but he'd had his hair cropped really close, and the sleeves of his purple-checked white shirt were rolled up to reveal thick, hairy wrists. He looked like an off-duty rugby player, which, judging by other guys in the offices, seemed to be the style du jour.

These days, our executives have to look butcher than our army, I thought. I felt positively effeminate with my suit jacket still on and my hair more than one centimetre long.

This wasn't my "Jake" suit, by the way. I'd written that off. Apart from anything else, I didn't want to keep coming across half-finished obscene poems in the pockets. So I'd nipped along to the Paul Smith shop in Paris and got myself a couple of grey suits that looked as conventional as a Rolls-Royce until I opened them up and showed off the psychedelic linings.

"La belle France get too French for you, then?" Charlie bantered. Like so many Brits, he loved to slag off the French and spend most of his holidays in France.

"Yeah, I actually started to miss Londoners."

"Sacré bleu, you poor sod."

The office doors were all glass now, letting natural light into the central corridor from the street. However, they'd been closed off with digicodes so you could see in but couldn't get in.

Charlie told me the code to my door, let me punch it in to get it memorized, and we entered a bright, white-walled room.

Three of the four desks in the office had laptops on them, and the laptops were being typed on by three people I didn't recognize—a young Indian guy, a black woman, and a Charlie clone. All of them, like Charlie, were in suit trousers and patterned white shirts.

"Guys, this is Paul."

I shook hands with Sanjeet, Marya and Tom.

Sanjeet was the coolest of the bunch—he had gelled hair, and one of those micro-shaving things going on with his sideburns, which tapered down into half-millimetre-wide dagger blades on his cheek. Marya came second in the cool stakes—she had very dark skin, black lipstick, and hid a slight plumpness inside a beautifully cut black trouser suit that accentuated her curves. She was, I noted, the only one who had her shirt untucked. Tom was ten years younger than Charlie but just as bald and stocky. His bottom shirt button was undone so I could see a tiny wisp of belly hair above his belt.

We all introduced ourselves briefly, and then the others sat back at their computers and carried on with their frenetic typing. It was a pleasant change from the traumatic day when I walked into my French office and came up against the four people who were going to make my life hell for the next nine months. Here, at least there would be no language barrier.

Or would there?

"Tom, mate, can you walk Paul through the settling-in bullshit?" Charlie said. "I've got to give the Beast a quick heads-up."

"Sure," Tom said. "Any news on my go-live yet?"

"What's the burning platform?"

"Well, I'm holding their feet to the fire on dates, but so far I've only got a soft launch, and it's February."

"Wo, showstopper."

What the fuck were they talking about? Didn't everyone in the company used to speak English?

2

"WHO'S THE BEAST?" I asked Tom when Charlie had gone. "It's what we call the CEO. Apparently when he took over, someone gave him an extension number that ended in 666 and he went apeshit. He doesn't look like the devil, though."

"Apart from the horns and the tail," Marya chipped in, without interrupting her typing.

"Is that why there are no phones?" I asked. So far, my desk was still totally bare apart from my laptop bag. The only phones in the room were mobiles.

"Didn't Charlie boy tell you?" Tom said. "We consultants just get a flat fee. You use your own phone. Up to you how long you spend on it."

"Right." It seemed sensible in an insanely puritanical way. The phones at Jean-Marie's company had devoted half their time to weekend plans, family problems, lovers' rendezvous and even premium-rate phone-in competitions. Well, mine had, anyway.

"Round-up's at nine. Done a flash report?" Tom asked me.

"No." I couldn't have done one because I didn't know what one was.

"Oh, OK." Tom went back to thumping his keyboard with his butch fingers.

And that seemed to be it. I was settled in.

"You're here for the famous frog project, right?" Marya asked me.

"Yeah. The not-famous-enough frog project."

"You broken the bad news to him yet?"

"No."

The breaking of a certain bit of Anglo-French bad news was basically the "problème" I'd been recruited for.

When I'd called Charlie, he'd said that the company was just about to get itself a French celebrity chef, and they needed someone to liaise with him.

"You've lived with them, you know what an awkward bunch of bastards they are," he said, showing that I wasn't the only British man who was crap at diplomacy.

Apparently, the chef was a genius with a sandwich, and Waterloo TM had signed him up as the (future) star who would bring an extra touch of class to the blue-cheese baguettes in the Voulez-Vous Café Avec Moi outlets.

The only problème was his name.

"You're going to have to get him to change it," Charlie told me.

"Why? What is it?" I asked.

"It's typically Breton."

"Yes?"

"His first name is the Breton version of Ian."

"What's that?"

"And his family name—well, there's a village in Brittany with the same name."

"Which is?"

But he wouldn't tell me on the phone. He preferred to send it over in an email. And when I read his message, I understood why.

My chef was called Yann Kerbolloc'h.

Yes, spoken with a British accent, it sounded like advice on how to resist rapists.

In French, though, it was perfectly neutral. Yann Kerbolloc'h was as innocent of any offence as a guy called Peter Burns wanting to be taken seriously in France. "Péter" means fart, "burnes" are bollocks. Welcome to France, Monsieur Fart-Bollocks.

And because no one in the company had dared to tell Yann about the problem, he was under the impression that we were going to print billboard-sized posters advertising our new "Yann Kerbolloc'h sandwiches." It was my first job to explain why not.

There was, therefore, a high likelihood that in the very near future I would be fending off a violent assault with a French baguette, but it was a risk I was willing to take, because having the job meant that I could meet up with Alexa whenever she wanted to check that I was being a good boy.

That was the deal with her. I was over here proving that I could behave—I could be there when she needed me, I could avoid trying to get my limbs wrapped round other women, and, most importantly, I could resist the compulsion to perform trios for voice and urine at three in the morning.

I wasn't sure whether there was going to be any sex included in the deal for the moment. But if the worst came to the worst, I could always resort to one of those lesbian-action movies.

"Anyone fancy a brew before the meeting?" I offered.

"Yeah. Hey, we were forgetting the most important thing," Marya said. "What mug can we give Paul, guys?"

"Actually, I've brought my old mug from when I worked here before." While I was sorting through the stuff I wanted to bring over from Paris, I'd found my old Waterloo Foods mug—plain white, with the slightly faded head of the Duke of Wellington pointing his beaked nose eastwards towards Belgium. I pulled it out of my bag and got an ironic-sounding "ooh" from Tom.

Sanjeet stood up to admire it. "Vintage," he said. "Look at this crap they gave us. Job lot of seconds, man." He picked up the mug standing next to his laptop. It was the same blue and pink as the corridor decor, inscribed with a dashing new "Waterloo" logo that had a little black TM hovering at its shoulder. But it felt light and fragile compared to my hunky old Wellington mug.

"Sanjeet will show you where the coffee and stuff is, won't you Sanjeet?" Marya shot a teasing look at Sanjeet, who immediately changed from a self-confident PR consultant to a sheepish schoolboy.

"Yeah, bloody Sanjeet here had a solo brew, didn't he?" Tom said, with real venom in his eyes.

"Only 'cause I didn't have one first time round, man," Sanjeet defended himself.

"So?" Tom said. "Solo brews are out of order. Anyway, you're forgetting something," he added. "Paul can't make a brew."

"Why not?" I asked. When I'd worked here before, refusing to let someone make tea for you was on a par with saying no to a blow job. It was just plain impolite.

"We've hit our limit, haven't we?" Tom said. "We always said we'd put a lid on the coffee club at twenty, and we're at twenty now. Sorry, Paul, nothing personal. You can be a visitor today, but after that you're on your own."

"We never had a limit when I worked here before," I protested.

"Yeah, well, it's all changed now," Tom said. "You know what they say, work for change or change your work. Sorry, mate."

So it looked as though I'd be taking two cases to the European

Court of Human Rights—first my request to translate "sandwich" into French, and now my appeal against exclusion from the Waterloo TM second-floor coffee club. Brussels was going to be much too busy to take on any new member states.

3

T HE DEPARTMENTAL ROUND-UP started late, which surprised me. I thought we Brits were supposed to be punctual. But no, it seemed that we were just as capable of being late for meetings as the French.

So it was ten past nine by the time we all sat round the oval table in Charlie's office.

Like the room where I'd just plugged in my laptop, it was very impersonal, a temporary home. You got the impression that Charlie could have packed away the photo of his wife and kids and vacated the premises in a matter of seconds.

He asked for, and got, two-minute reports from Tom, Sanjeet and Marya. This was what they'd been typing when I arrived.

They were working with the marketing people on similar projects to mine—an idea to sell own-brand coffee, a study comparing Voulez-Vous to American chains, and, most important of all it seemed, a consumer survey on whether "Waterloo" was the right name for expansion across Europe. There was another logo change in the air, with all the huge outlay that that would entail.

They discussed their problems in the same gobbledygook I'd heard them using before.

"We're not going to die in a ditch over that," Charlie would declare, or "Seems like we're boiling the ocean."

Everyone got their allotted time slot and no more. Two-minute update, maximum three-minutes discussion, and that was it. No one deviated from the agenda for a second. Massive problems of potential overspending and hopelessly missed deadlines were dealt with calmly and positively. No one came even close to getting as irritated as they had over who made tea.

Finally, Charlie turned to me. I was top of the bill.

First, we brainstormed about my chef's new name. Charlie asked me to let the others make some suggestions first.

"Let's start with some famous French names," he said.

"Napoleon," Tom pitched in immediately.

"Josephine?" Marya said.

"No, *living* French people, please," Charlie said.

Sanjeet opened his mouth to answer.

"And no footballers," Charlie interrupted. "No one would buy a sandwich made by a centre forward."

There followed a full minute's silence while everyone realized that they didn't know the name of a single living French male apart from footballers and "that president guy."

"Paul, rescue us, s'il vous plaît," Charlie pleaded.

I listed a few French stars. Every one of them was greeted with frowns of ignorance, including Gérard Depardieu—until, that is, I said him again as "Jay-Rar Dee-par-doo."

None of the names took Charlie's fancy, though.

"How about something food-based?" he asked.

"What, like Yann au gratin?" Tom suggested.

"Or Yann au vin?" Marya added.

"Yann Beaujolais Nouveau?" Sanjeet struggled to keep a straight face.

"Sorry, guys," Charlie said, "but you talking a load of Kerbollocks."

"Why don't I have a look at the Paris phonebook on the

Internet," I suggested. "I'll pitch you some ideas tomorrow morning."

Charlie approved this. I'd already used up my five minutes of fame and he still wanted to talk about how to sell my chef to the British public.

"What are his core competencies?" he asked.

"Cooking?" I ventured. I mean, what a question.

"Yes, Paul, he's a chef. Anything else?"

"He's French. I mean, that's why you hired him, right? He's French and he can cook."

Charlie grimaced.

Tom defended me. "Paul's right. Why bother with details?"

"Yes, but Jamie Oliver's blond. That TV goddess chick can lick chocolate. What's our man's USP?" Charlie asked.

"He can juggle courgettes," I said.

"He can?"

Actually, I'd made this up, but in the promo photos I'd been sent, Yann had had a pair of courgettes in his hands as if he'd been about to play the drums with them. Or juggle.

"Courgettes?" Charlie said the word as if this was not a vegetable to be taken seriously. He obviously needed to go and spend a few weeks with my ex-mother-in-law down in Corrèze.

"Scope for knob gags," Tom said approvingly. "Tabloid coverage. Sounds good to me."

Charlie shook his head.

As we left the meeting, he caught up with me in the corridor.

"You didn't have a written flash report," he said.

"No."

"Well I'm going to need one this evening."

"Right." I'd ask one of the others how to do that.

"And a resolution plan."

"OK." Whatever that was.

"With interim milestones."

"Yeah." Frankly, I understood French better than this.

"And remember that as a consultant you are both the owner and resolver of any issues."

"Of course."

"That courgette stuff was funny, but don't think you can wing it all the time."

"Point taken."

"Good. We're not a blame culture. But don't screw up."

And all this just because I'd agreed to tuck my shirt in.

4

B Y THE TIME I got back to my mansion that night I was bushed.

No, I wasn't living in the ex-Russian Embassy. But it was a real mansion—a beaten-up, white-washed and grey-stained block called Boscombe Mansions that had been converted from family apartments into a hundred bedsits for immigrant Londoners like myself.

The flats were above a parade of shops—Burger King, Starbucks, Kodak Express, a newsagent and a betting shop. This being the French ghetto, there was also a crêperie.

In the street there was a permanent smell of fast food in the air. Inside my building it was lemon disinfectant.

But the bedsit was only mind-numbingly expensive, as opposed to bank-breakingly expensive, and it was excellently located. You had to hand it to the French, I decided. If you've got to pick a place for a ghetto, South Kensington is not a bad spot. Just down the road from Harrods in one of the city's smartest neighbourhoods.

When I'd arrived there at the weekend, the first French things I'd seen were the consulate and the school, called, of course, the lycée Charles de Gaulle. Both were right opposite the Victoria & Albert and Natural History museums, a location that just about summed up France, I thought—style and science.

The consulate was typically provocative. Not only was it flying a tricolor, there was also a huge European flag hanging out over the road. I was sure that a few London cabbies would have crashed in fury on seeing that.

There was a whole street of French cafés, with a deli and a rotisserie, and round the corner was a wonderful French patisserie with a window full of gateaux. One of these had me drooling—a fluffy, creamy chocolate gateau with a wafer-thin collar of chocolate shavings. They don't know how to make gooey cakes, I thought, but you can't beat them at tarts and gateaux. It was like a mirror image of my tea room. The patisserie was bringing chocolate shavings to Londoners, while my tea room was taking goo to the French. I'd have to call Benoît and ask how the goo was going.

Something else reminded me of the tea room, too. There were French restaurants dotted all over South Kensington, and none of them had been forced to translate their menus.

The crêperie offered a "crème de marron" pancake, which was defined as "purée of sweetened marron glacé"—what the hell was that? I'd lived in France and even I didn't know.

Another place had "œuf de canard en meurette," which seemed to mean something like "dying duck's egg." Not a speciality I'd ever tried.

And at the bottom of that menu there was "potage paysanne," which I ought to have reported to the police. Stew of peasant girl? Were London's Frenchies really cannibals?

They hadn't seemed that way on the Internet.

There was, I'd discovered, a lively community of French expats living in London and chatting to each other on the Web. Sharing the good news that French freezer-food shops were opening up here, so they'd be able to get frozen foie gras for Christmas. Telling each other which bars to visit if they wanted to meet some of France's famous London-based footballers. And advertising accommodation to rent.

I'd had enough of sharing with French *Friends* fans, so I opted for the bedsit, which was in this "mansion" building owned and run by a Parisian management company. My new home was decorated with unstainable dark colours and indestructible materials, with a "kitchen" that consisted of a fridge with a microwave on top. It was as charming as a motorway service station, but it felt kind of monastic, which was the idea.

That evening, I sat down with a takeaway ratatouille (that hadn't been translated on the menu, either) from the French deli, and phoned Alexa.

She emailed me a photo while we were talking. It was another of her light-saturated colour shots of me, taken when I was leaving Yuri's house on the morning I got kidnapped by the Hulk. All you could see was my back. My hands were in my pockets, my legs looked as if I was about to kick out at a stone.

"What does it mean?" I asked. "That you were glad to see the back of me?"

She didn't quite understand the idiom. I had to explain it.

"No," she said. "I thought you looked like a man who is just leaving the building after having sex."

"Oh. Was that a bad thing?"

"No. It was flattering."

"Oh. Great. Brilliant." Though if she meant that our future sexual encounters would be limited to me getting shoved around by a Ukrainian bodyguard and then having coffee with her mum, I wasn't sure how keen I was. "What do you mean exactly?"

"Well, you come to London, you find my house, and afterwards you look like you have . . . how do you say . . . achieved something. Like having sex."

"Right. Though what I mainly achieved was making you cry."

She laughed.

"Why *did* you cry, Alexa?"

She laughed again. "One day I will tell you. But for now it is best that you do not know."

So she was going to play la femme mystérieuse, was she? I didn't know how much of that I could take. There was a distinct danger that London would rub off on me and that I'd get used to half-naked women whose idea of mystery was shouting "Guess whether I've got any knickers on!"

5

I'D BEEN IN the French ghetto for only two or three days when I was warned that I ought to leave the country.

It happened while I was trying to withdraw some cash from the local branch of a British high-street bank. The ATM recognized that my credit card was not English, and very diplomatically started to talk to me in French.

It wanted my "code personnel," and asked me "Combien voulez-vous?"

Everything was going fine until it came to the bit about "your cash is being counted," at which point the machine told me, "Vos espèces sont comptées," which was a tragic mistranslation. Basically it means, "Your cash is limited."

So every day, this machine was telling the expat inhabitants of the ghetto, and all the French visitors to this posh area of London, "You're too poor to stay here."

Maybe this was why the French always go on about how expensive London is. It's because whenever they try to withdraw some cash, the British bank tells them, "Go home, you French pauper."

It was typical—we Brits and French try so hard to send out positive messages. But we always get it wrong, and preserve this notion that we hate each other.

This was also the day when I was due to meet Yann the chef.

If it hadn't been for his name problem, I would have been

looking forward to it. I felt a kind of affinity with him, because we were both, in our different ways, French expats here in the UK, and we were both in the business of supplying "foreign" food to the masses. But we didn't get off to a particularly good start.

First, Charlie poked his head in the office.

"Paul, your raison d'être's here." He'd taken to using French phrases whenever he talked to me, and getting most of them wrong. Like, he'd been asking for my flash report by saying, "Come on, Paul, when are you going to donnez moi le flash?"

"Pardon?" I asked.

"Your chef is in reception," he said. "They've been trying to call you. Haven't you got your phone switched on?"

"Yes, of course." Though I'd been texting Alexa, so I'd ignored the incoming call.

I found Yann marching along the corridor, reading the office numbers out loud in French, incensed that none of them was the one he was looking for.

"Monsieur Kerbolloc'h," I called out, pronouncing the name in as un-English a way as I could. "Welcome to Waterloo." OK, that didn't sound too diplomatic when said to a Frenchman, but I don't think the historical reference even registered, because he was spitting mad about the way he had been treated down in reception.

"Ze girl, she is dronk," he said.

"Dronk?"

"Yes, she laugh non-stop. She as dronk too much beer."

Oh shit, I thought. And now she's probably photocopying his ID and sending it to all her mates. I'd have to call and put a stop to that.

"I tell her she is dissing me and must geev me respect. This is right, no?"

"Yes," I said. "She ought to have shown you some respect."

Though he'd have to learn that not all the English-speaking world operated exactly like a rap video.

To placate him, I offered to make a cup of coffee.

"Oh, not ze Eengleesh-style piss," he groaned.

I assured him that no, this was not piss, it was real espresso.

I'd started my own breakaway coffee club, buying an espresso machine that took one-dose capsules, and pinning up a notice welcoming anyone who wanted to join. Mine was going to be a simplified club, I announced. Even though I was a tea-room owner, my new club would be strictly no tea, no milk except for little catering capsules of cream like you get on aeroplanes, and no obligation to make a cup for everyone. You could either have it in your own mug (with DIY washing-up), or a recycled paper cup.

So far I had ten members, and I'd already had to go out to get a new box of espresso doses.

Yann refused to contemplate the indignity of drinking from a paper cup.

"The papp-air is for ze reading, not for ze drinking," he decreed.

He wasn't much happier with the chunky Waterloo TM mug I found him—"You English, you drink from ze bidets?"—but at least he agreed to use it.

"Zis is good, no?" he asked as we watched the coffee drizzle out. "I say ze coffee is piss, I say you drink from ze bidet. Zis is Eengleesh humoor. You insult everysing, no?"

So this explained it. He wasn't an arrogant git, he was trying to be English.

He seemed to be the type of guy who was generally trying just a little too hard. He had long, thick black hair, pulled back into a pony tail. His clothes were football-star casual—enormous sports anorak, superimposed sweat shirts, designer jeans, limited-edition trainers—but he walked more like a matador, as if a bull was permanently watching him for signs of weakness.

A handsome guy, though. He would look perfect on TV with his hair tied back and a chef's smock wrapped around his slim torso. Promoting him was going to be a doddle.

Once we'd changed his name.

Charlie had said I could use his office, to get a bit of privacy when I broached the thorny problème. So we sat on opposite sides of the oval table, and I totally avoided the subject.

Instead, I explained that English humour was impossible for non-Brits to do. We Brits can insult ourselves, but if anyone else does it, we think they're a jumped-up, know-nothing foreigner. If he wanted to please the Brits, I said, he should make some anti-French jokes.

"OK," he said, without batting an eyelid. It seemed he really wanted to succeed over here. He'd given up trying to be a celebrity chef in France, he told me, because they don't really have them.

"Ze chefs in Fronce, zey just do ze cooking and collect ze stars of Michelin."

What he meant, I thought, was that they don't have time to prance about in front of the camera explaining to the punters how to fry onions.

"And so zere is not celebrity cooking books. Ze French pooblishair, zey don want my book. And ze cooking television, it is only for ze satellite."

"So you want to bring authentic French cuisine to the UK?" I didn't really like to tell him that that was exactly what all our British celebrity chefs were trying to do already.

"Yes. Exactly. Real French food By Yann Kerbolloc'h."

"Right."

This was my cue, wasn't it? No chickening out. I took a swig of coffee, swilled it round my gums to summon up the required energy, and gave it to him straight.

He was understandably taken aback.

"Pull ze testicle?" he asked.

"Yes, tug on the ball, tweak the gonad. It's not your fault, though. It's just like a Brit called Peter Burns . . ."

But he wasn't listening. He was clearly watching a film of his life flashing by, with all the incomprehensible situations in English-speaking countries suddenly making sense. Including, most recently, the scene in reception.

"Just now, at ze entronce . . ." He pointed over his shoulder towards the stairs.

"I will speak to the receptionist," I promised him. "Now, I have some suggestions for you."

I gave him the list of names that I'd brainstormed with the PR team, and within seconds his look of despair had been replaced by a new determination.

"Yes," he said, placing a fingertip near the top of my list. "Zis is perfect. Real French food by Yann Lebreton. Perfect."

"Great."

"You know, some pipple say I am not real Breton because I av black air? Zey say ze Bretons av all orange air, like ze Celts. But I am real Breton. Now I am *Le* Breton. Yes."

He held up his hand for me to do a high five. We were back in a rap video again. I made the effort to stretch across the table and give him his high five, though. Le client est roi, after all.

We went to the office so I could introduce him to the other guys.

Sanjeet and Marya were at their desks, and dealt perfectly

with Yann's new name. It was as if Kerbolloc'h had never existed.

"OK. Who's got my mug?" Tom had burst into the office. His head swivelled in search of his prey, and he pointed down at my desk. "Paul! Bastard!"

I asked him whether he was implying that I had accidentally lent his mug to my guest and client, the chef Yann Lebreton.

"Yes. Hi, Yann, enchanté to meet you. Have you finished with my mug?"

Yann forced a hearty laugh, then stifled it, wondering what the hell was going on. Was this an example of English humour; he seemed to be thinking. But no, Tom was deadly serious.

"How can you tell it's yours?" I asked. "It's just a new Waterloo mug."

"No, look, the handle's a totally different shape. Much flatter. As your nose will be if you outsource it to your clients again."

"Here, use mine," I begged him.

"I don't want to use your smeggy mug. I don't know what disgusting germs you brought back from France. Present company excluded, of course," he added tactfully.

"Well, use a paper cup, then."

"What? For tea? You really are a foreigner, Paul. Have you finished?" He smiled at Yann, peered down into the mug and, deciding that the remaining centimetre of coffee no longer constituted an actual drink, relieved him of the burden of finishing it. "Anyone want a brew?" he offered. "Yann? Like to try some real English tea?" Now that Tom had his mug back, he was benevolence itself.

"No, sank you," Yann said, still slightly confused by the complexity of this English tea ceremony.

"Anyway, we've got to go downstairs," I said. "To the design studio." Yann was due to look at some poster mock-ups and give us some signatures to scan.

"OK, less go." Yann stood up, relieved at the chance to escape.

The design studio was the temporary home of a bunch of young, Mac-using music fans with an attitude. Putting them all together in one room had been a mistake, I thought. They had melded into a single organism of merciless cool.

Today, two of them were rocking to the deafening beat as they light-pencilled their creations on to screen, and Yann did not get off to a good start by asking them to "pliz put down ze museek."

I was going to wait and let them take the initiative themselves, but Yann had got in there first, and I wished he hadn't.

Paula, the graphic artist we'd come to see, was a denim-wearing Northerner who'd told me that she thought all Southerners were "basically ponces." She now eyed Yann as if she was counting exactly how many miles further south France was, before getting up slowly and turning the music down to background level.

The other designer, Karl, a hyper-trendy East Ender with a popstar haircut and a big-collared shirt, stopped work to assess the intruder.

Yann ignored, or failed to detect, their hostility. He was almost as cool as they were, I had to give him that.

"Merci," he said, and went to admire the large poster of himself on the wall behind Paula's desk. There he was, standing astride a Voulez-Vous logo in chef's garb, looking moodily creative and holding blank white tubes where his baguette creations would be scanned in.

"You wanna come and sign your autographs, then?" Paula held out the light pen.

"Autographs?" Karl asked. "You famous?"

"I am Yann Lebreton, ze chef," Yann pronounced, inviting Karl to compare the real thing with the poster on the wall.

"Never 'eard of ya. Is that yer real name?" Karl asked cruelly. I guessed he must have heard about the Kerbolloc'h problem.

Yann saw what was going on and wisely decided not to react. "Where I sign?" he demanded, grabbing the pen.

Paula opened up a file for him, and he began practising his new autographs.

"Voilà." Yann had performed five or six curly signatures on screen and stood up, satisfied with his new autograph. Then he suddenly looked puzzled. "Why you not use ze photo wiz ze courgettes for ze post-air?" he asked Paula. "Ah prefer zat photo."

"Oh, yeah. No, not a good idea."

"Wah not?"

"We need a photo with the baguettes," I said. "We couldn't use the courgettes."

"Anyway, I didn't think it was appropriate," Paula said.

"Pardon?"

"I saw one of your recipes in your press kit."

"And?" Yann sensed that something bad was coming, and he was right.

"And, well, your courgette recipe is bollocks, isn't it?"

"Bollocks?" Yann glowered at her, looking for a sign that she was taking the piss out of his name. But she wasn't. She was taking the piss out of his recipe. "Yeah, you know, crap," Paula said.

"Paula . . ." I begged, but there was no stopping her. This, I had come to realize, was the big problem with the consultant system. If you didn't think you needed the next contract, you could tell your client that he was crap and bollocks.

"What?" Yann had understood, but couldn't believe his ears.

"Yeah, the only way to do courgettes is to fry them in olive oil.

You serve the bloody things *raw*. I mean, tasteless or what? You should stick to sandwiches, mate. No raw courgettes in there."

Yann was looking like a deep-sea fish that has suddenly been hauled up from the ocean floor by a trawler. His gills were puffing, his body was unable to get a grip on this weird new world where he'd been dumped. A designer offering opinions on cooking, to him, a qualified chef with a diploma from a French cooking school? This sort of thing did not happen in his world. He didn't know, of course, that the upshot of having so many celebrity chefs is that we Brits are all cooking experts in our own way.

"Courgettes are baby marrows, aren't they?" Paula went on philosophically. "You've got to fry them to give them some flavour. So the only real question is, do you slice them thin straight across, or do you slice them thick at angles like you get at the chinky?"

"Chinky?" Yann asked.

"Yeah. Chinky. You know, like, don't take your minkey to the chinky?"

"Minkey?"

At this, I'm ashamed to say I laughed. Getting a Frenchman to quote Inspector Clouseau was cruel, but beautiful.

Yann pounced on me and began to rant. He had had "enurf." He was an important "partnair" for the company. I was supposed to be "cultiving" the partnership rather than laughing at him, as everyone in the company had obviously been doing for months already. My colleagues attacked him for using their teacup, and even attacked his cuisine. If I could not defend his image in the company, how could I defend it to the media?

Most of what he said was entirely justified. Though I'm not sure it was in my contract to have a courgette inserted where he threatened to insert it.

6

ALEXA LISTENED sympathetically to my troubles. She had a good laugh too, which I didn't mind at all, because it meant that she was trembling against me, her long, cool legs entwined in mine, her shoulder rubbing fragrantly against my face.

Yes, we were in bed together.

We had slept together.

But only in the eyes-closed, snoring sense that I'd tried out with Nathalie after getting trapped in the lift. This was a T-shirt-and-knickers-on stayover at my place, and I'd proved my point.

My point being that it would be great for Alexa to come and sleep with me.

At first she'd refused, but I'd explained that I meant literally sleep. I said that it would be a good test of how close we were. Spending a night together, just talking, snuggling up, enjoying each other's company in total privacy. If that was fun—as I was sure it would be—it would prove that there was hope for us.

It had taken me more than a week of cajoling and candlelit dinners, but she finally weakened. Or decided to give me a chance. She made me swear that there would be no sneaky attempts to exchange bodily fluids, and after a night out at a Kensington pub full of French people, she stayed over.

Lying close—but not too close—the following morning, I asked Alexa to explain her film idea to me. The idea

I'd supposedly inspired when we were at the Monet exhibition.

It sounded fun.

All the things about the French that drive other nations crazy can be explained by a love of lifestyle, she said. When they run a red light, they're not simply showing total indifference to the danger of killing someone—they just think that life is too short to spend minutes waiting for a light to decide what colour it wants to be.

"They might have a rendezvous with their lover, who is waiting for them in a big, bouncy bed," Alexa said.

"I'm with them on that," I said, but she was too into her idea to take it as a hint.

"And our president, for example. He was accused of corruption. What for? Not letting his friends sell drugs or armaments, but for spending too much money on *food*."

It all sounded very convincing, but how, I asked, was she going to make a film out of that?

"Simple," she said. "I observe the French, in different places, doing very everyday things, and I give the real significance of these actions. Like, even your old obsession with merde—I film a rich lady in Nice who lets her dog shit on the Promenade des Anglais. Why does she do this? It is simple—she does not want it to shit in her chic apartment because that would spoil her lifestyle, so she takes it to the nearest place, it shits, and she returns to her lifestyle."

I didn't like to tell her that chic ladies, in Paris at least, had actually started pooper-scooping. Although maybe, I thought, it had become a new part of the lifestyle—I scoop therefore I am.

I told Alexa about the shock of settling back into the British lifestyle, and especially the coffee-club war that was brewing out at Waterloo TM.

By now, a couple of weeks after my arrival, I'd poached sixteen members of the old coffee club, and had a total membership of thirty or so. Tom, who was in charge of the old club, was alternating between outrage and suicide. For a start, his milk-buying schedule was totally screwed. Pints would sit there in the fridge, passing their sell-by dates unopened. And when the kitchen had run out of washing-up liquid, he'd demanded to know exactly how many times we'd used his sponge and liquid to wipe the nozzle of our espresso machine.

I bought a bottle of washing-up liquid as a peace offering, but I couldn't help him with the milk problem, which would very soon—and he knew it all too well—be compounded by a coffee problem. Because all the coffee drinkers had come in with me, and Tom was now left with just a tea-drinking rump of a drinks club.

I said I saw no reason why we shouldn't co-exist, but Tom couldn't come to terms with losing his empire, and was often to be seen wandering the corridors, touting in vain for new members.

"You must send him to Paris to work at your tea room," Alexa said. She giggled, trembling against me in a way that made me want to postpone conversation for a while and concentrate on a more physical style of communication.

I gritted my teeth, though, and moved on to the least sexy subject I could think of—my long-distance battle with the French authorities.

Benoît had sent over a list of problems for me to deal with.

What, for example, was he supposed to do about the letter from the Minstère de la Francophonie rejecting the translated version of our menu?

After all my protests, I had eventually given in and sent them a menu with translations for such dangerously misunderstandable items as potato salad, cream and cup of tea. However, my laptop was British, and it would have taken me three hours per word to find all the accents. So I'd missed them out. My argument was that French customers weren't stupid. There was no danger that they would read "tasse de the" and think that they were going to get a cup of the English word for "le." Similarly, if I wrote "creme" instead of "crème," would Parisians leave the tea room shaking their heads in incomprehension about this accentless stuff that was served on top of cakes?

I didn't think so.

The linguists at the Ministère (note the accent) didn't agree and were demanding a retype.

"They're trying to drive me insane," I told Alexa.

"No, you can drive them insane," she said. "Type all your translations in—how do you say—big letters?"

"Capitals?"

"Yes. In French, when you type capitals you are not obliged to use accents. They will have to accept it and they will hate you."

"Brilliant." This was exactly the kind of girl I could spend the rest of my life with.

"Why don't we spend Christmas together?" I suggested on an impulse. If I'd thought about the idea first, I would probably never have dared to say it.

"Christmas Eve? Yes, everyone says the atmosphere in the pubs is great on Christmas Eve."

"No, I don't mean just go out for a drink. I mean the whole of Christmas. A week or so. What do you think?"

"Not with my mother and Yuri?"

"No, not here, not in London," I said. "Let's go away somewhere. The south of France, say."

"Hmm." She didn't sound keen.

"It'd be warm."

"It can be very cold."

"You'll need to travel around France to research your film, won't you?"

"Hmm." This was a more positive "hmm" than the first one. Her voice had actually gone up a bit at the end.

"Let's do some research together over Christmas."

God, it was hard not to squeeze her against me and hint that I'd love to do some other research, too.

"Hmm." We were back to a non-committal sound again.

"I could finance your film, you know."

This time she stiffened. "What do you mean?"

"Jean-Marie says he wants to buy my business."

"You don't want to sell it."

"No, but if I did, I could finance your film and you wouldn't need Yuri's money."

"I told you, I cannot take this responsibility for you screwing up your life."

I felt her inching away from me in the bed, and tightened my grip on her waist as much as I could without it being too aggressive.

"I wouldn't be screwing things up. I could sell Jean-Marie half the business—including half my debts, by the way—and let Benoît carry on running it. He's doing a good job. Then I could invest the money in your film. And I mean invest. If it makes a bundle, I want my money back with interest."

"I do not think it will make money. It is not Harry Potter."

"Don't do yourself down, Alexa. You're a star now. Beaubourg, the Saatchi Gallery. People are going to want to see your film. You're a good investment."

"So you only want me because I am a star."

"Hey, don't forget I knew you when you were a part-time waitress. I only noticed you because you kept dropping plates."

She elbowed me in protest. But it was, I felt, an affectionate elbow.

"Anyway," she said, "I am not the only star. You are the star, too."

"What do you mean?"

She was silent for a moment, composing her answer.

"That is why I cried."

"What is?"

"When you said you were happy that my exhibition would be at the Saatchi. You were happy for me. You did not think, yes, the photos of my face will be famous now. Sacha said, 'Huh, you want to make that English guy famous.' He did not think of me at all. You thought of me only, and this made me cry. I thought, yes, perhaps he really does love me, this silly Paul."

I know I'd promised that this would be a sleep-only sleepover. But there are times when a guy can't possibly keep his promises. And when a girl doesn't want him to.

E VEN THOUGH WE were back together again, my plans for Christmas didn't get any further. I was still keen to go away, just the two of us, but Alexa didn't want to talk about it. Seeing each other in London, with the safety net of her mum's place in Notting Hill, seemed to be all she wanted right now. All she was willing to risk, maybe.

I thought things were going really well. We were relaxed in each other's company again, and rarely missed an opportunity to spend an evening—and night—together. But Alexa always seemed to be waiting for me to screw things up again.

It was the office party that finally put the oil amongst the pigeons and the cat on the fire.

Like the coffee club, plans for the Christmas party provoked more conflict than contracts worth millions. Should it be a sit-down dinner or a buffet? Karaoke or just dancing? Smoking or non-smoking? One container lorry of booze or two? The argument had been raging long before I rejoined the company, with proposals and counter-proposals appearing on company notice-boards, in emails and in frequent conversations in the kitchen or at the local sandwich shop.

Finally, it was announced that, in order to make things more inclusive, the party would be a sit-down buffet, with karaoke followed by dancing, and that there would be smoking and non-smoking areas, and three oil tankers of booze. What's more, the menu was to be "created" by my very own star client, Yann Lebreton.

All of which sounded fine to me, except for the news that, instead of significant others, we would have to invite our clients, so that the company could set it all against tax as corporate hospitality. Which meant that it would be Yann who would be taking me to the ball.

So, on the last Friday before Christmas, we all came to work in clothes that we wouldn't mind getting covered in party stains. Lots of the women, I noticed, had put on strategic outfits. Formal-ish office wear on top, with signs of night-time hunting gear under-neath. Strapless tops beneath jackets, short skirts that were kept hidden below desks until party season was declared open.

The whole day felt like that moment before a football match when the players are lined up and the referee puts his whistle in his mouth.

The actual start of the party was an anti-climax, as we mingled beneath the glitzy paper chains in the function room, getting used to the taste of our tea-time shot of champagne, and making whispered jokes about what our MD, the Beast, would say in his speech.

The Beast himself looked nothing like the devil at all. He was a tubby little American guy who could have glued on a beard and been a perfect Father Christmas. He did his ten minutes of blah about all of us thinking outside the box and staying in the loop, and before we had finished applauding and whooping, he had buggered off back to the USA to let us get on with our drinking.

He would probably have been touched to see how whole-heartedly we put his words into action. It took no time at all for a large percentage of us to get out of our boxes and start dancing in loops.

The piled plates of cold food were largely ignored as people bounced out of their office personalities, yelled along to "I Will Survive," broke world records of tune-lessness at karaoke, and spilled out of the function room to wreak havoc in the offices.

I left Yann explaining cuisine theory to the cleavage of one of our marketing assistants, and took a bottle of champagne for a walk around the building.

In the kitchen on our floor, two guys from my espresso club were filling Tom's kettle with old, congealed milk, which I thought was a bit cruel. But hysterically funny all the same. Probably because the bottle in my hand was my second of the night.

In one of the offices, a woman was sobbing loudly, her mascara streaming down her face and on to the blouse of the colleague who was comforting her and making libellous insinuations about Sanjeet's sexual prowess.

On the staircase, I joined in a champagne fight between two gangs of auditors. The auditors were the biggest clan in the company. Everything was always being audited. Now, once they had sprayed every drop of bubbly from their bottles, they began to audit the contents of the fire extinguishers at each other, at which point I decided to leave them to it.

On my way back to replenish my alcohol supply, I found that the argument about Sanjeet had spread into the corridor. Marya was defending him against some rumour that I didn't quite understand—how could he be a virgin? No one over twelve in England is a virgin.

I decided to support Marya, and pitched in with a couple of people who had formed a "stop talking bollocks" group.

"Bollocks," we chorussed, and then started to sing, "What a load of bollocks."

I was in mid-bollock when I noticed Yann staring at me from an office doorway. He seemed to be angry about something, which was confirmed when he came over and began growling in my ear. He was only half-coherent, though. I guessed he'd been drinking.

Finally, I worked out that he was talking about his name, and the penny dropped.

"Oh, excuse-moi, Yann." I kissed him on the cheek to show how sorry I was, and explained the situation to my fellow bollock-singers. They had to stop insulting my guest.

"He's very sensitive about his bollocks," I told them. "He used to be a bollock."

This didn't calm Yann down at all. On the contrary. He started trying to strangle me, and I was forced to dodge out of his grasp and rush off in search of some more champagne to cool my aching throat.

After a quick trip back to the bar in the function room—which was now given over to the functions of food-throwing and butt-groping—I found myself in our kitchen again. Tom was rinsing out his kettle, and I hung around to sympathize with him. I suggested that it might be time for him to come in with my coffee club, and tried to lighten things up by making a joke about how his milky kettle would be producing cappuccino from now on any-way. Instead of laughing, he attacked me. Fortunately his kettle was plastic, and bounced almost painlessly off my head. But I thought it best to avoid causing any more conflict between our two hot-drinks factions, and skidded along the corridor in search of a hiding place.

In the photocopy room, I found Charlie, trousers down, showing that he hadn't read the email we'd received from the health and safety officer, requesting all staff to "refrain from sitting on photocopiers in case of glass-related accidents." Every Christmas, the message said, British A&E units were flooded with office workers who had somehow got shards of glass from broken photocopiers stuck in their buttocks.

Charlie was not a light guy, but the photocopier had obviously been built to withstand tough love, and black-and-white pictures of his balls and hairy arsehole were sliding out into the stacker.

He got down from the machine and, with his trousers and underpants still round his ankles, offered me the chance to flick through his artwork. Was I sure, he asked me, that I didn't want to check out his "London derrière"? He found this so funny that he started to choke, then gag, and only saved himself from asphyxiation by pulling out the A3 tray and puking into it.

Even in my slightly (well—very) intoxicated state, I wondered what exactly was going on here. Was I supposed to think, yeah, my boss is a great guy, he can get pissed with the lads. It'll be really funny tomorrow when people get strangely coloured 3-D bullet points on their photocopies.

Put it this way, I couldn't imagine Jean-Marie using that way of gaining respect.

Though to be fair, Charlie did redeem himself somewhat, because he used one of the sterilized wipes that the health and safety people had thoughtfully (and pessimistically) left by the photocopier to swab down the glass for the next sitter. If anyone did end up in A&E, the lacerations in their backside would at least be germ-free.

I wandered off again and homed in on the sounds of a fight outside the function-room doors. It was the old Sanjeet argument, which had now escalated. Two, no three, women—including the normally calm Marya—were bouncing off walls, ripping down posters and flattening plants as they tried to break their three-way clinch and land some decent punches. Sanjeet was standing nearby, doing his sheepish schoolboy thing, but with a small dose of glee thrown in. They were fighting over him, someone told me. He had been shagging two women, and had tried to break it off with one of them by telling her he had turned Christian and wanted to become a virgin again until he got married.

Sanjeet was suddenly pushed aside as Yann bundled his way out of the function room. He saw me and pointed an accusing finger that suggested he wanted to continue our earlier conversation.

I looked around for some means of escape, but fortunately, the gallant Frenchman in Yann was distracted by the sight of the snarling, flailing women. He waded bravely in to try and separate them.

Less than a second later he was lying on the floor with a bruise swelling visibly below one eye.

"Toi!" he shouted at me.

I went over to help him up, but only offered myself as a scapegoat. "C'est ta faute, ça!" he bawled. It was all my fault.

Lying there rubbing his cheek, he started to yell at me in French above the mingled noises of vintage disco music and female swearing. How was this going to look in his publicity campaign? He was sure to have a bruise. How could he go on television? The chef with a black eye—an "œil au beurre noir" as the French call it, literally an "eye with black butter."

I thought this was meant to be a culinary joke—chef, butter— and laughed, but this seemed to enrage him even more.

There was only one way to cool him down, I realized. I upended my bottle of champagne over his head and doused his fiery temper in fizzy French wine.

Yann au vin it was, after all.

8

In the Merde for Love

1

WHEN I WOKE UP, I was miraculously hangover-free. That's the great thing about champagne. If you drink nothing else, next morning your head is as clear as a bell. The French even have an expression for it—rester au champagne, they call it. It was another lifestyle idea that Alexa would have to film.

Anyway, thanks to champagne, I was perfectly sober as I made my phone calls at eight o'clock on the morning of Christmas Eve.

I told Charlie (who had already had a full English breakfast and been out mountain-biking) that I didn't think the future celebrity chef and I would be able to work constructively together after he'd chased me through every corridor and staircase in the building with a dish of grated raw courgette salad, and forced me to hide in the basement to escape a certain vegetable death.

Charlie agreed, and given that I was a consultant, we just had to un-sign our contract and I was free to concentrate on other things, like getting my life together.

I reached Jean-Marie at home and offered him the chance to buy a 49 per cent share in the tea room. He was delighted, and told me again that I'd made a real man of Benoît. He sounded so pleased that I thought he might even do his son the honour of not trying to sleep with Katy. What a great Christmas present that would be.

*   *   *

And then I called Alexa with a song.

"Come away with me." I didn't dare sing it, of course, in case I scared her away for ever.

We still hadn't made any firm plans for the evening, apart from agreeing that we'd do something together. Now I told her that I knew exactly what I wanted to do.

Romantic dinner in Paris, the night train south in a cabin for two, Christmas amongst the lemon trees. I'd already booked everything. I could hardly believe my luck at getting tickets on that night train. I seemed to be in favour with the gods again.

There was just one catch, I added—after Christmas together, we'd stay together. A week away, then look for an apartment à deux.

"You are giving me an ool-tee-ma-tomm?"

"An ultimatum? No, of course I'm not. Well, yes I suppose I am. We've got to stop this messing about, Alexa. It's doing my head in. I want you for Christmas and I'm offering you me. Presentation ceremony at the Eurostar departures board, Christmas Eve, three p.m. train."

"That's this afternoon."

"I know. You haven't got any other plans, have you?"

"No, not really."

"And you have a valid passport?"

"I don't need one. This is the European Union, Paul. Only you English need a passport. We French can travel with our identity cards."

But I didn't want to get into a debate about the Treaty of Maastricht. "Please be there, Alexa," I said.

"It is a big decision."

"Yes, it is. It's two big decisions. One each. And I've made mine. I want to be with you. It's the only thing I feel at all certain about right now."

So there it was. Suspense.

I could picture with perfect clarity how great it would be to see her walking towards me through the station crowd, a bag on her shoulder and a smile on her face. It was like hundred-metre runners who imagine themselves crossing the line and try to force the future to happen the way they want it to.

But I'm not an Olympic sprinter, and I couldn't stop myself envisaging what it'd be like if she didn't come and I was left standing alone with my two railway tickets. The message would be clear—I wouldn't get a second chance.

I honestly did not know which of the two visions would come true.

But then, I told myself, Christmas presents are supposed to be a surprise, aren't they?

2

LIGHTS WERE FLASHING. The departures board was getting anxious.

Travellers were scuffing towards the barriers, digging for passports in their pockets, holding out tickets like batons in a relay race.

I was standing to one side clutching my two tickets in my hand, scanning all the latecomers' faces and assuring the guy in the blue overcoat that I would go through the barrier as soon as my girlfriend turned up.

I could tell from his face that he thought I'd been stood up.

He had to be wrong.

But her phone was on voicemail. There was no answer at the house.

I re-checked the printout of the email I'd sent her with the travel details. It all seemed perfectly clear.

Although—give her the benefit of the doubt—she might have thought it was check-in at three p.m. rather than departure at three p.m. She might think it was OK to turn up at two fifty-five.

It was now two forty, ten minutes after the official end of check-in.

The guy at the barrier gave me one last chance, but I shook my head like someone giving up at an auction, and went to the ticket office to change the time of our departure for the next train, in an hour. This gave her till three thirty.

I left a message telling her what I'd done, carefully avoiding the question: where the hell are you?

The horror vision was coming true. Sometimes, when someone's late, I suddenly get this deep conviction that they'll never turn up. I can actually see them not turning up, if that's not a contradiction in terms. It's part of my masochistic tendency, I guess.

Now I resisted that conviction. I made myself imagine her rushing up the escalator from the Tube, or even strolling along totally unaware that she was late. She'd misread the email.

I wouldn't even be angry with her for making me wait and doubt.

I went to sit down at a coffee bar from where I could see the check-in barriers, and watched the minutes tick away on the big illuminated clock over the departures board.

I forced myself to wait five minutes between phone calls, but pretty soon it was three twenty-five. Now she was seriously late.

I only stopped trying Alexa's number when I noticed that my phone had disappeared off the table top.

Two kids had come by earlier, begging for money. They'd nicked my phone.

Fuck it, I thought. If a woman scooping up dog merde from a Paris pavement can be an omen, so can a disappearing phone.

She wasn't coming.

And I thought I'd worked out why. It was trust. She didn't think she could trust me. After all, what had I done the night before? Got roaring drunk and tried to drown my client in champagne. As far as she knew, I'd probably tried to shag someone on top of the photocopier. And then this morning I'd chucked in my job. Was that being reliable?

No, it wasn't, and she'd got cold feet.

She wasn't coming.

It was one minute to the end of check-in. I took a last look across at the escalators, then left Alexa's ticket with a steward and went through.

3

I FELT NUMB. It's like when you've bashed your head against the corner of a table, or (I guess) been punched by a woman at an office party. After a while, the actual pain becomes less acute. It settles down to a background ache, and you just sit there and let the bruise grow.

I could feel the bruise growing inside me now, deep blue, as big as the dent in Florence's dad's car all those months ago. There was nothing I could do to stop it.

I hardly noticed the night falling, and the tunnel taking me back to France.

I knew the Paris metro well, so I got from the Gare du Nord to the Gare de Lyon on autopilot.

I'd booked a table at the Train Bleu restaurant, the big brasserie in the Gare de Lyon, where for the past century travellers have dined before getting on their night trains to the south.

"Une personne?" the air-stewardess-style hostess asked me.

"Oui." It felt as though I was betraying Alexa by denying her existence. Should I have said I was waiting for someone else to join me? Or was it her own stupid fault for not being there? Guilt and resentment sloshed around in my stomach like an indigestible meal.

The hostess gathered up a menu and wine list, and escorted me to my table.

It would have been the perfect place for a Christmas Eve tête-à-tête. This was a brasserie with style. My seat was carved wood, like a church pew, except that it had a brass overhead-luggage rack, where I slung my coat and my solitary bag. The ceiling was a magnificent travel version of the Sistine Chapel, with various angels apparently setting off on their holidays, including one naked woman who was letting every curious traveller peer up between her legs. She was probably on her way to one of the nudist beaches—the île de Ré, maybe. No, wrong railway station. The walls featured huge murals of places that you could go to from the Gare de Lyon, including the kind of Mediterranean landscape that I'd hoped to be waking up to with Alexa the next day. Every other square inch of wall and ceiling was ornately embellished with gold scrolls, chandeliers and Christmas garlands.

The menu was just as cruelly festive. I ordered six oysters, a filet de sandre (river fish) in a caper sauce, and a bottle of champagne. Not that I had anything to celebrate. It was more a case of wanting to get painlessly drunk.

I slurped the oysters down, remembering the night over a year ago when I'd had them for the first time at Jean-Marie's place and thought they tasted "like bronchial mucus." Now I bit through the grey-green flesh and wished that Alexa was here so that I could tell her the story about that dinner with Jean-Marie.

I only just managed a smile when the couple at the next table raised their glasses and wished me "joyeux Noël."

Mine wasn't going to be joyeux, though. I was reminded yet again of that stuff Alexa told me the first time we split up—about "joie" and "tristesse" and how she didn't think I was capable of real joy. Well, now I knew she was wrong. I was definitely capable of joy. I would have felt pretty damn joyful if she'd turned up at the station rather than dumping me on Christmas Eve.

The couple at the neighbouring table were from Lyon, they told me. They had a hairdressing salon in Paris and were treating themselves here before getting on a TGV and joining the guy's family for Christmas.

Where was I going? they asked.

"Menton," I told them, "on the Italian border."

"You have friends or family there?"

"Friends." I didn't want to spoil their Christmas Day with flashbacks of this lone English guy taking his depression down south for the festive season.

4

THE FRENCH RAILWAYS have moved the non-TGV night trains out of the Gare du Lyon, and my train was going from the Gare d'Austerlitz, a short taxi ride away.

As I looked for the platform number on the departures board in the big, bustling station hall, I had a sudden irrational surge of hope. She might have caught a later train after all, and come straight here from the Gare du Nord. She could be here now, amongst all these people shuffling around with their bags full of Christmas presents for their families.

But no. It was time to stop kidding myself.

I gave Alexa's ticket to the carriage steward, and went to crash out in my lonely little cabin.

It wasn't much smaller than my bedsit, where we'd so recently spent the night together. The walls were covered in beige Formica, the colour Alexa's shoulders had been back in September. There were two bunks, a fold-out mirror, a tiny round sink, even a porcelain flask in case you got caught short in the night.

It would have been such fun, I thought. This dolls' house bedroom, rattling southwards through the night, the two of us making the most of the vibrations from the rails and using only one of the beds. Then, on Christmas morning, pulling back the curtains to watch the sun rise over the Med.

*   *   *

When the train lurched forwards, a part of my brain listened out for someone shouting, "Stop the train, I want to get on!" or for a woman banging on all the cabin doors, asking if a Paul West was in there.

But no, there was just the sound of the wheels clicking faster and faster over the rails, and a crackly voice listing all the stations we'd be stopping at before I had to get off.

The first of these was just south of Paris, a town that was almost close enough to be a suburb of the city. The platform was dark, wet and almost deserted. No one would get off here, I thought. It would just be a pick-up stop.

So I was surprised to see a group of five people walking away from the train. Two of them had peaked caps on—railwaymen. Two were young guys in baseball caps. And one was a girl with a leather jacket, who was struggling wildly, hanging on to a large rucksack with one hand and trying to thump one of the railwaymen with the other.

5

A LEXA?
Alexa.

"Alexa!"

I was up out of my seat and shouting her name. I ran along the corridor, fought my way out of the door and tumbled down the steps on to the low platform. The cold, foggy air slapped me in the face.

"Alexa!"

I starting running towards them. I was going to look a right jerk if it wasn't her, I realized.

"Alexa!"

I could hear what was going on now. The girl was trying to explain something in French, the railwaymen were repeating "Oui, oui, c'est ça" in the cynical, disbelieving drone that French people use when they don't want to listen to you.

"Alexa!"

She turned towards me.

"Paul!"

With one huge tug she was free, and we grabbed each other like two people sharing a parachute.

"You didn't come," I said.

"Why didn't you wait?" she asked.

"I thought you'd changed your mind."

"No, of course not. The Tube stopped in the tunnel," she said.

"There was an electricity cut. And I couldn't phone until I got out—the London Tube is too deep." She pulled away and looked me in the eyes. "You never answered."

"My phone was stolen," I told her.

"I took the first train to France, and a taxi from the Gare du Nord. And I ran to the train just in time. But I had no ticket. The contrôleurs thought I was with these two boys. They refused to look for you."

She hugged the breath out of me again, and I realized that she'd been going through exactly the same kind of torment as me. She must have thought I was ignoring her calls because I was mad at her. She thought I'd given up on her. Well, she was right about that.

"Je t'ai attrapé," she said. She'd caught me. She clung on even harder.

I pulled her against me and took a deep breath of her perfume, as if I had to make sure that this wasn't one of my mirages or hallucinations.

"When I got on that train alone, I thought I'd lost you," I told her.

"No, how could you forget? I'm a French girl. We're always late."

There are times when you just don't want to let go of someone, and this was one of them. But we both knew that it would be rather difficult for us to climb back on to the train if we were hugging each other.

Only trouble was, when we finally felt reassured enough to let go, we saw that the ticket collectors had gone, the train was moving out of the station, and we were alone in the gloom of the empty platform with the two kids in baseball caps, who were still laughing together about how close they'd come to getting a free ride down south.

"Stop!" I shouted as loud as I could, but the locomotive didn't seem to be listening.

We jogged alongside the train for a few yards, until we realized that we weren't going to be able to follow it all the way to the next station. Not with Alexa's bag slowing us down.

"Merde," Alexa groaned. "Hey, where's *your* bag?"

"On the train."

"And your ticket?"

"On the train."

"But you do have your passport on you?"

"No."

"And your credit card?"

"No."

"Then you're really in the merde, aren't you, Paul?"

I looked at her standing there in her battered leather jacket, her hair ruffled by the rush of air from the departing train, her eyes wide with concern for me.

"No," I said. "Because I've got you."

EPILOGUE

E LEVEN THIRTY P.M., Christmas Eve, commissariat de la Police Nationale, Jouay-sur-Seine

"Nom?" the night-shift policeman asked me.

"Paul West."

"Pool . . . ?"

I spelled it out for him, and he keyed it one-fingered into his computer.

"Time and date of theft?" he said, his finger poised.

"Well, I'm not sure that they have been stolen yet."

"Uh?"

"I left them on a train."

"We thought that it was best to report it now, just in case," Alexa added, trying to clear up the confusion.

But the policeman had stopped listening. He was gazing at his computer screen as if he'd just found out what he was getting for Christmas.

"Paul West?" he asked.

"Yes."

"Driver of a Renault Vel Satis? Owner of a tea room with a non-translated name?"

Oh, merde.

ACKNOWLEDGMENTS

The author would like to thank everyone who contributed in any way—deliberately or accidentally—to the success of the whole *Merde* adventure, and especially those who threatened physical violence if they didn't get thanked.

Those people are, in no particular order of violence: E, L, S, SL, K, K, M, C, LF, SW, AB, CW, EC, B, NH, NB, PF, DL, MTL, VC, BG, IA, AS, ER, LR, CD, JL&V, JR&J, IM, BS, CW, LG, SR, G, M, P, C&P, Y, SM, MB, JR, JS, AZ, S, V, V, F, C, BP, JR, SC, AB, BE, EB, SF, L, N, DC, MD, AP, GC.

If I've left you out, I'm really sorry. Get in touch and I'll send you a book and a grovelling apology.

Stephen Clarke lives in France. He has experimented with Gauloises, pétanque and suppositories, but only as research for his writing. He likes to spend his free time sitting on café terraces trying to think up a clever answer to the question "Did those things in your books really happen?"

His first book, *A Year in the Merde*, which introduced Paul West, was first self-published in 2004 in Paris, where it became a word-of-mouth bestseller. It was published by Bloomsbury in the U.S. in 2005 and has now been translated into fourteen languages, including French.

The text of this book is set in Fournier. Fournier is derived from the *romain du roi*, which was created toward the end of the seventeenth century for the exclusive use of the Imprimerie Royale from designs made by a committee of the Académie des Sciences. The original Fournier types were cut by the famous Paris founder Pierre Simon Fournier in about 1742. This Monotype version dates from 1924. Fournier is a light, clear face whose distinctive features are capital letters that are quite squat in relation to the lowercase ascenders, and decorative italics, which show the influence of the calligraphy of Fournier's time.